DWIGHT DAVIS

DWIGHT DAVIS

The Man and the Cup

NANCY KRIPLEN

EBURY PRESS

First published in Great Britain in 1999

1 3 5 7 9 10 8 6 4 2

Ebury Press
Random House · 20 Vauxhall Bridge Road · London SW1V 2SA

Random House Australia Pty Limited
20 Alfred Street · Milsons Point, Sydney · New South Wales 2061 · Australia

Random House New Zealand Limited
18 Poland Road · Glenfield · Auckland 10 · New Zealand

Random House South Africa (Pty) Limited
Endulini · 5A Jubilee Road, Parktown 2193 · South Africa

Random House UK Limited Reg. No. 954009

www.randomhouse.co.uk

Papers used by Ebury Press are natural, recyclable products
made from wood grown in sustainable forests.

A CIP catalogue record for this book is available from the British Library.

ISBN 0 09 186850 5

Designed by Lovelock & Co.
Printed and bound in Great Britain by
Mackays of Chatham plc, Chatham, Kent

CONTENTS

To David

PREFACE

T his book is a joint biography – of a man and of a piece of metal. But what a piece of metal. The Davis Cup, the piece of sterling silver that was Dwight F. Davis's legacy to the world of international sport, holds within its ample bowl a century of tennis history. Dwight Davis's life holds within its 66-year span a half-century of political, diplomatic and social history.

Both Dwight Davis and the cup that bore his name were indefatigable travellers, and this in an era before airplanes made crossing the world's continents and oceans fast and easy. After the cup's initial launch, the two, the man and the cup, followed different, though equally interesting, paths through the years. From time to time these paths would cross briefly and then swing off again in different arcs through the decades.

There are certain sporting trophies that transcend the immediate athletic event – that in their physical, gleaming, silver (usually) selves bestow upon our sports-mad culture historical grace. There is, possibly, a faint resonance from the past in their varied shapes – a reaching back through our collective memory to the bowls and urns of precious oils presented with great ceremony to winning athletes in ancient Greece.

Architectural critic Herbert Muschamp has written about 'the designed object' that is considered 'not just a work of visual art but a medium of communication, an instrument more powerful in its own way than a written manifesto'. I. Michael Heyman, secretary of the Smithsonian Institution, says there is a 'power of objects, of real things, to move us in ways we can barely articulate, stimulating memory, evoking emotions'.

BEGINNINGS

I say 'I am going to have a game of tennis.' But what I
really mean is, 'I am going to have a wonderful time under
the sky, in the sun. I am going to rush around, feeling the
motion of the air and the movement of my body through
space ... For a while, for me, the world will not exist ... I
shall lose myself in the fun of the game, in competition
which seems real but is not important. I am going to play.'

Helen Wills Moody
New York Tribune, 25 October 1938

CHAPTER 1

BEGINNINGS

B oston was getting hot again. Though the previous afternoon's rain had temporarily cooled off the city, another heavy blanket of stifling August air was beginning to press down relentlessly on Copley Square and the narrow streets of Beacon Hill. Suffocating tendrils of heat curled along the banks of the Charles and up its tributary, the accurately if inelegantly named Muddy River, as it twisted and turned through the Fens.

At the outer reaches of Boston near Brookline, an area many Boston residents still thought of as 'out in the country', Muddy River ran, for a time, alongside the tracks of the Boston & Albany Railroad. Twenty-six trains a day carried people back and forth between the palm of central Boston and the finger of suburbs and villages stretching out to the west.

On this Wednesday afternoon, 8 August 1900, more passengers than usual were climbing down from the early afternoon trains at Brookline's Longwood Station. Their destination was just a three-block walk from the station: a large grassy field at the intersection of Longwood and Brookline Avenues, the verdant grounds of the Longwood Cricket Club.

At Longwood, as at most of the other cricket clubs which dotted America's East Coast, the sport of cricket had been gently elbowed onto the sidelines by another English import, lawn tennis. And it was for lawn tennis – an international tournament, the first of its kind – that the crowds were gathering on this August afternoon. Some Boston newspapers were even calling it a World Championship, brushing aside the fact that only two countries were participating, the United States and England.

During the next three days three American men and three Englishmen would compete in a variety of singles and doubles matches. The country winning three out of these five matches would take possession of a splendid new silver bowl which had been donated by one of the young American players. A native of St. Louis, Missouri, and a recent graduate of Harvard University, he had turned 21 just one month earlier. His name was Dwight Filley Davis.

Engraved on the large silver bowl Davis had donated was its official title: International Lawn Tennis Challenge Trophy. But almost from the beginning it would be known simply as the Davis Cup.

The sport of tennis and baby Dwight Filley Davis both had made their first appearance in St. Louis in the year 1879 – a bit of interesting symbolism, perhaps, but a coincidence of minor significance since Davis would say, many years later, that he actually learned the game at a summer resort on the East Coast.

In 1879 St. Louis was America's sixth-largest city and had, among other cosmopolitan appurtenances, the services of a British Consul. It was he who first introduced the game of lawn tennis to the city, and a few years later there was a sprinkling of courts around town, both privately owned and at clubs.

Lawn tennis – imagine. What a change from the rough, scrappy river town that the first Davis had found when he arrived in the 1830s. Sam Davis had come from Brookline, Massachusetts. The western part of the continent was opening to settlers. St. Louis, the one-time French fur trading post on the banks of the mighty Mississippi, was well situated to provide the blankets, farm tools, iron stoves and pots and pans that homesteading families would need as they rumbled west on the Oregon and Santa Fe trails.

A popular trail guidebook told travelers to 'toughen their wagon and have at least six mules, with spare harnesses and parts'. As for food, they were advised to pack 'coffee, beans, bacon (often stored in a barrel of corn meal), spices, flour, sugar and fruit'. That was besides shoes, cradles, churns and school books, of course. Stores in Missouri trailhead towns such as Independence, St. Joseph and Westport (later part of Kansas City) were ready to supply those beans and harnesses. And enterprising Easterners such as Sam Davis were ready to supply merchandise to those stores.

In 1835, 26-year-old Sam Davis had joined J. R. Stanford of St. Louis and David Griggs of Boston in a partnership to sell merchandise in St. Louis. Their store, Stanford & Davis, was on Commercial Street, a few blocks from the Mississippi River. Sam Davis married Caroline Tilden and by 1840 Davis's two original partners had been replaced by two brothers-in-law, John Tilden and Eben Richards. The firm was now Davis, Tilden and Richards. In the 1850s came a new building, new partners, and a new name, Samuel C. Davis & Co.

Appetites continued to grow for western land and, later, western gold. The streets and hotels of St. Louis filled with travelers and traders, speculators and gamblers. Daily, steamboats left the levee to head west on that other 'trail', the Missouri River, which emptied into the Mississippi just north of St. Louis. And sometimes the boats were so loaded down with passengers and goods from St.

Louis wholesalers (such as, of course, Samuel C. Davis & Co.) that water sloshed up over the side guards.

Three sons were born to Sam and Caroline Davis. Samuel Craft Davis Jr., was born in Massachusetts in 1841 or 1842. The younger two, however, were born in Missouri – John Tilden Davis, born 18 September 1844, and the baby, Charles, born in 1849 or 1850, who died a few short years later.

With the business doing well, the Davises, like other affluent St. Louisans, could afford to move away from the row houses stretching west from the river and into a neighbourhood of grander homes being developed about a mile further inland.

Lucas Place was a six-block development stretching between 14th and 17th streets, with a park on the east end to keep out through traffic. In the mid-1850s Sam moved his growing family into 1522 Lucas Place, the third house to be built on the fashionable new street. Though there had long been fine homes for the town's leading citizens, before 1850 they had tended to be mixed in with more humble dwellings and sometimes even commercial buildings. With Lucas Place, St. Louis became what it would be even a century later, a place of Places: residential enclaves of elegant homes within the city but not wholly of it, often with restricted access to sometimes private streets.

On Washington Avenue, a few blocks away from the Davis home, was the fledgling new school which had recently changed its name from Eliot Seminary to Washington University and which now combined a collegiate division with its academy or preparatory school. It was from here that John Davis was graduated in 1863 at the age of 19.

The summer before his senior year at school, John got a look at a bit more of the West. He made a three-month journey on a wood-fired packet boat up the Missouri River to Ft. Benton, deep in the vast Nebraska Territory and only 50 miles or so from the Canadian border. 'I have determined to make a collection of fossils and minerals to present to the University,' he wrote solemnly in the journal he kept of the trip. He observed, listened to and questioned his fellow passengers, including an old Indian trader and a Sioux war party which visited the ship for about two hours. He saw antelope and elk and bear and thick herds of buffalo that covered both banks of the river for miles and miles. He proudly demonstrated his prowess with a gun – though with some embarrassment when buffalo slaughter took place on a Sunday. (Bales of buffalo robes were among the main items the packet was transporting back to St. Louis.) And when the boat would stop at forts or towns he would dash into the settlement to get a newspaper with the latest accounts of Civil War action back in 'the states'.

In 1865, Sam Davis Sr. moved back East to run the Boston end of the business, leaving his 21-year-old son John and an older partner to run the operation in St. Louis. Sam Jr. was in Boston studying law at Harvard, from which he had already received an A.B. degree in 1863. (Sam Davis was admitted to the bar in Massachusetts in 1867 but would practise law only a few years before an early death in 1874.)

In 1867, John Davis was named a partner in the St. Louis store. It was a big year for the young man. In February 1867 he had married a St. Louis girl named Maria Filley (pronounced Mar-I-ah, long 'I'). The two families, the Davises and the Filleys, had long been friends. During the next 12 years three sons were born. The first two sons got Davis family names – John Tilden Davis Jr., born in 1868, and Samuel Craft Davis, born in 1872. But the third son, born 5 July 1879, was given a name from his mother's side of the family: Dwight Filley Davis.

Filley was a name of note in St. Louis. Back in the 1830s Dwight Davis's maternal grandfather, Oliver Dwight Filley had been the first of the Filley boys to arrive in St. Louis from the East. Oliver and his brother Giles were from Connecticut; their cousin Chauncey was from New York, as were his brothers Edward and Samuel. The Filleys, like Sam Davis, were among the many young men – self-reliant and ready to take risks – who, after some business experience in the East, had hurried to the 'Great West' looking for greater opportunity.

Oliver Filley was, by trade, a stove and tinware manufacturer. By the late 1850s he was said to be among St. Louis's growing number of men of substantial wealth. But politics interested him as well. He was in the circle of younger men who supported Missouri's powerful Senator Thomas Hart Benton. He was one of the founders of what would become the Republican Party in Missouri. During the tumultuous pre-Civil War years of 1858 to 1860 he served as mayor (some said reluctantly) of St. Louis. Three years later, his cousin Chauncey also served as mayor.

Yet by all accounts Oliver Filley did not let civic prominence and prosperity go to his head. While Filley was mayor, Edward, Prince of Wales, a young man of 19, happened to pay a visit to St. Louis. Public note was taken of the fact that the mayor, who had an aversion to wearing gloves, was not willing to change his sartorial ways even when accompanying England's future king to official functions.

But darker days filled much of his term of office. As calls to abolish slavery and the secession of the Southern states tore apart the nation, the border state of Missouri went into convulsions. Many of the early settlers had been Southerners and had brought slaves with them into the Missouri Territory. And in 1821 when Missouri had joined the Union as a state, it was as a slave state (balanced by the new free state, Maine, in what was known as the Missouri Compromise). Though slave holding was generally limited to the southern and western parts of the state, as late as 1861 slaves were auctioned on the steps of the massive stone St. Louis courthouse.

A large crowd at the final auction 1 January 1861, showed that there was no more public tolerance for the practice by purposely holding down the bids. No slaves were sold and, writes historian James Neal Primm, 'no one ever again tried to sell human beings at auction in St. Louis'.

Supporters of the South (including Missouri's Governor Claiborne F. Jackson) pushed for secession. Other citizens wanted a neutral Missouri, still in the Union, if possible, but not in a war. A third highly vocal group, including Oliver Filley, was determined to keep Missouri in the Union and join the North on the battlefield, if necessary. A strong anti-slavery position was taken by the Union, the anti-slavery newspaper Oliver Filley helped found (and which years later after mergers and name changes would become part of Joseph Pulitzer's *St. Louis Post-Dispatch*).

St. Louis was a pile of dry twigs waiting for a match. Some citizens were even suggesting that if Missouri seceded from the Union and joined the Confederacy, St. Louis should secede from Missouri. Volunteer units and home guards formed, drilling secretly at night in warehouses and factories – including Giles Filley's stove foundry –where floors were sprinkled with sawdust to muffle the sound.

Rumours of plots and intrigue hung like smoke in the air over downtown street corners and drifted into households like that of the Filley family at 76 North 6th Street. By now Oliver Filley and his wife Chloe (also originally from Connecticut) had seven children, three boys and four girls. The Filley daughters, according to family legend, played a small part in one of the dramas. Forces supporting the South, so the story went, were at one point poised to take over St. Louis. If Oliver Filley sent his daughters to school, that would mean he did not know about the plot. If he kept them home, that meant the plot had been discovered. Filley did know – but sent his daughters to school anyway. This confused the plotters, who were then exposed and captured.

In March 1861 Abraham Lincoln, from Missouri's neighbouring state of Illinois, was inaugurated as president of the United States, and in April, shots were fired by rebel soldiers against government troops at Fort Sumter in South Carolina. The American Civil War had begun. The gunfire was echoed a month later in St. Louis.

The powerful Committee of Safety, of which Oliver Filley was a leader, had given approval for Union-supporting troops to make a pre-emptive strike against the secessionist camp in Lindell Grove, a wooded area on St. Louis's western outskirts. Townspeople came out to watch, matters got out of hand, and in a disorganized shooting melée 28 people were killed and others wounded.

On another occasion, however, Oliver Filley, strong Union supporter though he was, went to the very visible aid of a possible Southern sympathizer. In late 1862 Filley traveled to Washington to see President Abraham Lincoln and deliver a letter and petitions concerning a certain Dr. Samuel McPheeters. Some weeks earlier, it seemed, the Reverend Dr. McPheeters had been dismissed from his pulpit in the Vine Street Church, upon orders of the federal Provost-Marshal.

St. Louis was still under martial law. Wealthy Southern sympathizers were being assessed to help support southern Unionist refugees pouring into the city. In some cases Southern sympathizers were being banished from the city if they too publicly cheered rebel battlefield wins and Union losses.

Dr. McPheeters protested that he had done none of that – that he, in fact, continued to lead prayers for the president and the government and, like other community leaders, had taken an oath of loyalty which he had no intention of breaking. Yet even if he were secretly a Southern sympathizer (as was Mrs. McPheeters), the federal government, wrote the president, had no business telling churches who should be in their pulpits.

'When an individual, in a church or out of it, becomes dangerous to the public interest, he must be checked; but the churches, as such must take care of themselves,' Lincoln reiterated in a letter to Filley a year later (the McPheeters problem had stubbornly refused to go away). 'It will not do for the United States to appoint trustees, supervisors, or other agents for the churches ... I will not have control of any church on any side. Yours, respectfully, A. Lincoln.'

Eventually, more than 100,000 men from Missouri (including 8,000 African-Americans) served in the Union Army. Another 90,000 served in the state militia, loyal to the Union. And nearly 30,000 men of Missouri fought with the Confederates. On 11 January 1865, three months before the war ended, a constitutional convention convened by the state legislature and meeting in St. Louis's Mercantile Library Hall, officially abolished slavery in Missouri by a vote of 60 to four. At last the war was over. Missouri, the scene of bitter fighting, had, nevertheless, remained in the Union, one of five border slave states to do so.

The normal rhythms of life resumed. Like the city of St. Louis itself, the Davis firm prospered in the post-Civil War expansion of America's West. And it was not alone. Many other wholesale dry goods firms in the city were thriving.

The city's wholesale dry goods district had moved up from the river to Washington Avenue, and it was here, on the northwest corner of Washington and Fifth Street (later Broadway) that Samuel C. Davis & Co. constructed a new five-storey building in 1871-73. It was 'the most imposing structure in St. Louis', proudly, if not exactly impartially, proclaimed an anniversary pamphlet published by the firm a few years later.

The new building had five elevators and, on its two outfacing sides, 'a remarkable expanse of window surface'. These windows, along with high ceilings and electric lights (powered by an engine in the basement), made the store the 'best lighted building in the city', important, of course, when customers were choosing which fabrics to buy for their retail stores or clothing factories. 'Delicate tints require a pure, steady and abundant light to distinguish them.'

From the new building poured forth a cornucopia of goods to be shipped by boat, train and wagon to stores and manufacturers in 25 states, as far north as Minnesota and as far south as Texas, as far east as Ohio and as far west as California.

Dress fabrics of gingham, satin and pongee; upholstery fabrics of silk brocade, mohair plush and jute velour. Brussels lace for curtains, mousseline for nuns' veiling, worsted damask for church cushions. And from the fourth floor notions department, sewing baskets, ribbons, buttons, hoop skirts, umbrellas, perfume, clocks, violin strings and harmonicas. (The grocery and shoe departments had long since been sold.) The firm had branch offices in Boston, New York, Paris, Manchester, England, and Aachen, Germany. It employed 135 people.

In St. Louis there was a certain social pecking order depending upon where a family's money came from, and today's newcomers became tomorrow's old guard. 'Beaver-skinning, real estate speculation and banking, in that order, were genteel sources of income', St. Louis historian James Neal Primm would later write. 'The grocery trade and iron-smelting were all right it one's grandfather had started them; but lager beer would never do.'

The Davis family might not include any French trappers but its burgeoning fortune rested on more than just hoopskirts and harmonicas. John Davis had extensive investments in real estate and banking. His property holdings in St. Louis alone were estimated a few years later at more than $1 million, including the store. There were also real estate holdings in Chicago, Boston and New York.

He was a director of several banks, railroads and a company that built bridges across the Mississippi River. It was said, with admiration, that he would not agree to become the officer of any corporation unless his holdings were significant.

Of course, all over the country shrewd businessmen were amassing wealth in the laissez-faire, expansionist climate of late 19th-century America. 'Robber Barons' reporters and historians would later call the unprincipled rogues among them. In St. Louis the pejorative term was 'The Big Cinch' for those who bribed officials, rigged contracts and otherwise happily gouged each other and the public. John T. Davis, however, seems never to have been listed among them. Despite his wealth, his good name seemed to remain unsullied.

He had the reputation of being a man of modesty and compassion. The specifics of his charities, however, like the specifics of his financial holdings, he kept private. What was known was his great interest in and support of his school, the growing Washington University, and his church, the Second Baptist.

In 1882 Sam Davis, the firm's founder, died in Boston, and his son, John Davis, officially took over as head of the company. A year earlier, in 1881, Maria's father, Oliver Filley, had died in New Hampshire. After having gone West to make their fortunes, both of Dwight Davis's grandfathers had returned to the East Coast of their boyhoods for their final years.

CHAPTER 2

'O QUEEN OF SCHOOLS'

For nine years the large clock high atop the imposing, three-storey, no-nonsense brick building at the corner of Washington Avenue and 19th Street had been monitoring the arrival of students. Some tardy, some prompt. Some reluctant, some eager. And now in September 1888, young Dwight Davis joined the 350 boys who climbed the stone steps each weekday morning to enter St. Louis's Smith Academy.

The academy, a preparatory school affiliated with Washington University, only recently had begun admitting boys younger than 11. (Dwight had turned nine earlier in the summer.) And then, only if they had 'sufficient knowledge of reading and writing to enable them to commence the study of Arithmetic and Geography'. These young scholars were to be 'placed under the immediate charge of competent ladies', said the school's catalogue, possibly to reassure concerned mamas that their small sons would be eased gently into the sometimes gruff male academic world.

The school was just a few blocks' walk from the Davis home at 2123 Lucas Place. John Davis, Dwight's father, served on the school's corporation board. Dwight would spend seven years here.

In 1879 the academy had taken the name of St. Louis businessman James Smith, donor of funds for the present building. However, the academy, like Washington University, had actually been founded in the 1850s by William Greenleaf Eliot, a respected St. Louis Unitarian minister and educator.

The school would later be saluted in a class graduation poem by Eliot's grandson, Thomas Sterns Eliot, who was in the Smith Academy class ten years behind Dwight Davis but whose older brother, Henry Ware Eliot Jr., was in school with Davis. Wrote young T. S. Eliot, in one of the poem's 14 stanzas:

We go; like flitting faces in a dream;
  Out of thy care and tutelage we pass
  Into the unknown world – class after class,
  O queen of schools a momentary gleam,
  A bubble on the surface of the stream,
  A drop of dew upon the morning grass.

The school's effect on Eliot, however, was anything but 'momentary'. Many years later, when the celebrated poet revisited his home town, he would say that he received the most important part of his education at Smith Academy.

The Eliot family motto was *Tace et fac*, 'Be silent and do'. If indeed William Greenleaf Eliot, who died in 1887, had woven this motto into the fabric of the school's culture, it may not have been particularly helpful to his grandson, the future poet who was, after all, expected to communicate, not be silent. But it may have been perhaps instructive and reassuring to Dwight Davis, who was, by most accounts, shy, quiet and reserved, at least later in life. Two other of William Greenleaf Eliot's laws were self-denial and unselfish service to the community. Though there seemed to be no particular trace of the first in Dwight Davis's later life, a seed of the second of these – public service – may well have been planted at Smith Academy.

Dwight, the young student, was particularly strong in geography, sometimes a bit shakier in arithmetic. In addition to launching young minds on a course that would lead eventually to Macaulay, Cicero and Herodotus, Smith Academy cared about the development of young spines. Boys were admonished not to rest their feet upon the rungs of chairs and to stand in a respectful attitude when reciting.

The informality of the deportment and posture of the student body, in fact, had been a cause of concern to an earlier chancellor of Smith Academy, who had come from Phillips Exeter in the East. 'The students are mostly from St. Louis, and some of them have been accustomed to bring altogether too much of the democracy of their homes and of the streets into the school-room,' he wrote a friend at his former school. 'It is a new revelation to their parents that their sons are my boys during school hours, and that they cannot leave their classrooms without my permission, even though a carriage and servant may be waiting particularly for them at the gate.'

Later there seemed to be a prickly regional pride in the school's vision of its educational mandate. 'We are not dominated by any eastern Universities, and ask of them neither direction nor dictation,' emphasised a school pamphlet. 'Our business, briefly stated, is to prepare the boys of St. Louis to pass any university examinations anywhere.'

By the time Dwight Davis was in his final year, tuition had risen to $75 for each of two five-month terms. Despite continued prosperity and obvious affluence, the Davis family was 'careful' with its money. Education, of course, was on the list of worthy expenditures. Dwight's two older brothers had preceded him to Smith Academy before heading east to Harvard. It was said that though the girls of St. Louis found the Davis boys great fun and good dancers, they had trouble getting girls to accompany them to one of the young set's favorite dance pavilions in town. Everybody knew that if you went with one of the Davis boys you had to come home early because they were only given enough money to take their dates on streetcars – and the last streetcar left the pavilion at 11 p.m.

Stinginess was a family characteristic which later generations would laugh about. The story was told about the time old Sam Davis had been extremely ill, yet was able to rouse himself long enough to scold the nurse for giving him his medicine out of a good silver spoon rather than a plain everyday one.

St. Louis continued to expand. There had even been a movement in the late 1860s, more or less serious, to move the nation's capital from Washington DC to the more central location of St. Louis. (Congress was not convinced.) Dwight Davis was growing up in a city that saw itself as a national power, a comer, even if it had not been able to overtake its great rival Chicago as leader of the country's midsection. In 1866, following the Civil War, the population of St. Louis had been 204,327. By 1890 the population had more than doubled to 451,770. St. Louis was now the nation's fourth largest city, after New York, Chicago and Philadelphia.

But growth – in population, in commerce – had its downside. Noisy streetcars, crowded neighbourhoods and above all, smoke. This was soft coal country. Like other cities in the Ohio and Mississippi valleys, St. Louis was fueling its drive forward with soft, cheap bituminous coal. Train engines and factory smokestacks coughed out the black stuff. It darkened the limestone and granite of proud new buildings downtown. It settled on clotheslines of drying laundry and in the nostrils of sleeping children. The cities of the plain 'are more or less enveloped in smoke', said *Harper's New Monthly Magazine* in 1884, 'pouring forth vapours as if they were but the mouth pieces of some fiery subterranean activity'.

Hyperbole, perhaps, but it was nevertheless time, decided many wealthy St. Louis families, to move again, away, if possible, from the centre city's commerce. There was, of course, a certain irony to this. 'Private streets were introduced to provide [the] mercantile elite protection from the uncontrolled spread – blighting, noxious and foreign – that their industry had generated,' commented a later architectural historian.

Lucas Place might be conveniently close to young Dwight's school, but the Davises decided to move farther west in the city. Their new home would be built in an area where two private streets were being developed in a one-time cattle pasture just north of the city's enormous 1,400-acre Forest Park. Along the area's eastern edge ran the unpaved road called Kingshighway, a remnant of the city's early days as a French settlement when this 'royal' road separated the king's lands from those farmed in common by the villagers.

The new enclave was called Westmoreland Place and Portland Place, and it consisted of six city blocks. John Davis bought three adjoining lots on the north side of Westmoreland Place and three more just behind these on the south side of Portland Place. It was the largest chunk of contiguous pieces of property owned by one person in the new enclave. With the purchase came the signing of lengthy covenants which would, hoped property owners, protect the area from unwanted encroachments of the outside world. 'A private place is not created unless the creators are interested in protecting the welfare of the homeowners, and the welfare of the residents of Westmoreland and Portland was not left to chance,' commented Julius Hunter, a later historian of the area.

Unlike Lucas Place with its small gardens and tall, narrow houses which still clung close together almost in East-Coast row house style, Westmoreland and Portland would eventually have many houses which could only be described as palatial. And in an area of grand houses, the Davis house would be among the grandest.

In 1892, as the typical, steamy St. Louis summer moved into fall, work was well underway on the Davis house at 17 Westmoreland. It was the ninth home to be constructed of the 90-odd houses that would eventually be built on the two private streets. Next door, at 21 Westmoreland, was the area's very first house, a sombre, stolid, rather plain brick Queen Anne-style house designed by architects Peabody, Stearns and Furber for stockbroker/banker Henry Newman. The same architectural firm had designed John and Maria Davis's house, but the two structures could not have been more dissimilar.

The Davis house was an Italian Renaissance palazzo-style residence, a fashion that had become popular for mansions on the East Coast during the past decade. The elegant, three-storey building had tall curved windows along the second floor. On the first floor, in the front, a central loggia with three graceful arches stretched between the extending east and west wings. The vault ceiling of the loggia was covered in a patterned mosaic.

The house was built of Missouri granite. The blocks of granite were not rough-faced and grey like those used in some of the other houses (and in the Davis stable). Instead, the long blocks of stone had been sawn smooth so that the house gleamed a distinctive, soft pink. (This pinkness was eventually darkened, of course, by smoke from neighbourhood chimneys as well as the heavily soot-laden air from the rest of St. Louis, which had the effrontery to drift over into this rarefied area.) Sawing the granite had been spectacularly expensive; part of the reason, some would say later, that this was probably the most expensive house to be built in Westmoreland and Portland Places.

Through his architects, John Davis also contracted with the firm of landscape architect Frederick Law Olmsted, most famous for his design of New York City's Central Park. By early 1894, Olmsted, Olmsted & Eliot – in recent years Frederick had turned much of the firm's work over to his sons – had landscaping designs ready. John Davis, however, was not to see the maturing through the years of the formal flower beds outside the dining room, the massed plantings in the front, and the trees on the side lawn of his new home. At sunrise on 13 April 1894, he died in his home on Lucas Place.

Davis had been at his desk at the Samuel C. Davis & Co. on Saturday, just six days earlier, and then had ridden out to see how the Westmoreland Place house was progressing. The following day he had become acutely ill and had gone into a coma on Thursday, the day before he died. For some time, it was learned, he had been suffering from Bright's Disease, a kidney ailment. He was 49 years old and his youngest son, Dwight, was 14.

The funeral was held on Sunday afternoon at the Second Baptist Church, with Dwight, his eldest brother John T. Jr., and his uncle John Filley among the family members in the front pews with Maria Davis. Sam Davis, her middle son, who had graduated from Harvard a year earlier, was touring Europe and had been cabled the news.

The Gothic limestone church, in which John Davis had been an active member, was crowded, with an overflow of attendees even outside in the churchyard. Twenty-one honorary pallbearers and eight active pallbearers (the latter all heads of departments at Davis Co.) accompanied the flower-covered coffin to the front of the church. The choir sang 'Watchman, Tell Us Of The Night' and the two Davis boys heard the minister talk about their father's charity and religious life.

Clubs and organizations to which Davis had belonged passed laudatory memorial resolutions. His death was 'a calamity' for the people of St. Louis, said the resolution passed by standing vote of the board of governors of the St. Louis Club, of which Davis had been president. Among other things, the resolution mentioned that he had been 'fortunate in his domestic life to an uncommon degree'.

A letter in the newspaper from a Davis acquaintance extolled the deceased's personal character. 'The refinement of his tastes sprang less from the cultivation of his intellect than from the unblemished purity of his heart. His speech was blameless, his imagination clean; I do not know how he used his fortune, I do know how he used his character. He helped create in this great city an atmosphere of simple manliness, integrity and spiritual purity.'

About that fortune of 'the merchant prince' there had been much speculation in the newspaper obituaries. Business associates were quoted as valuing the investments, the extensive real estate holdings (in St. Louis, Chicago, Boston and New York) and the Davis Co. and its merchandise at somewhere between $15 and $20 million. The morning and evening newspapers agreed that he was, in fact, the richest man in the state of Missouri.

After some speculation around town about whether or not a will existed and if it did exist, whether it contained any large public bequests, a will was filed for probate after Sam Davis returned home. The simple one-and-a-half-page document, written in John Davis's own firm, flowing handwriting and dated the previous November, divided his estate between his wife and three sons.

And so, her husband of 27 years suddenly dead before his 50th birthday, Maria Filley Davis picked up the pieces of her life and proceeded on. She moved into the magnificent mansion on Westmoreland Place and her youngest son entered his final year at Smith Academy. Much of the new area was still barren and empty, though young, spindly trees and a few bushes had been planted in the central parkways which ran down the middle of both broad streets. But construction continued, houses were completed and more families moved in.

As a widow, Maria Davis would not feel isolated in the neighbourhood. Already living there was plucky Corinne Dyer, from one of the old French families, who had built 38 Westmoreland for herself and her six children only three years after her husband died. A half-dozen or so other widows also had moved (or would soon move) into the new area. 'In some cases,' pointed out historian Julius Hunter, 'they had brought substantial family fortunes to their marriages.' They might be in mourning, but they could still have coffee together.

And there was family nearby. Maria's younger brother, John Filley, had built a house in the next block at 40 Westmoreland for his wife and three children. And her sister Ellen (who had married John Davis's cousin Tilden Richards) had a son Dwight's age who came to live at 17 Westmoreland for part of the year the two boys were in the sixth and final year at Smith Academy. There was, of course, plenty of room.

Maria also kept busy with the St. Louis Woman's Club and the Wednesday

Club. Such organizations – sometimes community-service oriented, sometime earnestly literary and cultural – responded to yearnings for intellectual stimulation in an era when women of a certain class were often expected to limit their interests to family, home and church. A 'window' in Sarah's tent, a member called a similar club in a similar Midwestern city. Also, it was decided that Dwight, who had graduated from Smith Academy in the spring of 1895, would not head for Harvard right away (he had just turned 16 that summer) but would live at home another year and enroll in the freshman class of nearby Washington University.

In the summer, when St. Louis turned limp in the humid, river-bottom heat, Maria Davis and her youngest son, Dwight, headed east to the Atlantic Ocean. For several seasons she had been meeting her Boston sister-in-law, the widow of John Davis's older brother Sam, in Magnolia, Massachusetts. Magnolia, a small resort town popular with a number of St. Louis families, was on the North Shore, just north of Manchester-By-The-Sea, Massachusetts. The area was sometimes called Boston's Gold Coast. Maria's sister, Jeannette Morton, with her children, often spent summers there as well, and they, like other young members of the family, were delighted when Dwight's older brother Sam would arrive aboard his large boat and take everyone out for a cruise.

The Davises stayed at the Oceanside, a huge, billowy Victorian juggernaut of a hotel with shingled turrets and a veranda one-sixth of a mile long. There, one could stroll, enjoy the brisk, cool breezes and greet summer friends – possibly Loose, the biscuit king from Chicago or members of the Heinz family from Pittsburgh. All this was fine enough for older ladies but how was a growing, active teenage boy to pass the summer?

As a matter of fact, this was lawn tennis country, this stretch of summer resorts northeast of Boston, running from Nahant up to Gloucester on Cape Anne. After all, there were those who insisted that it was in Nahant in the summer of 1874 that tennis had first been introduced to America. It was then, many claimed, that 22-year-old James Dwight of Boston and Harvard, had laid out a court on the front lawn of the Nahant house of his uncle, William Appleton. James Dwight and his cousin, Fred Sears, wanted to try out the racquets and hard rubber balls from a boxed set of Major Walter Wingfield's new game *Sphairistike* (Greek for 'ball games') or lawn tennis, which had been purchased for the Appletons by their son-in-law in London.

Others claimed, just as stoutly, that the game first had been introduced into the United States on Staten Island in 1874 by a young woman named Mary Outerbridge who had picked up her *Sphairistike* set on a trip to Bermuda. Either way, through the 1870s and 1880s the new game was growing in popularity along the East Coast, including Boston's North Shore summer resorts.

On tennis courts at the Oceanside – once the fog lifted, that is – guests could play within sound of the crashing Atlantic breakers a few blocks away. (Said a bit of doggerel in the *North Shore Breeze*, '"The fog has gone" the bell hop cried/The guests ran out the door/One fleeting bit of blue they spied/The fog had gone – for more.') It was at Magnolia in the summer of 1894, the summer that his father died, that Dwight Davis first took up the game.

A left-hander, he learned the sport quickly. Just an easy bicycle-ride away from the Oceanside was the Essex County Club in Manchester, which Dwight's family had joined in 1893, the year two clay (dirt) courts were laid out. After testing the local competition, young Dwight was ready to move further afield. The next summer, 1895, he entered the tournament at the Hotel Wentworth in New Hampshire. George Wright's annual event at the New England resort was extremely popular with players, who were entertained at dances in the evening, and vacationers, who watched the action on the tennis courts from the hotel's long porch. Davis lost in the first round in singles, and he and Beals Wright lost in the preliminary round in doubles.

Apparently unfazed, Davis entered the national championships three weeks later at Newport. The sport was young, the apprentice period was brief and enthusiastic newcomers were welcomed. In fact, 50 of the 82 entries were making their first appearance in the Nationals in 1895 – 'a swarm of youngsters' one tennis writer called them.

Since 1881, the Casino in Newport, Rhode Island, had been the site of the United States National Lawn Tennis Association's men's singles championships. The Casino, built in 1880, was an all-purpose polo, croquet, court tennis and lawn tennis facility for the summer people of this historic town, including the residents of the elaborate 'cottages' that lined the cliffs above the ocean.

Entering the country's top tournament a year after taking up the game was one thing, winning was another. At the 1895 championships, the 16-year-old Davis did not make it out of the preliminary round, though he did win one set. (Joe Wear, a fellow St. Louisan and Smith Academy classmate, made it through to the second round.)

The following summer Davis was back out on the competition circuit again, a little taller and a year older. On occasion, however, there were still flashes of a schoolboy's anger after defeat. After a close, first-round loss in the Canadian Championship to a player from Boston, the frustrated Davis 'could not even remember the score', wrote J. Parmly Paret, a player who also wrote about tennis for a variety of newspapers and magazines. 'He had got over his "grouch" before the evening was over, however,' reported Paret who had begun keeping an eye on the new competitor. 'Young Davis is very strong in overhead play ... To keep him away from the net means to prevent his clever left-handed smasher of which many an older and better player might well be envious.'

Things went a bit better at the US Nationals in 1896 and Davis won his preliminary round match. In the next round, however, he came smack up against the likable Robert Wrenn, a 23-year-old from Chicago and Harvard, who had already won the national singles title twice. At one set all, Davis was within one point of taking the lead but the third set slipped away. Wrenn won the match and went on to win the title.

Two other young players competing in the 1896 championships were Malcolm Whitman from Boston (Brookline, actually) and Holcombe Ward from New Jersey. Whitman, tall, handsome, light-haired and patrician, was the son of a successful textile manufacturer. In the fall he would be returning to Harvard for his sophomore year. His hair as well as his tennis would be immortalized in his class poem:

... His locks are so pretty and curly and fair,
That the girls always watch him at tennis and swear,
They could stand his bad playing just to look at his hair ...

Holcombe Ward, six months older than Dwight Davis, was small, dark-haired, quiet, studious, and the son of a textile merchant. He was from South Orange and had gone to St. Mark's. He and Davis would be members of Harvard's freshman class, the class of 1900, or, as a class scribe would later put it more melodramatically, 'the last class of the dying century'.

CHAPTER 3

A SERVE IS BORN

I n the spring of 1897, as the end of their freshman year at Harvard approached, Dwight Davis and Holcombe Ward were engrossed in a new research project. Their 'laboratory' was not on the campus in Cambridge, however. Their work was being done across the river in Brookline, on the tennis courts of the Longwood Cricket Club.

In practice matches against Malcolm Whitman, Ward was getting beaten regularly. (No surprise, really. Whitman had broken into the USNLTA's rankings of the top ten US players a year earlier.) One reason for his defeats, Ward decided, was the weakness of his (Ward's) serve, which Whitman pounded back at his feet before he could reach the net to volley.

In order to prevent this, Ward began testing a new serve – the ball hit high in the air, with a twist of the racket which would carry the ball from one side of the racquet to the other, and a strong follow through which propelled the server forward towards the net. Davis observed his friend's innovation and pointed out the effective bounce the ball would take if focused power were applied at just the right moment.

As the summer tennis season progressed Ward and Davis continued to tinker with and refine the new serve. When all was working right, the ball's curve through the air and high bounce gave the server more time to rush forward and get positioned at the net. Whitman was already using a 'reverse twist' serve, striking the ball upwards from right to left which made it break to the receiver's right. It was effective, but different from the one Ward and Davis were working out.

In later years tennis writer Parmly Paret analyzed the difference in the three men's twist serve. Whitman's, though slower, still spun the ball so rapidly that it took on an oval shape as it crossed the net and took a high, sharply angled bounce. Ward and Davis used a harder, faster delivery. Ward's serve would break in sharply to the receiver's body, crowding him back from the ball. Davis's serves, because he was left-handed, would bounce off in a still different direction. 'There was a constant hesitation and suspense in waiting to return the ball, as the amount of curve and behavior of the bound varied from time to time,' wrote

Paret, who played all three at Longwood and elsewhere. During doubles matches against Ward and Davis, he added, it was more important than usual to keep track of who was serving.

It could be said, with only slight exaggeration, that what Germany was to music and Italy was to art, Boston/Cambridge was to American tennis in the 1890s. It was the place that a young man with a serious interest could find others of like mind, a place for honing skills, a place of cross-pollination.

Not that tennis was the only factor or even the deciding factor in Davis's choice of Harvard. Both of his older brothers were Harvard graduates, as was his father's older brother, Sam, who had died in Boston before Dwight was born. The faculty roster rang with names of academic brilliance – the philosophers Josiah Royce and George Santayana, for instance, and William James, whose watershed *Principles of Psychology* had been published a few years earlier.

Some at Harvard, however, lamented what they considered an excessive emphasis on science at the expense of the humanities. They saw an intellectual climate dominated by students content with a gentleman's C who spent long weekends in New York or rushing off to 'brutal sport'.

'Art is left to languish and die,' complained Henry Eliot, another of the St. Louis Smith Academy graduates who was also at Harvard. An Eliot cousin would later write that at Harvard the study of classics was dead 'because they never helped to build bridges, manipulate markets or fight battles'.

Harvard might not have suited the Eliots but it apparently did suit Davis. Here he could learn both in the classroom and on the tennis court, though hardly a venue of 'brutal sport'. He went out for baseball and played on the sophomore football team. He joined the right clubs – Institute of 1770, D.K.E., Hasty Pudding, Alpha Delta Phi (serving as president, Ward was treasurer), which made him part of what Harvard historian Samuel Eliot Morison would call 'the Institute-Pudding-waiting club-final club crowd'.

Sometimes it must have seemed questionable to Davis's family whether he was spending much time in the classroom at all. His grades were, in fact, horrible. Nothing in his recommendations from Smith Academy had predicted this. 'An excellent boy, a good student,' one teacher had told Harvard admissions when asked about his character and ability. His Greek teacher at Smith Academy had been a bit more cautious. 'Certainly of average ability, sensible – in spite of his great wealth – of quiet tastes and habit.'

By the end of his sophomore year at Harvard, Davis's gentleman's Cs were keeping company with several Ds and an E. He was informed that he had been dropped to the class of 1901 and would be required to repeat his sophomore year. This was, apparently, not uncommon. There were pre-printed lines on the school's official grade record reading 'Dropped to class of ...' and 'Restored from class of ...'Things were going better for Davis in tennis. The Harvard Lawn Tennis Club, with a motto, naturally, in Latin, had been formed in 1884, and to handle the sport's early burst of popularity 30 courts had been laid out. Nearly half of the courts were sacrificed to the construction of a new residence hall, but by the mid 1890s, when Davis arrived, 22 courts had sprouted on Jarvis Field, making 'no college so rich in tennis courts,' said the USNLTA's *Official Lawn Tennis Bulletin*. By 1900, President Eliot would announced in a report on the university's athletic programs, that 790 men played lawn tennis, as compared with 640 who rowed and about 250 each in baseball and football.

But it was not so much the facilities (since many of the serious students of the game belonged to Longwood anyway) as it was the concentration at the school of good practice partners and match competitors. 'It is extraordinary how Harvard University continues to figure in the distribution of tennis honors,' wrote *Harper's Weekly*. 'It has been so from the days of R. D. Sears down to the triple championship of Bob Wrenn.'

'The Harvard group', writer Paret called Whitman, Ward, Davis, Beals Wright and Leo Ware, in an retrospective article a half century later. He might well have included William Clothier (US singles champion in 1906) who was only two years behind Ward and Davis in college. Paret labeled the Harvard group's years of dominance, 1898-1906, one of the 'two golden ages in the history of American lawn tennis'. Wrote Paret, 'In college at the same time they played constantly with each other and developed features of play that have lasted to this day'. (The other golden age, said Paret, was the Tilden-Johnson era of 1915-1930.)

This, then, in those pre-Harry Hopman, pre-Nick Bollettieri days, was how young American players were learning the game. They played each other incessantly, at practice and on the summer circuit. They played with and listened to five-times doubles champion Dr. James Dwight as he emphasized the serve and playing at the net. Dr. Dwight also had experimented with different training diets; he recommended cold oatmeal between sets. (Though sporadic health problems might have kept Dr. Dwight from practising medicine, they did not stop his participation in tennis.)

Young players dutifully watched their tennis elders at events such as the special exhibition tournament at the Essex County Club where 'old-time tennis cracks' such as Dr. Dwight, Oliver Campbell and Dick Sears, came out of retirement 'to show the present generation how the game was played'. (Former American champion Campbell was an elderly 24 at the time.)

They stood on chairs and perched in trees at Newport (after being ousted in the early rounds) to see over the heads of the crowd and watch the experts on the championship court. They wrote and read about strategy and stroke production in new tennis publications as well as in the general press. They analyzed one another's games and dissected, sometimes in numbing detail, such things as the technical role of shoulder, elbow and wrist. (Ward, for one, kept scrapbooks jammed with articles about technique.)

And constantly they peered across the Atlantic to see who was saying what and how the sport was progressing in Great Britain, the land of its birth. The *New York Times*, for instance, picked up from an English newspaper Dr. Joshua Pim's comments about the level of play in the United States. America had good players, said Pim, but they didn't pay enough attention to the 'fine points' of the game and, besides, their backhands were weak.

In 1898, four years after he had started to play, Dwight Davis's tennis career began to blossom. And it was doubles that first propelled him into prominence. The hours of practice were paying off for Davis and Ward, now a regular doubles team. Early in the season they had gratifying wins in front of their respective 'home' crowds, winning the New Jersey state doubles championships at Orange, Ward's home town, and the Magnolia Invitational on the courts of the Oceanside Hotel, where Davis had learned the game.

In mid-July came their biggest win to date, which sparked a modest controversy. The National Doubles Championship was actually a playoff between the winners of the Eastern doubles tournament and the Western tournament, played in Chicago. Davis and Ward decided to go for the Western title. St. Louis, after all, was legitimately, geographically West (even if St. Louis boys, like Davis, often joined Harvard's Southern Club).

Ward and Davis won, and some people – identifying the players more with college than home town – were outraged. 'East versus West in the double event was a misnomer,' complained *Harper's Weekly*. 'If it is really intended that this event [the national doubles championship] should have a genuine sectional flavor, it is surely absurd that the spirit of the law should be so glaringly violated. Ward and Davis should not have been permitted to enter at Kenwood [Chicago].' (Properly chastened, the pair qualified by playing in the Eastern tournament the following year.)

At Newport in August 1898, the champions of the West met the champions of the East, who just happened to be Whitman and Wrenn. Doubles never had been and never would be Whitman's strong suit. Earlier he had tried to team up with Brookline neighbour and frequent practice partner Leo Ware. They did not 'hitch well', said one observer.

The Westerners won the match and, therefore, the opportunity to challenge the holder of the national doubles title for the past two years, Leo Ware and

George Sheldon. In this, as in many tournaments, the previous year's winner 'stood aside', that is, did not have to play through the ranks but waited to play the winner of the 'all-comers' in the challenge round. This time the more seasoned players won. It was a five-set heartbreaker with Ward and Davis three times coming within one point of winning. The effort was good enough, however, to bring the pair of 19-year-olds to the tennis world's attention. That attention continued through the week as Davis, the tall, dark-haired young unknown from St. Louis and Harvard, steadily played his way up through the rounds of the 1898 National Singles Championship.

The galleries of fluttery, pastel-gowned young socialites and their straw-hatted escorts, buzzed with extra excitement. There would be a new champion this year – one of the four players in the semi-finals: Whitman, Ware, Davis or W. L. Bond from Chicago. Last year's champion, Bob Wrenn, was not defending his title. He had returned only recently from several months in Cuba with Teddy Roosevelt's Rough Riders. In fact, he would not even be showing up at Newport at all, spectators were disappointed to learn, since he had recently been taken ill again with malaria picked up during this Spanish-American War service. However, fellow Rough Rider Bill Larned, a semi-finalist in 1897 and number two in the national rankings behind Wrenn, had come to watch the matches at Newport and received an enthusiastic reception. (Satirist Finley Peter Dunne's fictional Mr. Dooley had even commented that the US Army was made up of 'injineers, miners, plumbers, an' lawn tennis experts'.)

On Sunday, 22 August 1898, a larger crowd than usual appeared at the Casino for the semi-finals. It would be Davis versus the Western 'expert' William Bond and, on the grandstand court, Whitman versus Ware. Despite a splashy win the previous day over veteran Richard Stevens, Davis was considered a slight underdog against the tenth-ranked Bond. But Davis's speed and passing shots held the day. He won in a 'brilliant' four-set match which the *New York Sun* called 'by far, the best sport of the day'.

Monday's final match for the championship pitted Davis against the seventh-ranked Whitman – two members of the 'younger generation of experts', said the *Evening Sun*. (It was probably the first time Davis had been boosted in print into the lofty ranks of 'expert'.)

The match began in late morning. Possibly nervous at playing for the country's championship, Davis made many early errors. At last he settled down, however, and began taking game after game from his more experienced opponent. He drove hard from the backcourt, taking the ball at the top of the bounce with a big sweeping stroke. Whitman liked to follow his serve into the net, but Davis's overhand twist motion (later generations would call this top spin) made the ball difficult to volley as it dropped suddenly just inside the lines. One side, then the other side. When Whitman did make a return, Davis often rushed to the net and smashed it.

Three games all, then 4-3, 5-3 and Davis had won the first set 6-3. He then took the first game of the second set – seven games in a row. The large crowd, sniffing an upset, cheered as the scorer hung up blue ball after ball on Davis's side of the scoring rack. By the end of the first set, the steady, conservative Whitman was muttering under his breath, exhorting himself to stay with his own calculatedly cautious game, to continue to follow his serve into the net and to wait for this flurry of 'miracle' shots to pass.

While Davis's hot streak lasted, said one seasoned observer, no one could have stopped him, 'not even Wrenn or Larned'. Whitman later would call this 'six of the most perfect games from the back of the court I have ever seen'. But like a spent rocket, the brilliant display suddenly sputtered out.

Shots that Davis had earlier placed so surely, now plowed into the net or out of bounds. And the more the younger player pressed, the more errors he made. Whitman won the next three sets and the match, 6-2, 6-2, 6-1. 'It is here that Whitman's skill lies,' wrote Holcombe Ward a few years later. 'While he himself does not seem to be playing especially well, it is always his opponent who is playing poorly, and who is throwing the match away on what seem to be inexcusable errors.'

Could Davis 'have combined the length and pace of his strokes against Stevens and the accuracy and steadiness of his play against Bond, the result of the match might have been much different', said one press report. 'But Davis is a very young player and this is his first big championship match.'

The *New York Journal* was not as charitable. The match for the singles title, which took less than two hours, 'was distinctly poorer' than that of the previous year, said its article the following day. Whitman, 'a new star ...' on the 'lawn tennis firmament', had not even had to play his best game since Davis was so erratic and unsteady.

Sweet vindication for Davis, however, came two months later at the Intercollegiate tournament at New Haven. This respected tournament, begun in 1883, was having trouble even getting many schools to enter because of Harvard's power. In the first round Whitman and Davis again faced each other.

After losing the first set, Davis, ever the risk-taker, pounded Whitman with fast, deep drives that this time stayed in. He finished off the final set 6-0 by returning Whitman's last serve with what the *New York Sun* called a nervy, punishing 'ace' – a term used for any clean winner, not just a serve. It was a 'disastrous end for his [Whitman's] highly successful season', said the newspaper. (Leo Ware actually went on to take the title in four sets, defeating Davis who apparently had injured his foot.)

At season's end Whitman was ranked number one among American players, and Davis, who had started the year ranked 22nd, was ranked fourth. And though Davis's ranking would climb to second in 1899 and 1900 (behind Whitman), and though, in the spring of 1899, he would be regarded by some experts as the most promising of all the younger generation of players, he would never again, as it turned out, get as close to winning the American singles championship as he did in 1898.

Doubles, though, that would be a different story.

CHAPTER 4

THE 'OULD MUG' SPAWNS A CUP

E arly in the 1899 tennis season the doubles team of Holcombe Ward and Dwight Davis received a scolding.

It seemed that a few weeks earlier, at the conclusion of their third year at Harvard and immediately following the Massachusetts State Championships, Davis had invited Ward to come along on a three-week cruise on the 70-foot schooner his brother had chartered. That meant three weeks away from tennis courts. This was the reason, one publication grumbled, that 'the famous colt team from Harvard' seemed out of practice at Orange, New Jersey. (Nevertheless, they managed to avoid losing any of their matches.)

After a few weeks back on land, however, they soon regained their doubles form, with wins at Magnolia, Longwood (the Eastern Doubles title) and Southampton. Davis won the singles competition at the first two tournaments as well. As always, Ward and Davis continued to look for ways to give their doubles game an edge. They would spend hours drilling on their specialties, the high, offensive lob, hit with 'back-twist' to make the ball drop just inside the baseline, or 'stop-volleys' which dropped a ball cold, right on the other side of the net. This was, of course, particularly effective against backcourt players.

It paid off in August at the nationals at Newport. Ward and Davis won their first national title, the US doubles championship, defeating Leo Ware and George Sheldon, the pair who had ousted them a year earlier.

After Newport, *American Lawn Tennis* looked at the new national doubles champs and suggested that other doubles teams also pair up early in the season and play the whole summer together. 'We do not recall any other holders of the double championship who have shown such excellent teamwork or who have developed the possibilities of the double game so far.'

As new kings of the hill, Ward and Davis were both asked to write about their approach to the doubles game. The two best returns of service, wrote Ward in William Patten's *Book of Sports*, were a high lob over the server's partner's head or 'some sort of a "drop" stroke' to the server. 'Return the ball at the server's feet, follow it to the net and kill the server's necessarily weak return.'

Wrote Davis in a long article in *Golf and Lawn Tennis*, 'A general rule, which of course will be changed to suit different conditions, is to keep the same distance between you and your partner all the time; for instance, if your partner is driven out to the side of the court five or six steps, follow him up, and thus protect his court for him until he can get back into position.'

Davis also touched on the psychological as well as the technical: 'Study your partner's every expression. Learn just what to say to him at the right time and have perfect trust and confidence in him. If he is nervous, overconfident, or indifferent, speak to him quietly and try to conquer these moods.' (A British writer, poking fun at these earnest comments in a London tennis magazine, lost his rhetorical edge by getting his Dwights mixed up and erroneously crediting the comments to Dr. James Dwight.)

At the 1899 national championships, Davis did not fare as well in singles. He lost a chance to challenge Whitman again for the championship by going down to defeat in the final round at the hands of none other than the dapper, mustachioed 29-year-old writer/player, Parmly Paret. Nevertheless, many predicted great things for the 'strapping, kindly-looking' young Davis, who had 'a bounding elasticity in his step, a firm grip in his hand'. He might be generally serious and reserved but that reserve disappeared on the tennis court. 'The Harvard Cyclone', one sports writer would dub him as he and his 'slam-bang aggressive' style of tennis exploded into the top ranks of US tennis players.

Also in 1899, Davis won the US National Intercollegiate title both in singles and (with Ward) in doubles. These collegiate wins (and the new national doubles title from Newport probably didn't hurt) at last brought tennis a measure of the respect Harvard traditionally paid to higher profile campus sports such as football. Both Davis and Ward were voted that most coveted Harvard symbol, an H. A small H, to be sure (though a major H would eventually be awarded retroactively to Intercollegiate tennis winners), but size didn't matter. The pair 'took a vicious pleasure' in wearing their white sweaters with the small red H, especially when Mac Whitman and Leo Ware were around, Ward reported later, 'as they had defeated us in two previous Intercollegiates'.

Davis's tennis might be thriving but some were becoming concerned about the overall health of the game. Tennis in America, after a first rush of interest following its introduction in the mid-1870s, had dropped in popularity. Some claimed it was that other new outdoor passion, golf, that had stolen the affection of the sporting crowd. Whatever the reason, by 1899 membership in the United

States National Lawn Tennis Association had dropped from a high of 106 clubs to just 56.

Now, at the end of the 1899 season those who cared about the new game thought that a series of matches between outstanding young players on the East and West Coasts might be just the thing to freshen interest in the sport. Therefore, Dwight Davis, Holcombe Ward and Malcolm Whitman, plus 19-year-old Beals Wright who also played regularly at Longwood and was Interscholastic champion, had all headed for California in August 1899, shortly after the conclusion of the national championships at Newport.

Accompanying them was Beals Wright's father, George, formerly a famous shortstop for the Cincinnati Red Stockings, the country's first all-professional baseball team. When the team's manager, George's older brother, had moved the team east, George had become a Boston Red Stocking. These days George Wright ran a Boston-based sporting goods firm, Wright and Ditson, which billed itself as 'the largest makers of lawn tennis supplies in the world'. Among its products was the *Longwood* racquet, which sold for $4.

The matches at the Hotel Del Monte in Monterey, California, in early September were immensely successful. The Easterners were quickly invited to travel up the coast and play more matches in Oregon, Washington and British Columbia. Finally, however, it was time to head back East. Harvard's fall term would begin 28 September. Davis and his teammates boarded the train for the long trip back to Boston impressed with the goodwill, good fellowship and enthusiasm for the game of tennis produced by these matches between East and West Coast teams.

Onto the fertile ground of these warm, positive feelings about the benefits of inter-regional athletic competition fell seeds from another important sporting event. Newspaper readers everywhere, including Dwight Davis, were avidly following the preparations for the competition between England's *Shamrock* and the United States's *Columbia* for the venerable yachting prize, the America's Cup.

Interest, that late summer of 1899, was particularly high. The previous America's Cup competition in 1895 had been an unsavory event, marred by disputes and allegations of cheating on both sides. A 'fluke, foul and fizzle', said the press. Everyone, including the sporting public, seemed eager for the 'magic' to return to the cup. An 1899 event that was particularly exciting and sportsmanlike would wipe away this temporary tarnish from the famous silver flacon.

Columbia had been launched in June 1899, at Bristol, Rhode Island. Upwards of five thousand spectators had been on hand to see the big, pristine white hull, bedecked with flowers from stern to hawse pipes, slowly slide into the water in the summer evening twilight.

Owner of the *Shamrock* was a colorful, competitive Irishman who had made his fortune in the tea trade and was a pal of the Prince of Wales. His name was Sir Thomas Lipton, 'Sir Tea', as he was sometimes waggishly called. 'I think I'll have a shot at the ould mug,' he was reported to have told friends. The 51-year-old Sir Thomas (his title was all of a year old) had not been a racing yachtsman though he did own the *Erin*, a fine steam yacht. Nevertheless, he was the very picture of nautical style, with his natty blue, spotted tie, his bushy moustache, his yachting cap jauntily angled just so. Lipton had lived and worked in the United States for several years as a boy. He knew and liked America and Americans and they, him.

At last, in early August, the *Shamrock* left the waters of the Clyde and sailed for New York. With towing help from the steamer *Erin* and strengthened by a temporary protective girdle of braces and stringers, the *Shamrock* crossed the Atlantic in a record 15 days. America was delighted to have Lipton arrive. He and the *Erin* were even asked to lead one of the lines of ships in a parade up the Hudson River as part of the tumultuous welcome home festivities for Admiral Dewey and the heroes of the Spanish-American War's Battle of Manila Bay.

In early September, at about the same time that Dwight Davis and his fellow tennis players were making the long train trip back across the continent, the official American trials were being held. It was perfunctory, really. The *Columbia* was the only new boat built in the US to defend the cup. As expected, the *Columbia* won the official trials, twice beating *Defender*, leftover from 1895.

The actual challenge races were held in mid-October over a course out to the Sandy Hook lightship, 30 miles off the tip of Long Island. *Columbia* won the first race. *Columbia* won the second race. And three days later, on Friday, 20 October 1899, a young Italian inventor named Marconi, aboard a steamer at sea, used his newfangled invention to send to newspaper men waiting on shore the first news bulletin ever transmitted by wireless telegraph. *Columbia*, he reported, had won the third race. The cup would stay in the United States.

Lipton was gracious in defeat and was quickly proposed for membership in the New York Yacht Club. His disgruntled predecessor four years earlier had complained, 'I am not sure that I like international contests ... I think they tend to demoralize sport by turning it into a serious business in which national prestige is at stake, and to convert amateurs, playing a game for the game's sake, into professional specialists struggling for their country's sake'.

But Lipton obviously did not feel this way about international competition – and neither did young Dwight Davis, who, like thousands of other Americans, had been avidly following the newspaper accounts of the defence of the America's Cup. If an international trophy could spark such immense interest in yacht racing, could not an international trophy do the same for tennis? Davis, already impressed with how the Pacific Coast tennis matches had strengthened relationships between East and West, now 'put two and two together', as he would later explain it.

'If team matches between players from different parts of the same country arouse such great interest and promote such good feeling,' he thought, 'would not similar international contests have even wider and more far-reaching consequences?' (George Wright, in his later years, would say that he too had suggested a trophy to young Dwight Davis – whom he knew could well afford it – on the western trip. The idea could well have gotten some general discussion among the travelling party.)

And there may have been other subconscious influences. Just three years earlier, in 1896 (after a slight pause of 1,500 years), a modern revival of the ancient Olympic games had been held in Greece. Another Olympics was scheduled for the summer of 1900 in Paris. The 1899 Paris Exposition Year also seemed to be inspiring various athletic teams to travel overseas. This 'rage', commented the *New York Times*, extended even 'to the bowlers of the country'. Certainly the whiff, if not of sporting socks, of interest in international sporting competition was in the air.

When he arrived back in Boston, Davis confidentially talked over his idea for an international tennis trophy with Dr. James Dwight, his tennis friend and mentor and president of the 18-year-old United States National Lawn Tennis Association. At age 47, the short, slim, dapper Dr. Dwight was the grand old man of the sport in America – if such a young sport could be considered to have a grand old man. Having competed in England himself ('the plucky American' English newspapers called him), he had been pushing the cause of international tennis competition for several years.

English players, as well, had occasionally competed on this side of the Atlantic, beginning in 1880 when an Englishman, O. E. Woodhouse, travelling in America, unexpectedly wrote from Chicago to see if he could play in the Championship of America at the Staten Island Cricket and Baseball Club. Initial questions about the level of the visitor's game were resoundingly answered. He surprised the Americans with his unusual new overhand serve and won the tournament.

In fact in 1897, two years before Dwight Davis's America's Cup-inspired epiphany, Dr. Dwight had written the English Lawn Tennis Association saying that the USNLTA would contribute to transportation costs if some leading English players wished to come to play in America. That this might be interpreted as a slight smudge on the purity of the sport bothered him just a bit, however. 'I own I have always had great doubts of the propriety of paying expenses of players, but to the extent named, we are willing to go,' he added.

Three had come from England later that year. Harold Mahony (an Irishman), Dr. W. V. Eaves (born in Australia) and H. A. Nisbet all had won or been runners-up at Wimbledon. Eaves and Nisbet ended up playing each other in the finals of the US Nationals at Newport, having mowed down all Americans except for Bob Wrenn who defeated Eaves in the challenge round. There was no question, therefore, about Dr. Dwight's enthusiasm for Dwight Davis's suggestion of an international trophy for competition, this time on a formal team basis, country versus country.

First public announcement of the offering of a 'perpetual challenge cup' for a new competition between countries came on Saturday, 13 January 1900. But there was an element of mystery. In a long, enthusiastic article on its sports page the *Boston Herald* announced a bit pompously that 'the *Herald* is not at liberty to announce the name of the donor at this time; suffice it to say that he is one of the foremost followers of and participants in the game in this country'. Prophetically (if a bit convolutedly) the paper added, 'When the effects of his generosity are evident in years to come, his rank for this will be even higher than his ability as a player will some day assure him'. Others speculated that USNLTA treasurer Richard Stevens, of Hoboken, was the mystery donor.

Shortly after this public announcement, Dr. Dwight, as president of the USNLTA, sent a letter, dated 16 January 1900, to the secretary of the British Lawn Tennis Association:

Dear Sir,
I beg to call your attention, as Secretary of the L.T.A., to an experiment which we are making that will, I hope, increase the interest in lawn tennis. One of our players here has offered us a Cup, to be a sort of International Challenge Cup. I enclose the conditions in a rough form. I trust that we shall both take a deep interest in them for many years to come.

I am very anxious that some of your better players should make us a visit this summer, and I hope that, should they come, your Association will see its way to challenge for the Cup. You can easily understand that we thought it necessary to require the Governing Association of a country to make the challenge to prevent a series of stray challenges from players good and bad who might be coming to spend a month here. In yachting, the expense prevents the possibility of too much competition for the right to challenge. In lawn tennis it would be different.

I hope, as I said before, that the scheme will prove a success. It might do a great deal for the game here, and possibly even with you it might be a help. In any case I trust you will do what you can to give us a lead in the matter.

Please accept my sincere sympathy and good wishes in your present troubles! [probably a reference to the Boer War]. I have eaten your salt too often not to feel very strongly for the anxiety that you all must feel.

With every wish for better times, Believe me,
Very truly yours,
James Dwight,
Pres. U.S.N.L.T. Assoc.

On 9 February 1900, the annual meeting of the United States National Lawn Tennis Association was held at New York City's Waldorf-Astoria Hotel. Officers re-elected included two Longwood men, Dr. James Dwight (president) and Palmer Presbrey (secretary). Dwight Davis was chosen as a new executive committee member, one of three nationally-ranked players on the five-man committee. In addition to the election, the group had some other business. It was formally presented with a new trophy by Davis, an 'international cup' for tennis competition between nations – a 'blue ribbon trophy of lawn tennis', reported the *Boston Herald*. After much discussion, it was decided that formal acceptance should be left up to the executive committee which, at its meeting on 21 February, duly voted to accept the new trophy. (Interestingly enough, this formal acceptance came more than a month after Dr. Dwight had already written to England.)

Just to get it all set up properly, Dr. Dwight had enlisted the legal advice of no less a person that the recently retired secretary of state (under President Grover Cleveland), his friend Richard Olney, who also happened to be a tennis player. Olney worked with Dr. Dwight, Davis, Ward and Palmer Presbrey in the drafting of the regulations for competition for the new trophy. From England came suggestions from W. H. Collins, president of the Lawn Tennis Association.

Challenge for the cup must come from the governing association of the country challenging, stated the suggested rules presented to the USNLTA. Players must be members of clubs belonging to that association, citizens of the country challenging and amateurs in good standing. In the event of two challenges, the governing association of the challenged country would decide which to accept.

Matches would consist of four singles matches between two players of each country and one doubles match. The doubles teams did 'not necessarily' have to be composed of the people who were playing singles, so therefore a team could consist of two, three or four players. If no country challenged for five years the cup would return to the cup donor – unnamed. This trophy, said the *Herald*, would 'bear the same relation to this sport as the America's Cup to yachting'.

The rules stipulated that a challenge for the cup must be received by 1 May to guarantee acceptance, but by mid-March Dr. Dwight had received back a letter from the English Lawn Tennis Association issuing a challenge. In its lengthy report on this development the *New York Times* now referred to the trophy as the 'Davis International Cup', while an article on tennis in the spring *New York Tribune Illustrated Supplement* shortened it, possibly for the first time, to 'Davis Cup'.

Back in Boston, Dr. Dwight went to work on tournament arrangements. Dwight Davis was taking care of supplying some sort of appropriate silver trophy.

SHAPING THE CUP

A massive gilt statue of an eagle, its wings outspread, perched above the second-floor windows of the building at 147 Tremont Street. It looked as if it might, at any minute, abandon its weighty responsibilities as jewellery store emblem and fly to freedom in the Boston Common across the way. The building was a handsome one – six storeys of limestone, with carved stone arches above the fifth-floor windows and, on top, an ornate frieze. Below the eagle was the name SHREVE, CRUMP & LOW CO, commonly shortened to just 'Shreve's' by the Bostonians who shopped there for elegant brooches, japanned trays, and sterling silverware.

In a city in which antiquity was revered, Shreve, Crump & Low had the proper credentials. The store could trace its history back to a late 1700s watchmaker and jewellery store owner who once had a shop across from Paul Revere's. The Low family were merchants in the China trade; the first Shreve was the son of a sea captain. It was this firm that had supplied the silver vase presented to Daniel Webster by the grateful citizens of Boston in 1835.

By the late 1800s Shreve's was well established as a supplier to Bostonians of the accoutrements of the Good Life. Smart striped awnings shaded the first floor windows on two sides of the building at Tremont and West Streets. It was here in these street level windows that some of the more spectacular items sold by Shreve's were sometimes proudly displayed – tennis trophies, for instance. The large silver Longwood Bowl (valued at $500) had been on view to the public in Shreve's windows. And it was here at Shreve's in the winter or spring of 1900 that the order was placed for Dwight Davis's new international tennis trophy.

Unlike the ewer-shaped America's Cup, the tennis trophies with which Dwight Davis was familiar tended to be either two-handled loving cups or silver bowls, and it was the latter shape – basically a large silver punchbowl – that was decided upon for the new trophy.

Shreve's, however, like many fine jewellery stores, was a purveyor not a manufacturer of elegance. A variety of companies manufactured the jewelled rings and bracelets and the fine porcelain plates which were displayed in the store's low glass counters. And the silver – the gleaming vases, the forks and spoons, the heavy trays, the elegant, swan-neck-spouted teapots, all made from that lustrous, magic and malleable metal, aptly described as 'moonbeam-coloured'.

To make this large sterling silver bowl for the new tennis competition Shreve's selected a firm in nearby Concord, New Hampshire, the William B. Durgin Co. Durgin, though one of the smaller American silver manufacturers (Gorham and Tiffany were the industry leaders), had a strong reputation for quality.

William Butler Durgin, the man, had been born in 1833 at Campton in the foothills of New Hampshire's White Mountains. His father was a farmer, yet farm life held no attraction for young William. Instead, at age 16 he went off to Boston to become apprenticed to the silversmith Newell Harding, the largest spoonmaker in New England. By the early 1850s, with about $200 in savings, plus, possibly, a small loan from his father, Durgin was ready to go into business for himself in his native state.

Durgin headed for Concord, the state capital, a bustling town of 8,500 people, some 50 miles down the Pemigewasset and Merrimac valleys from his birthplace. Manufactured here were stage coaches, most particularly the famous Concord coach, the elaborately trimmed, bright coloured, high-wheeled vehicle used by Wells Fargo and others to open up the American West. Yet despite the coach business and the ample waters of the Merrimac which ran along the western edge of town, Concord was not, nor would it ever be, one of the large, thumping New England mill towns. When William Durgin arrived in town, many of its residents were farmers, and much of the town's commerce was the trading they did along Main Street. It was on Main Street, near the Free Bridge Road, that Durgin first opened a small shop. The year was 1853 and he was 20 years old.

It was not unusual for former apprentices to strike out on their own at an early age, concentrating, like young Durgin, on spoons rather than the more difficult hollow ware which required more elaborate – and expensive – equipment. There had been silversmiths in Concord before, and when Durgin arrived at least two of them were making spoons, though as a sideline to jewellery. Durgin bought their tools and went to work.

Ironically, just as Durgin was getting started, the big firms in the American silver making industry were moving into more advanced production methods for making flatware. By 1854 in Providence, Rhode Island, for instance, John Gorham had installed a drop press powered by steam. But up in Concord, Durgin doggedly worked away using the old methods. It was laborious and slow, emphasised a contemporary magazine article about the early silver industry: 'Two men by exceedingly hard work and sometimes violent exertion could make in a day two dozen of their rough teaspoons, no two of which were alike in shape or weight.'

Despite the relative simplicity of making spoons (compared to making hollow ware), there was still equipment necessary to the forming and working of silver. Some of that equipment was at first too expensive for Durgin to own himself – a pair of rolls, for instance. It was a common sight in Concord to see the young newcomer, a bar of silver over his shoulder, walking down Main Street to Walker's Saddlery Co. There, with the help of a couple of strong local lads, he would flatten the silver into thin sheets using the saddlery company's powerful, hand-turned rollers.

Back in his own shop, Durgin, using the muscles and brawn of 'a good, husky man who could hit straight and true' as one early Durgin worker put it, handled the punches and sledge hammers used in 'bowling up' spoons by hand. His helpers knew him as 'a stickler for the graceful bend and the correct proportion of the handle to the spoon'. He insisted that the bowl of the spoon have the proper thickness at the 'toe' where most of the wear naturally comes. But these workers came along later. At first it was just William Durgin himself, making spoons and then putting on jacket and hat and selling them.

Young Durgin was married in 1854 at age 21, and four years later the first of his children, a son, George Francis, was born. Business prospered as well, with Durgin gaining a reputation for doing work of high quality. In the mid-1850s he leased a lot on School Street and there, within the shadow, almost, of the graceful dome of the New Hampshire State Capitol, built a new small shop. Nine years later that structure too had been outgrown, and a new three-storey brick building was erected at the same location. At street level it had a pressed metal facade of columns and arches painted white, a style popular in town. In large letters above the third floor windows were the words:

DURGIN'S
SILVERWARE MANUFACTORY

At first Durgin used only the basement and part of the first floor, renting out the rest. As business expanded, so did the need of floor space. By the mid-1870s many of the tenants on the lower floors had departed and their space taken over by machines and workbenches and the company's 18 or so workmen.

In the basement were the polishing and finishing rooms. On the first floor, at the rear, silver was melted, rolled, cut and shaped. At the front of the first floor were the engraving department and a large walk-through storage vault with 75 black walnut drawers. Knife blades were plated on an upper floor. And for a time there was, on the first floor, an elaborate sales room with frescoed walls and ceiling.

By this time almost all American silversmiths were using the sterling standard for their silver (seven and a half percent copper). But earlier, Durgin, like other silversmiths, had worked in coin silver (ten percent copper). Occasionally the connection between coin and spoon had been immediate. At one Concord wedding, after the groom had paid the minister 25 silver dollars for his services, the minister turned and gave the coins to the bride as his wedding gift, with the instructions that these be made into spoons. Durgin was happy to oblige.

William Durgin was, according to observers, a shrewd, careful man of good character and habits, doing a good business, with products that enjoyed the best of reputations. He could also be very firm about things he considered important. For one thing, Durgin refused to advertise. The quality of his pieces was enough, he felt, to bring in customers. Another principal: only solid silver would be manufactured in his plant (knife blades, of course, didn't count).

Since the 1840s many American silver makers had been making silver plate – pieces in which thin coatings of silver were transferred by electric current onto a base of another metal, such as copper, tin or nickel. Not Durgin. Around town it was said that, at a time when he could have used the business, Durgin had turned down a $10,000 order because the customer, a Boston department store, wanted silver plate rather than solid silver.

Gradually the Durgin line of goods expanded. Soup ladles and other pieces of flatware were added, as was hollow ware: sugar baskets and gypsy kettles, then teapots, trays and fancy dressing table sets. Later there were even rings and teaspoons made of gold, as well as an extremely popular line of souvenir spoons.

The old 40-ounce iron pot which Durgin himself, and later, apprentices, had used to melt down the silver over a charcoal fire was replaced by new equipment for melting the bullion and converting it into bars. Gradually machinery filled the brick building – finishing lathes and then rolling mills. When the first drop hammer was installed, curious Concord residents came by the factory on School Street to see this marvellously noisy and powerful manufacturing innovation which was speeding up production immensely by allowing the use of dies to do the cutting and shaping formerly done by hand.

In 1876 Concord, like towns big and small all over the United States, celebrated the nation's 100th birthday. An unlikely participant in the town's gala two-mile-long Fourth of July parade was one of Durgin's impressive big rolling mills, ensconced in a place of honour in the red, white and blue bunting-draped Durgin Co. unit.

Engravers, chasers, finishers, apprentices – by 1885 some 60 men filled Durgin's brick building, working at the benches and machines, racing down the stairs at noon and popping out onto School Street like peas out of a pod. Workers chuckled about one of the boys from the polishing room who would eat his lunch on nearby Park Street then saunter over to the fancy Eagle Hotel a block away and pick his teeth on the front steps, as if he had just finished eating there.

At about this time Durgin, whose health was not always of the best, began turning over more and more of the day-to-day management of the firm to his 27-year-old son George, who had started with the company as an apprentice after graduating from Phillips Academy, Andover. George, too, proved to be a skilled, conservative manager, and business continued to grow. Several travelling salesmen were put out on the road, to spread the word about Durgin's quality solid silver, initially to cities along the East Coast and then, later, throughout the rest of the country.

There was a pervasive English influence at Durgin's 'shop' (an English term William Durgin preferred to 'factory'). For a time he insisted on importing stub files from England. However, the most important thing Durgin imported from England was men – die-cutters, engravers, spinners, designers. Though many English craftsmen also worked for other American silver manufacturers, there were enough of them at Durgin's that the company was sometimes known locally as 'the English shop'. For several years Durgin even had a cricket team, disbanded when not enough competition could be located.

One of these overseas recruiting trips occurred in the summer of 1887. In early June Durgin and a company associate sailed for England to hire skilled workmen. After arriving Durgin ran an advertisement for craftsmen and designers in a British newspaper. Among those who responded was a 22-year-old art instructor named Rowland Rhodes.

Rhodes was born in 1865 in the Staffordshire town of Newcastle-under-Lyme. He was the son of a marble mason, a maker of monuments in this industrial town of ironworks, collieries and potteries in the English Midlands. As a boy young Rowland had been allowed to work with his father's tools, and by the time he was 13 he had carved a piece of his own, a Madonna and Child of marble. At the completion of the course at the Newcastle School of Art, the boy was awarded a scholarship to study in London. He attended the National Art Training School (later the Royal College of Art) at the South Kensington Museum (now the Victoria and Albert Museum) where he was awarded, in 1882, the silver Queen Victoria medal.

By the time of William Durgin's 1887 recruitment trip to England, Rhodes had finished the three-year course at South Kensington and was teaching drawing and painting at an institute in the northern industrial Lancashire town of Preston. However, Rhodes had a 'spirit of travel', as his wife was later to put it, and when the American offered him $10 more a week in wages and a fare-paid trip to the United States, the young man accepted.

Rhodes settled into life in Concord, became active in a local Methodist Church (his father had been a lay Methodist minister) and became engaged to a girl from nearby Chichester, New Hampshire. For two years he designed and modelled silver pieces for Durgin but then decided to return to Europe for additional formal training.

In the winter of 1889 Rhodes arrived in France, working first as a labourer at a foundry in order to learn techniques of metal casting and then enrolling at the Julien Academy in Paris. He perfected his French by chatting with the children who played about his studio, and on Sundays he would travel to nearby villages in the picturesque countryside to preach, much as his father had done back in Staffordshire.

Among the works he completed during this period was a two-foot-tall statue of an Egyptian playing the harp, cast in bronze using a new French process. Another life-size plaster work, entitled 'Youth's First Recognition of Love', was exhibited at the Grand Salon in Paris in 1892 and, a year later, in the United States at the Columbian Exposition in Chicago.

In 1892 Rhodes returned to Concord and the Durgin Co. At the time of Grover Cleveland's election as president, leading silver manufacturers in the country were invited to submit designs for new White House silver. Chrysanthemum, an intricate pattern designed by Rhodes for Durgin, was the one selected, winning out over those submitted by other companies, including such industry giants as Tiffany and Gorham.

Yet despite his successes at Durgin and the financial security which this provided, Rhodes still had ambitions to have his own studio. A compromise presented itself. In 1893 he moved to New York, working half the week for Durgin (which now had a New York office) and the other half at his own studio on east 13th Street, two doors from Broadway. A printed announcement was sent out informing the New York carriage trade that 'Mr. Rowland Rhodes (sculptor)' bringing 'letters of introduction and high commendation from some of the most eminent Art Patrons in Europe' was open for business. 'He is now fully equipped and ready to take commissions for sculptural work of the highest grade, Architectural, Figure Work, Portraiture, &c., and respectfully solicits your patronage.'

Alas for Rhodes, the timing was wrong. The second Cleveland administration was a period of economic hard times. Among the things people were not buying was commissioned sculpture. Despite the brave, optimistic announcement, patrons did not appear at the little studio on East 13th Street in sufficient numbers. Two years after arriving, Rhodes told his wife that it was time 'to get in out of the wet for awhile'. The 30-year-old artist, a sturdy man with a square, dependable face edged by a reddish beard, and his patient New Hampshire sweetheart had married on Christmas Day 1894. They returned to Concord in June 1895.

For the next five years Rhodes again designed and modelled silver pieces for Durgin, while continuing with his own art work on the side. Among the projects he had begun was a series of statues depicting famous New England characters. In 1897 the first of these, entitled Cy Prime, was cast in bronze.

Yet despite Rhodes' efforts in sculpture, his dedication to his studio art, his plans for further study in Italy, it was one of his projects for the Durgin Co. which would become (Rhodes undoubtedly would have been astounded to know) the most frequently viewed of any of his works and eventually one of the most famous pieces of silver in the world.

Now, in 1900, Rhodes began work on Dwight Davis's silver bowl. Under Rhodes' practised pencil, the design for the new sporting trophy began to take shape. Squared lines across the top of a piece of white drawing paper marked off the general dimensions of the bowl. Small dots, placed precisely with callipers, staked out the general swell of the side curves. Instead of a smooth rim, the top edge would be gently scalloped by a dramatic Georgian border of clusters of primroses and acanthus leaves, that traditional bit of shrubbery favoured as a decorative detail by English silver designers.

The primrose motif would be repeated around the bottom third of the bowl, this time combined with tiny buds and tendrils, with all descending into a sea foam effect around the foot, or base, of the bowl. Circling the foot would be more clusters of small flowers connected with gentle waves or scrolls. And how much silver would be required for all these fanciful embellishments – and the large bowl which they decorated? In pencil, at the top of the drawing, were preliminary calculations: 186 oz plus 30, for a total of 216. Also written in pencil was the number 414, the Durgin file number for this piece.

Despite the tendrils and shells and primroses, Rowland Rhodes' design was almost Puritanically restrained in comparison to some other trophies of the period. It was an age of trophies and commemorative cups and bowls for all kinds of major and minor occasions – patriotic, romantic, athletic. Designers and silvermakers pushed the compliant metal to decorative extremes.

A few years earlier the *Official Lawn Tennis Bulletin*, had, with only slight hyperbole, gleefully written about the trophies a 'crack' could expect to collect 'monumental vases and ewers, standing precariously on crossed rackets, and chased round with a confusion of nets and balls'. There were, continued the article, 'magnificent soup-tureens, with covers hardly lifted by the figure of a Mercury-like tennis-player violating first principles, with neither feet on the ground nor eye on the ball, unless it were an especially high lob ...' A tennis trophy made by Gorham for the High Rock Club in New York state took its motif from James Fenimore Cooper's *The Last of the Mohicans*: Indian war feathers decorated the rim of the cup.

At the William B. Durgin Co. where Rowland Rhodes was finishing the design for this new international tennis trophy, business was thriving and the firm expanding. In fact, the silver industry in general had been growing all through the last part of the 19th century. For one thing, silver was plentiful. Out in the Nevada Territory in the early 1860s, the bluish sand found at a site claimed, for a time, by a prospector/sheepherder known as 'Old Pancake' Comstock, had turned out to be silver ore. The resulting outpouring of silver from the Comstock Lode, the world's richest silver deposit, and the opening of mines in other areas in western United States meant plenty of raw material for silver manufacturers back east.

Also the latter part of the 19th century was a boom time for the establishment of American fortunes. The Whitneys, the Vanderbilts, the Carnegies and their only slightly less prosperous if more anonymous peers around the country (such as the Davises of St. Louis) were eager to fill their homes with the gleaming pieces of utility and extravagance which Durgin, and other silver companies, produced. The Durgin trademark, a sedate Old English D encased in a simple oval, as 'substantial as the rock ribbed hills' of New Hampshire, as a later observer put it, was becoming known not only in America but abroad.

Now, as the 19th century prepared to roll over into the 20th, there were sometimes as many as 120 employees at Durgin, and extra space had been acquired in the building across the street. (This business of the new century provided a topic for good-natured arguments in the finishing room and other departments: when, exactly, did the new century begin – on 1 January 1900, or 1 January 1901?)

From the one product, spoons, with which William Durgin had first started, the company's line had expanded into a mind-boggling variety of pieces. In some flatware patterns, brides could order 161 different pieces of table silver, including such items as asparagus tongs, terrapin forks and three different sizes of cucumber servers.

So it was here, in the four-storey brick building in the centre of Concord, midst the terrapin forks and bon-bon dishes, that Dwight Davis's trophy began to take tangible shape in metal. The bowl and its base were to be two separate pieces, with the bowl ending in a long plug which fitted snugly down into the base. An experienced 'spinner', probably William Morton, pressed a flat, thick disk of silver against a spinning wooden form. Because of its size, the huge disk needed frequent annealing, and the metal glowed red as heat was applied to keep it malleable. Slowly the shape of a large bowl began to emerge.

Elsewhere in the building other skilled craftsmen converted Rowland Rhodes' pencil lines into engraved, hand-chased and repousséed decorative details. In the casting department liquid rivers of silver were poured into carefully shaped moulds. The resulting large clusters of flowers, leaves and swirls were then applied to the top rim of the bowl and the outer edge of the base. At some point in the process it was decided that some of the decorations on the side of the bowl in the original design would be omitted in the final rendering in silver, leaving a wide area around the curve of the bowl free of decoration. In the finishing shop, workmen scoured, burnished and polished the large bowl to a bright, gleaming lustre.

As the bowl neared completion there was undoubtedly the usual satisfaction in the shop areas as well as in the business office at the front of the building that a large, specially designed order was turning out well. The usual satisfaction but apparently no more than that. Four years later, when a lengthy newspaper article about the Durgin Co. would list the special pieces of which the firm was particularly proud – a Karl Bitter-designed gold cup 'for one of the country's most eminent bankers', a silver prayer book cover for the dowager queen of Italy – no one would think to mention this particular trophy.

At last it was finished, a handsome, two-piece punch bowl, standing 13 inches high, 18 inches across at the top, ten inches across at the base. Stamped on the underside of the base were the marks STERLING and SHREVE CRUMP & LOW CO. and a small eagle. Only the imprinted file number 414B (showing that this was the second part of piece number 414) officially marked its Durgin origins. The inside of the bowl was lightly washed in gold, and around the lip on the inside, were etched, in flowing, Art Nouveau lettering, the words:

INTERNATIONAL LAWN TENNIS CHALLENGE TROPHY
PRESENTED BY
DWIGHT F. DAVIS * 1900

The cup was ready for the 60-mile trip down to Boston and its first appearance on the international sporting stage.

CHAPTER 6

RACQUETS AT THE READY

D wight Davis had managed to graduate with his Harvard class in June 1900 after all. His doubles partner, Holcombe Ward, also received his A.B. degree, but then his timely graduation had never been in doubt. Davis had buckled down in his fourth year (technically his junior year) and actually earned two Bs, neither in economics, however, though this was the academic subject he liked best. The country's future secretary of war did manage to receive a C in military and naval science.

Harvard wits had taken a shot at Ward and Davis and tennis in their traditional class poem:

… The most difficult one of the bard's heavy duties,
Is choosing the first of this class full of beauties,
For all are so handsome and all are so fair,
Which faces are fairest 'tis hard to declare,
Dwight Davis, the tennis Apollo, some think
Is most handsome, but there's other ice on this rink …
There's Holc Ward, the child wonder, who wins every set,
Though his great play in tennis is drives to the net …

Throughout the summer preparations continued for the August international matches. It finally had been decided that Longwood would be the site. Like Longwood Avenue, the Longwood Cricket Club had taken its name from the extensive, 600-acre estate in Brookline and Boston belonging to those eminent and wealthy Bostonians, the Sears family. (This Sears money came from one of the early Boston sailing/merchant fortunes. Proper 19th-century Bostonian eyebrows would have raised slightly at the thought that later generations might think this Massachusetts Sears family had something to do with that other Sears, that mail-order catalogue person from somewhere out west.)

The estate had been developed and named in about 1840 by David Sears, who, as a young man back in 1811, had visited Paris when Napoleon was in power and had become an admirer of the French emperor. The original Longwood was the house, located on the Longwood Plains on the island of St. Helena, in which Napoleon lived in exile until his death in 1821.

In 1877 the Longwood Cricket Club had been formed when some two dozen local cricket enthusiasts began renting this corner of the Longwood estate as playing fields for $40 annually. A year later the club had acquired two sets of tennis rackets and laid out its first grass tennis court. The new sport of lawn tennis had, so to speak, wriggled its head under the cricket club's tent. Appropriately enough, one of Longwood's enthusiastic young players of this new game was Richard D. Sears, grandson of David Sears.

Playing for the United States in the international matches would be the current national singles champion, Malcolm Whitman, and the US doubles champions, Davis and Ward. Davis, ranked number two in the US, would also play the other singles match. Confirming the accuracy of his number one ranking, Whitman had just defeated Davis in the finals for the Longwood Cup.

In the fall Mac Whitman would begin his second year at Harvard Law School. Now that undergraduate days – and frivolities – were behind him, Whitman was under considerable pressure from his father to give up tournament tennis. 'When I was a child I spake as a child … when I became a man I put away childish things,' his father would often intone.

Yet Whitman would be available for the American team because he had marshalled his arguments and convinced his father to let him play the circuit this one final summer season. He already had two legs up on several trophies, he pointed out. A third win would mean permanent possession. Of course, once the senior Whitman had relented, like any proud father he had taken great pride in his son's summer successes, sending him money for celebration parties after important wins.

On Saturday, 4 August 1900, four days before the international matches were scheduled to begin, the Cunard Line's *Campania*, carrying the three-man British team, docked in New York. Only one of the British players who walked down the gangplank had the dashing flair Americans expected to see in international sportsmen. Ernest D. Black, a 27-year-old Scot who now lived in the north of England, was tall, darkly handsome and athletic looking. He sported an imposing, bushy black moustache and had a taste for broad-brimmed, Panama 'Planters'' hats, cocked jauntily up on one side. He was the current champion of Scotland and Yorkshire.

The other two men on the team were shorter and looked more like accountants than sports champions. Herbert Roper Barrett, 26, was, in fact, a London solicitor. Earlier in the summer Roper Barrett (he generally used his middle rather than his first name) had won the Belgian singles championship. But his real game was doubles. This year he and a partner had finished second in the doubles competition of the Lawn Tennis Championships at the All England Lawn Tennis and Croquet Club, that prestigious tournament more simply known by the name of the London suburb where the club was located, Wimbledon.

Oldest and the best known of the trio was Arthur W. Gore, 32. A slim, wiry man, 'Baby' Gore had first played lawn tennis as a child on the sands of the pretty French resort town of Dinard in the late 1870s. Like Black, Gore, too, wore a bold dark moustache, though his was waxed up into small neat curves on the ends. Gore had first competed in the lawn tennis championships at Wimbledon in 1888, and though now, in 1900, his hairline was beginning to recede slightly, his tennis ability was not.

Gore had won the All-Comers at Wimbledon in 1899, only to be beaten for the final championship by one of the famous Doherty brothers, Reggie. Earlier this summer Gore had finished third at Wimbledon (runner-up to Sidney Smith in the All-Comers). Even more significantly, he would go on to win his first English national championship at Wimbledon a year from now, in 1901. One tennis writer later would call him 'a striking instance of lawn tennis longevity'.

Before they left London the three were given a private luncheon by the LTA and presented with white satin caps embroidered with the Royal Standard. They were also given a sendoff in verse, in a parody of Macaulay's 'Horatius at the Bridge' in *Lawn Tennis and Croquet* by the anonymous scribe, W.A.B. It praised 'The Dauntless Three' who had stepped forward when the Doherty brothers declined to be part of the challenging team:

> ... for since we lack the brothers twain,
>   What hope to win the cup?
> Then out spake brave Goratius,
>   The back court player great;
> "Lo every man upon this earth
>   Gets beaten soon or late;
> And how can man play better
>   Than facing fearful odds
> For the honor of his country,
>   And the old lawn tennis gods?"

... Then out spake E. D. Niger,
A Yorkshire man was he;
"Lo, I will be the second string,
And singles play with thee!"
And out spake Roper Barrett,
Of Gipsy club was he:
"I will abide, at right hand side,
In Doubles with E. D." ...

A small notice in *Lawn Tennis* suggested that tennis players come to Euston station at noon on 28 July, to give Gore and Barrett a patriotic send-off as they caught the boat train for Liverpool, where Black would join them. Apparently the send-off party was slim. The next week's edition carried a 'very amusing account' by 'A. Nanias', which sarcastically painted a picture of a mob farewell scene: 'Tens of thousands of spectators lined the route ... The police with their Jubilee medals (these are always worn on important occasions) pinned on their heaving bosoms, directed the enormous vehicular and pedestrian traffic with their usual tact and care ... The enthusiasm of the crowd knew no bounds ... The mob yelled itself hoarse with delight, the massed bands playing "God Save the Queen" and "Yankee Doodle" at the same time with brilliant effect.'

Jubilee medals indeed. And on top of being practically ignored, Barrett apparently crushed a finger in the door of the train on the way to Liverpool. (Six months later the slight was still not forgotten. 'Although lawn tennis players at home can hardly be accused of showing overwhelming enthusiasm when their representatives go abroad to defend the national honour – to America, for instance,' wrote *Lawn Tennis*, commenting upon a legitimately hearty send-off for an Australian team heading for New Zealand.)

The English team captain, Gore, was ranked fifth in England, Black was ranked sixth and Barrett, 13th (though rankings were said to be not as important in England as they were in America). Actually, there had been a few raised eyebrows at the makeup of the English team. Where was Smith, the man who had beaten Gore at Wimbledon in June? Where was Nisbet, who had played in America earlier and was Barrett's partner as Wimbledon doubles runners-up? And, of course, where were the Doherty brothers? Between them they held both the English singles and doubles titles, though it was said that the younger Doherty, Laurie, had temporarily stopped playing singles because of poor health. (It was learned later that the Dohertys also just did not like ocean travel.)

Some would later insist that the English contingent had been affected by England's involvement in the Boer War in South Africa, yet of the top English players, only Dr. W. V. Eaves was known to be serving there. And for that matter, the Spanish-American War had affected the careers of at least two seasoned American players, Bill Larned and Bob Wrenn.

As much as anything, however, it probably was that English tennis authorities simply were not too concerned about the level of tennis competition their players would meet in America. Even in the US many still automatically genuflected before the supposed superiority of European tennis. Just a year earlier one American veteran had suggested that American tennis teachers needed to go abroad and 'learn the game ... and then come over and teach our young players the proper way to make strokes'.

On hand in New York to greet the English team was, appropriately enough, the former American champion, Ollie Campbell, who himself had competed in England in 1892. The three British players were expected to go straight to Boston after their arrival so they could practice on the unfamiliar courts. To the amazement of their American hosts, the trio instead headed for Niagara Falls, hardly on the way. Later, some said that the British team still thought the first matches were to start two days later than the actual schedule or that they did not know whether or not practice courts would be made available to them.

Others said that since Barrett had to head back to England at the end of the week, he was eager to use what brief time he had to see the spectacular falls, always popular with foreign visitors. Whatever the reason, the 'Dauntless Three' viewed the falls on Sunday and judged them to 'beggar description'.

After their side trip to Niagara Falls, the British finally arrived in Boston on Monday morning. They rested briefly at their University Club lodgings and then headed out to Brookline and the Longwood courts for some practice. With the challengers on hand, at last the modest little ceremony could take place that would become, in later years, a glittery, featured part of Davis Cup competition, the draw.

CHAPTER 7

THE FIRST MATCH

O n Monday afternoon players and officials, some in tennis clothes, some in work-a-day mufti, gathered on the front porch of the Longwood clubhouse. Clubhouse? Some visitors had been known to smile and raise an eyebrow upon hearing the term applied to the Spartan building which stood to one side of the two main courts. In its earlier life the long, low building obviously had been a farm shed of some sort, though in recent years it had been fancied up a bit with the addition of a simple porch and shutters at the windows. Inside were such other amenities as lockers for the players and a shallow bathtub.

Participating in the draw ceremony were the captains of the two teams, Arthur Gore for the British, Dwight Davis for the Americans. Both held floppy, cloth tennis hats upside down. Between them stood Holc Ward, who reached into the tennis hats and pulled out slips of paper on which were written the names of the players. In the two singles matches on the first day it would be Ernest Black against Dwight Davis and Arthur Gore versus Malcolm Whitman. The following day's doubles would pit Black and Barrett against Davis and Ward. The third day would be two singles matches again, a reverse of the first day's pairings. The winning team would be the one which won three of the five matches.

As the drawing for match pairings concluded, those who had carefully watched the English at practice and already knew something of their games, shrewdly realized that the Americans had, in fact, been lucky in the draw. Like would play like in the first two matches. The two dashing, brilliant, though sometimes erratic players (Black and Davis) would play one another. The two steady, strong, all-around players (Whitman and Gore) would play each other. Davis's effectiveness in rushing to the net might have a better chance against Black than against a strong baseliner like Gore who delighted in passing a man at the net with hard, carefully placed shots. Though Davis would eventually have to play Gore, an early win would be a great morale boost for the US.

The Boston newspapers suggested that the English visitors, though becomingly modest ('good fellows – they would say nothing as to their chances'), were, in fact, rather confident. 'While the English players are not out and out in declaring that they will win the trophy, they are satisfied that they will make a good showing,' said the *Boston Post*.

The *Boston Herald*'s man watched Monday afternoon's practice and told his readers the next day that the Englishmen were all 'hard hitters, driving the ball fast and low, and very accurately. They waste no time in rallies and their kills are quickly and accurately made'. *Boston Globe* writer Fred Mansfield wasn't above politely hinting that the visitors might, just might, be underestimating their competition. This was indicated, he said, by their 'ill-advised' arrival in America and Boston so close to the time of the match's beginning. 'While it would be manifestly unfair to attribute to the visitors any undue confidence in winning,' he continued, 'their lack of reasonable training on American courts to adequately prepare themselves for the international matches is suggestive.'

The tiny, weekly *Brookline Chronicle*, had supreme confidence in the hometown players. 'There is not the slightest doubt that our team of doubles will win and little fear that the single men will fall.' In New York, where the matches were also being followed, the *Times* had taken the safe path of predicting 'very close tennis'.

The Americans' secret weapon would be their booming hard, twisting serves. The English players, who still served straight and flat, later would call this the 'screw' service. Black, the first of the visitors to face this new serve, though a hard, fast server himself, would be described as 'dumbfounded'.

But the Americans' diabolical new way of getting the ball into play was still an unknown hazard, possibly not even unveiled at Monday's practice. Actually, as the time for the matches approached, it was probably surface not service which caused the English players concern. These Americans played on longer grass, for one thing. Even at Monday's practice, before there had been rain, the visitors found the courts not as fast as those they were accustomed to, though there were polite mumblings that conditions were very even, don't you know.

Tuesday's soaking rain not only postponed the start of the matches but made the courts even slower. (The visitors from England could not have been totally unhappy with the rain, however, since it postponed the start of the match and gave them an additional day of rest after their recent travels.)

Neither the efforts of the Wednesday morning sun nor of Longwood's English-born groundskeeper/cricket coach, John Isaac Chambers, had made much difference. Ike Chambers, a champion cricket bowler from Nottingham hired by Longwood 16 years earlier, had brought with him great knowledge of how to grow and maintain a fine 'English' lawn.

It was he who had laid out Longwood's first permanent lawn tennis court. His normal tools in caring for the courts were a three-ton iron roller and sturdy horse. Now, on Wednesday, he and his helpers could have used a three-ton sponge. The

Boston Herald would admit in its next day coverage that the courts were 'not of the best'. However, insisted the paper, 'the arts and wiles of a thorough groundsman were utilized to the limit, and nothing more could be done'.

A bespectacled 38-year-old, Richard Sears, was serving as referee for the day's matches. As last-minute checks were made to ensure everything was ready, Sears surveyed club grounds much changed from those early days when cricket matches first replaced hay as the crop on this corner of his grandfather's estate. In addition to the ten or so grass tennis courts, there were also several clay or dirt courts.

Around the two, side-by-side championship courts on which today's matches would be played there was grandstand seating, part of it covered. Rows of sturdy, wooden, straight-backed chairs provided other seating for spectators. A thick line of trees along the edge of the property provided always welcome shade.

Steadily the spectators continued to arrive, not only by train but by Brookline Avenue trolley, horse-drawn cab or even in the new noisy, snorting motor cars – 'bubbles' they were calling them over in Newport, Rhode Island. Not surprisingly, the matches had produced keen interest from English expatriates living in the Boston area.

It was a well-dressed crowd – men in straw hats, high collars, ties and suit coats. Despite a summer-long campaign around the country from those pushing sanity in summer dressing, not many men in this area had been seduced into discarding their suit jackets in favor of the infinitely cooler 'masculine shirtwaist'. This was, after all, Boston, *The Late George Apley's* Boston. As one newspaper was to chide a few days later, '… Boston men sometimes lack the courage of their convictions in sartorial matters. They prefer to wait and see what Chicago and Long Island City will do in regard to the shirtwaist vogue before taking any rash steps themselves'.

The ladies, and there were many of them in the crowd, rustled into the covered grandstands and reserved box seats in splendid dresses of silk or long skirts of linen and shirtwaists of batiste. At the US championships at Newport one player had commented on how distracting the attractive, colourfully-dressed ladies in the gallery could be. Even English player Roper Barrett, who would later grumble about almost all aspects of this international competition, would comment that 'the spectators were most impartial and the female portion thereof not at all unpleasant to gaze upon'.

Though some women might be at Longwood only as a decorative ornament on the arm of a tennis-loving escort, others had a lively interest in the sport and were, in fact, enthusiastic tennis players themselves. Longwood currently listed 25 women (the limit) among its nearly 200 active members. The ladies had the use of the courts only in the mornings – but, of course, not holiday mornings.

The starting times of Wednesday's two matches had been staggered (one to begin at 2.30 p.m., the other at 3.30 p.m.), but at least part of the time they would be going on concurrently on the side-by-side courts. Palmer Presbrey, tournament manager, and a group of other officials walked around the two courts, carefully checking the condition of the turf. At 2 p.m. the courts were pronounced playable, though a bit heavier than usual, and the players were notified. The Englishmen, reported onlookers, 'marvelled considerably at the conditions of the turf under the circumstances'.

And now, as the afternoon shadows began to lengthen, the participants in the first match – Dwight Davis for the United States, Ernest Black for England – walked onto one of the courts. The 1,200 spectators settled into their seats, and the match began.

Black tossed the ball and served. And Davis, the donor of the cup, the originator of what would one day be the world's best-known international sporting competition after the Olympics, got his first chance to put a racket on the ball.

He hit it out.

CHAPTER 8

'WITH WEEPING AND WITH LAUGHTER'

Ernest Black, the Scot, was as dashing in play as he was in appearance, the crowd at Longwood soon realised. He placed his shots well, driving hard from the back of the court, though he seldom came to the net. He had a strong, effective first serve and a particularly fine backhand. Dwight Davis, however, did manage to win the first game.

Now it was Davis's turn to serve for the first time. The ball twisted and curved. Black, observed one tennis writer, 'watched its gyrations with an expression of blank amazement'. Black's team-mate, Roper Barrett, watching from the sidelines, was equally astonished. It took some time before those watching with Barrett could convince the Englishman that it was not just the soggy ground causing the peculiar bounces but something new Davis was doing to the ball.

As the set progressed, however, Black became a bit more comfortable with the serve, and Davis lost his service three times and finally the set 4-6. There was a storm of applause for the visitor's win. It was the theory of tennis writer Parmly Paret that left-handed players started slowly. It is unclear how large his sampling was since left-handed players like Davis still seemed to be a rarity.

Davis settled down and took the next two sets 6-2 and 6-4. But Black, down only one set, was still in the match. In the fourth set he continued to cover the court well and force the pace. Both players scrambled to get balls that appeared to be unplayable. Davis's game held, however, as he combined aggressiveness with accuracy (not always the case when he played), pulling ahead, finally, to win the set 6-4 and the match, three sets to one. After the first set he had lost only one of the games he served. The crowd was enthusiastic. It had been 'grand tennis', said the *Boston Herald*.

'International Championship singles – Dwight F. Davis, United States, defeated E. O. Black, England, 4-6, 6-2, 6-4, 6-4', read a newspaper summary the following day. In future years this linking of player with country – whether in print or in pronouncements from the chair – would prove to be among the most profoundly satisfying aspects of Davis Cup competition for players in this normally individualistic sport.

Meanwhile, as Black and Davis had been playing their final set, Malcolm Whitman, for the US, and team captain Arthur Gore, for England, had begun their match on the adjacent court. Now it was Gore's turn to experience the new American serve, Whitman's 'rattlesnake'. As the 'egg-shaped lump' left Whitman's racquet and crossed the net, a puzzled Gore quickly switched his racquet from one hand to the other, then 'finally wound up by letting the ball escape him altogether', reported the *Boston Morning Journal*. Slipping on the wet ground in smooth-soled shoes did not help. (Neither Gore nor Black wore cleats, unlike the Americans.)

This was not as exciting a match as the one between Davis and Black had been, and Whitman won easily in straight sets. American tennis writers did have compliments for the visitors, however. They did not lob excessively, they did not fuss about line calls, they did not worry about stray balls elsewhere on the court and they kept the game moving along quickly by not dawdling between points or taking 'any elaborate care of themselves between the sets'. The Englishmen had waited patiently on the sidelines while the Americans, as was their custom, went into the clubhouse for 'a rubdown and a brush-up' between the second and third sets. (A pointed comment, undoubtedly, on the common American tournament practice of allowing a seven-minute rest after the second and any succeeding sets.)

Though players from both countries had to deal with the same playing conditions, pointed out one writer, the slow, soggy courts were harder on the British since they relied on ground strokes and, unlike the Americans, seldom came into the net.

The next day, Thursday, the doubles match pitted Davis and Holcombe Ward against Black and Barrett. With better weather, the crowd was even larger, and the overflow included more than 100 standees on the high sidewalks outside the grounds.

After a slight delay while the net was changed and enough linesmen were rounded up, the match at last was underway. It soon became apparent to spectators that the style of doubles played by the two teams was quite different.

The English team played much of the time between the service line and the baseline. From the backcourt they hit hard driving shots, and Black's strokes and general verve were as impressive as they had been the day before. The galleries enthusiastically applauded his cross-court volleys and other spectacular shots. Though Barrett's strokes were weaker – particularly his serve – he was very quick to see, and take advantage of, holes in the opponents' defences. He appeared to have a better grasp of the doubles game.

The Americans, on the other hand, rushed to the net at every opportunity, pounding volleys at angles beyond their opponents' reach. How gratifying, pointed out Mansfield in the *Globe* the following day, for former champions Richard Sears and Dr. Dwight to see the success of this both-men-at-the-net tactic which they had pioneered, at least in the US.

Ward and Davis played smoothly together – Davis, for once, was the steadier of the pair – while Black and Barrett at times were undecided about who would try for a ball. Ward and Davis did much 'smashing' of high balls (always a crowd pleaser), while Black and Barrett had much less success with this shot.

And again, of course, there was the edge from the Americans' serves. They never lost a service game. Sometimes they used a new strategy (later players would call it the 'I' formation) of having the net man stand on the same side of the court as the server. The aim was to cut off cross-court returns of serve and generally confuse the opposition. It did. At the end of the match, which had included 'brilliant rallies', the United States had won in straight sets, 6-4, 6-4, 6-4. The win was decisive but the competition certainly had not been one-sided, decided observers. It had been a 'thrilling contest', closer, in fact, than the score might indicate.

Three points had now been secured by the United States team. 'Davis International Tennis Cup Will Therefore Stay at Home', said the headline in the *Boston Post*. As would be the case often in future Davis Cup contests, the two final singles matches to be played might salvage a bit of pride for the losers but would make no difference in the outcome. It would be a reverse of the first day's singles, Davis against Gore and Whitman against Black.

Except for the Friday afternoon's heat (blistering), the playing conditions had begun to resemble what the visitors were used to – ground dry, grass clipped close. Gore's game benefited. Davis managed to win the first set 9-7 but the points were long and the play seemed very even. Against Gore's solid backcourt game and accurate passing shots Davis's favourite spot (at the net) was not producing the points it had on the previous two days. Yet unlike Whitman in his game against Gore two days earlier, Davis showed no inclination to stay back himself.

In the second set, leading 6-5, Gore sent three shots sizzling past Davis at the net. The Englishman was within one point of taking the set. But Davis dug in and placed the next four balls out of Gore's reach. It was now 6-6. Both men had begun to show the effects of the heat and the long rallies. Each player continued to hold serve until the score stood at 9-9. Whitman and Black prepared to start their match on the adjacent court.

But then the rains came. Suddenly, in torrents. Spectators who, minutes earlier, had been resplendent in summer finery, crowded dripping and bedraggled onto the porch of the tiny clubhouse. Others headed for the small barn to seek shelter from the downpour with the horse who pulled the grass roller. Officials held hurried consultations with one another and with the captains of the two teams, who happened to be playing one another. Since the winning of the trophy had already been determined, it was decided that the rest of the competition would be cancelled rather than postponed. Barrett had to leave; Gore and Black were scheduled to play in an exhibition over the weekend at Southampton.

To Americans, of course, the first competition for the new international trophy had been a spectacular success, proof of how far the country's tennis had progressed. An unabashedly jingoistic drawing in one Boston paper showed a giant silver bowl being towed off the tennis court by two tiny American players while the third player sat on the rim waving an American flag. Three other players, bowing slightly in apparent obeisance, stood on the sidelines watching it go, a limp Union Jack at their side.

Friday evening another Davis Cup tradition began – the concluding banquet at which competitors, mellowed by good food and wine, toast each other, the game and the overarching value of international competition. The evening's festivities were at the Somerset Club, that most exclusive retreat of Boston's Beacon Hill Brahmins. After many toasts, speeches and stories, the English team left on the night train for New York. The next day Barrett sailed for London and Black and Gore travelled to Southampton where Gore easily defeated Richard Stevens and Black lost to Bill Larned. (One account of the match said Black's poor showing was certainly understandable given the previous night's revelries.)

Then it was on to Newport and the US national championships for more testing of American vs. English styles of play. In the third round of the championships Gore defeated Holcombe Ward in a match on the grandstand court (probably with no little satisfaction, though the two had not played at Longwood). For a time it had looked as if Ward, using short shots that dropped just over the net, had discovered how to neutralise Gore's hard passing shots from the back court which had given Davis so much trouble during the cup competition. But Ward ran out of steam in the fourth set and the ever-fit Gore was able to outlast the younger player, an ability he would demonstrate all through the remaining years of his remarkable tennis career. (He would win both singles and doubles titles at Wimbledon in 1909 at the age of 41.)

In the fourth round, as (bad) luck of the draw would have it, Gore and Black ended up playing each other, with Gore defeating a somewhat lethargic Black decisively in three sets. Gore next faced George Wrenn Jr., who had just defeated his older brother (and former US champion) Bob Wrenn, still suffering from the effects of malaria. The younger Wrenn defeated Gore in a match that *Golf and Lawn Tennis* called 'the sensation of the tournament', but it took five sets.

Whitman, who retained his national title, also played a 'practice' game at Newport which attracted some interest. He defeated Black 6-2, 6-4, 6-4 in the match-up which had been rained out at Longwood.

As autumn arrived, tennis racquets were laid down and pen and paper picked up as weapons of choice in the continuing controversy of American versus English play. Once they reached home, the English players had unloaded their frustrations at the conditions they had found in the competition for the new international trophy. The Americans had been unfair in changing the days of the matches, complained Gore, who even went so far as to predict there would be no more challenges for the trophy. (An LTA committee issued a report reviewing arrangements and said there was no basis to this complaint.)

American balls were too soft. (The English publication *Lawn Tennis and Croquet* published a diagram showing the path of Ward's and Davis's serves, in which the 'erstwhile round' tennis balls which had become 'eggified' were carefully drawn in the shape of tiny eggs). The grass was too long. The courts were slow and rough (having been 'eaten away by ants'). The nets sagged and swayed in a way that would have brought a blush to the face of any English hostess staging a tennis garden party, etc. etc. etc.

And the serves. They were a 'cruel surprise', in fact, 'the English were surprised more than they were beaten', wrote a certain 'S. Apphira' in *Lawn Tennis and Croquet* (probably Gore, using a coy nom de plume). The representatives from England 'outplayed the Americans at all points of the game except the service'.

Nonsense, responded American tennis writer Parmly Paret who was asked by *Lawn Tennis and Croquet* to give an 'impartial' American viewpoint. Paret had himself been competing elsewhere during the international cup matches, but he had carefully observed Gore and Black at Newport, meticulously analysed their records and had even played a two-set practice match with Gore. (Gore won.)

Only three Americans – Whitman, Davis and Ward – used the twist serve, said Paret. But other players also had beaten Black and Gore while they were in America. The balls, weather and court conditions admittedly were different from those in England, but they had not changed materially since 1897 when Mahony and Nisbet had played in the US. Mahony and Nisbet were on the English selection committee. Why had they not better prepared their players? No, concluded Paret, the English players had lost because of overconfidence and the superiority of the American style of play.

Too many excuses were being made, admitted an English writer in *Lawn Tennis and Croquet*. 'Such excuses are neither dignified nor just. *Qui s'excuse, s'accuse*. The plain facts are that our men could not return the service, and were handsomely beaten by men, who, on the play, were too good for them.'

Meanwhile, Laurie Doherty, not exactly a disinterested observer, was carefully saving an article quoting British tennis authority Eustace Miles who had apparently witnessed the Longwood matches and had criticised the defeated team for showing up without knowledge of or preparation for the American game. 'Even the Messrs. Doherty will require the most careful training in this before they come over,' warned Miles.

Interestingly, several of the elements that had been factors in the outcome of the first Davis Cup competition would surface again and again in future cup challenges. Overconfidence, for instance, and dissatisfaction with the condition of the host country's courts, and possibly most important, the inability of a country (or its tennis association) to convince its leading players that they were needed and that patriotism outranked personal convenience.

As the *Brookline Chronicle* had written a bit plaintively at the conclusion of the first Davis Cup matches, 'The representatives which England has sent over come to us with the best of records, but it does not seem possible that these are the most expert players which that home of tennis can produce'. And of course they were not.

Clarence Hobart, however, a top-ranked American player in the early 1890s who had played in England, agreed with much of the English assessment. The English had better equipment and for the most part ran tighter, better organised events, he said in a long letter to the American *Golf and Lawn Tennis*. Why should not the tennis associations of both countries develop common standards? (The letter was eagerly reprinted in England.)

In the end, points for wry good humour went, hands down, to the English. The *Lawn Tennis and Croquet* scribe W.A.B, again with a nod to Macaulay's 'Horatius at the Bridge', concluded the epic he had begun before the English team had departed for the US:

Stout Niger lost to Davis
By three fierce sets to one;
And Barrett and the former,
By Ward and D. were done;
From Whitman brave Goratius

Took not one single set;
And the proud Queen's man's tennis friends
Wished they had never bet.

And in the night of winter
When ancient players score
With the long story of the times
When they were to the fore;
When by the cheerful fireside
 Snores loud the pussy-cat,
And the contented pug-dog
Snores louder (for he's fat);

When the goodman mends his racket,
And (for fear of stoutness) bants;
When the goodwife's needle merrily
Sews patches on his pants;
With weeping and with laughter
Still is the story told,
How our Goratius lost the match
In the brave days of old.

Back in America, the September issue of the United States National Lawn Tennis Association's publication published an effusive tribute to Davis. 'The generous Harvard player is even now ... trying to arrange for another international challenge for next season,' said the article. 'Every indication points to another season of increasing success next year ... For this bright outlook we may thank the donor of this new International Cup, and the official organ takes this early opportunity in recording its sincere gratitude to the "noblest Roman of them all".'

Not quite Horatius, but close.

CHAPTER 9

OFF TO ENGLAND

I n late summer 1900, following the international matches, Davis and Ward won their second national doubles title. It appeared that the time would soon be ripe for the American pair to take their racquets and stop volleys to England and test their game against the fabled Doherty brothers. There were rumors that Whitman would go over for Wimbledon the following summer as well.

'Most welcome news', said the English publication *Lawn Tennis and Croquet*. 'The first year of the new century would indeed be memorable in the history of the game. We must devoutly hope that nothing will interfere to change the plans of the Americans.' (Except for Germany, which celebrated in 1900, all enlightened Western nations were properly celebrating 1901 as the first year of the 20th century.)

Davis, despite his doubles success, had again run into a wall on his way to challenging for the national singles title at Newport. He went down in five sets in the third round before another left-hander, the fourth-ranked Beals Wright. Young Wright's game was constantly improving, and he seemed to be mastering the return of the fearsome twist serve.

In September, Dwight Davis, accompanying Gore, had arrived in England on the first leg of a post-graduation tour of Europe. In England there was much interest in his visit, particularly since he had entered the important, season's end tournament at Eastbourne. Now, chuckled the English tennis press, we shall get a chance to see just how effective this new American serve is with proper balls on proper courts.

As for the rest of Davis's game, 'It is the opinion of Americans who have seen him play that, if he happens to have one of his days, he will make even R. F. Doherty sit up if he meets him, while if he happens to be off-colour, he may be beaten by any first-class man. (Rankings in both countries divided players into classes.) He is essentially a brilliant player, and as such is bound to vary considerably,' wrote *Lawn Tennis and Croquet*.

In London Davis and Gore played some practice matches on the covered wood courts at Queen's Club and on the centre court at Wimbledon. Gore won handily both times, though it was admitted that Davis had never played on wood before and that he seemed to miss his spikes on the grass at Wimbledon. (Back in America, tennis writer/player Parmly Paret was uneasy about Davis's losses. 'I wish you would tell me more about what Davis writes you,' he said in a letter to Ward. 'Did Davis mention these sets with Gore, and did he use the twist [serve] at all against him there? Does he say why he was beaten? I presume lack of practice, but they are making capital of it.') Down in Eastbourne, as it turned out, Davis did not meet Doherty but instead played ex-Wimbledon champion Harold Mahony, whom he 'disconcerted ... very considerably by his service'. It was the opinion of observers, however, that the unsettling effects of the Davis serve were not quite so pronounced with the harder English ball. Nevertheless, English players would just have to get busy and work up their own version of the new serve, said *Lawn Tennis and Croquet*, 'unless indeed they are all content to remain behind in the race for progress'.

Following a 7 February 1901 meeting in New York at the Hotel Waldorf-Astoria, the United States National Lawn Tennis Association announced that international lawn tennis was now 'established on a firm basis. The International Challenge Cup as generously given by Dwight F. Davis has been accepted by the USNLTA under a deed of gift ...'

This was a common procedure with tournament trophies. In fact, tennis magazines published blank USNLTA deed of gift forms to facilitate such formal transfers of ownership – and responsibility. Chief among the latter was monitoring whether the requisite number of tournament wins (often three) had occurred before a player claimed permanent possession and headed home with an impressive piece of silver packed in his suitcase along with his dirty laundry.

Davis and Ward, for instance, had two legs up on the famous pair of cups presented by Colonel John Jacob Astor in 1890 for the national doubles championship. A third win would give them permanent possession of the historic trophies, said to have cost $2,000 and to be the most valuable prizes to be won on the tennis court. Trophies mattered. Greedy 'mug hunting', however, was frowned upon, that is, the practice of top level players entering lesser tournaments just to collect the silver.

Dwight Davis's big silver punch-bowl, of course, would never be retired, would always circulate from winner to winner, as had been made clear in the deed of gift. Instead, Dr. James Dwight arranged for competitors in the international matches to receive miniature silver 'pots', as he called them, Lilliputian replicas, two inches in diameter, of the large bowl.

While the Davis Cup was officially received by USNLTA, its donor was still enjoying his graduation tour abroad, his first trip to Europe. He had spent the winter fox hunting in England and playing somewhat desultory tennis exhibitions on courts with picture postcard settings along the French Riviera, including Nice, where the tennis courts were next to a bull ring.

Cannes had been abuzz with news of a dramatic change: tournament matches were being played on Sunday for the first time. 'Naturally,' noted *Lawn Tennis and Croquet,* 'only those players wishing to play are put on, and the remainder are perfectly justified in observing that to play on six days of the week is quite enough.'

Davis explained that he had not practiced enough in recent weeks to enter any tournaments. 'He is one of those players who takes a month or two to get into form,' said *Lawn Tennis and Croquet.*

Whenever Davis had the chance, he promoted the coming summer's challenge match for the new international trophy. The level of tennis was rising in several European countries, particularly Holland and Belgium, but also in Sweden, Germany and France. However, no one seemed to anticipate a challenge from any place but England, which as expected, sent a challenge from London 12 February 1901. Nevertheless, the American tennis association said it could not reply until the first Monday in March, since until that deadline, 'any country has the right to enter the lists'.

'The Englishmen are very keen over the international matches and would rather win them than our championship at Newport,' said Davis in an interview upon his return to the United States in early March. He also gave assurances that he carefully had not used the reverse twist serve at all or volleyed much, in order to keep those strokes under wraps until the next international competition. Yes, he said, he thought the Dohertys were likely to come this time 'but they dread the ocean trip'.

Davis himself, it seemed, had no such aversion to ocean travel. After attending the USNLTA executive committee meeting in New York in early March, he made a quick trip home to St. Louis, then returned east in late April and sailed back to England.

Meanwhile, Holc Ward, operating at a slightly different financial level than his doubles partner, was getting advice on travel costs from Parmly Paret, who had played in Europe three years earlier. A five-week trip could cost $250 'if you did not take a wheel or a camera', Paret wrote to Ward. Three weeks could cost $200 'with close economy'.

Ward joined Davis in England several weeks before Wimbledon. Malcolm Whitman had not made the trip after all, having retired from competition for the year. Ward brought with him three of Wright & Ditson's *Davis* model racquets.

Davis himself had taken six. The racquets, which retailed for $8, were in short supply since they were very hard to make 'owing to the difference in thickness of the frame at the throat from the *Pim*', George Wright had advised Ward. The senior Wright had further advice for Ward. 'Lookout my boy and do not let the Englishmen get on to Dwight and your twist service and your style of play,' he wrote. 'We want you to keep it up your sleeve to make good use of when you play the International Matches in this country as it's here all the honours are to be gained.'

It was, of course, impractical advice. Holding back while playing exhibitions was one thing. Holding back while playing for the English championship – and as the first current American title holders to compete at Wimbledon since Oliver Campbell in 1892 – was quite another. At last here was a chance for Ward and Davis to test their game on English turf, with English balls, against England's best.

It was the chance to see this new American approach to the game which brought a record crowd of spectators to the Wimbledon grounds on Worple Road in the last week of June 1901. The Americans had entered the doubles competition only, declining to play in singles or mixed doubles. They were limiting themselves to doubles, 'with the characteristic determination of Americans to do their absolute best in the thing which they are striving for', explained USNLTA official Palmer Presbrey, who had shown up in London expressly to see the challenge round match (if all went according to form) between the Americans and the Doherty brothers.

Concentrating on just one event, however, drew the criticism from some 'that by reserving themselves entirely for the Doubles, they were making rather too much of a business of the affair', wrote *Lawn Tennis and Croquet*, with fine old British disdain for trying too hard. 'The very thought of Mr. Davis in a Mixed Double is enough to make one's mouth water,' added the publication.

Ward and Davis moved easily through the early rounds and won the All Comers, losing only one set in four matches. Their court attire raised British eyebrows slightly, particularly their customary black shoes rather than Wimbledon white. In his summer straw hat with band (what many men in the stands were wearing), dark shoes, dark belt, and white shirt with sleeves rolled up, Davis looked a bit like a young bond salesman who had just taken off his tie and jacket and decided to play a bit of tennis on his lunch hour.

English tennis writers relished the chance to see the new American game – and players – first-hand. They noticed that the doubles pair carefully stayed together on the court, moving together when they rushed the net, rather than taking a position of one up and one back. Davis, wrote one English observer, had an overhead volley which was 'almost the fastest we have ever seen. He seems to use his racket like a kind of flail; he puts plenty of wrist-snap into the stroke ... He kills more balls than any other when he gets them over, as he generally does.

'Moreover, he has the power of taking the ball anywhere, either while it is rising, or while it is falling, or while it is at the top of its bound. He moves his body very little, and relies largely on his wrist ... The result is that he might play very badly if he were off his day: the wrist angle is far less reliable than the body angle. But Davis very seldom is off his day. He has a splendid eye. Ward is a neat player but not nearly so brilliant as Davis.' However Ward, added this observer, seemed better able to manipulate the twist serve than his partner. In one match, said another article, 'it was a case of Davis, Davis everywhere; and this was enough'.

Again there was the strange positioning of the netman when his partner was serving. This produced formations 'so peculiar and so varied that it is impossible to describe them in detail', wrote *Lawn Tennis & Croquet*, though it decided to try. 'Roughly speaking, when the first service was from the right hand court, an inch or two from the centre of the baseline, the man at the net was parallel to his partner and in a crouching position; when it was from the left court, again close to the centre, the man at the net was about half-way along the left court. There were all sorts of subtle variations according to whether the service was to be fast or slow, direct or reverse, or at some distance from the centre line. In every case, the man at the net was always very much in the way' of the return of serve.

At mid-afternoon on Tuesday, 2 July 1901, the tarpaulin was pulled off the centre court (it had rained earlier) and under an ominously grey sky, the two Americans and the defending champions, R.F. and H.L. Doherty began to play.

Reginald Frank (Reggie) Doherty was 28, his younger brother, Hugh Laurence (Laurie) was 25. They had won the doubles championship the previous four years, and Reggie also had been the Wimbledon singles champion since 1897, though this year he had lost the singles title to none other than Arthur W. Gore. (Laurie Doherty would bring the singles title back into the family the following year and hold it from 1902-1906.) They were truly playing on home turf, having both been born in the suburb of Wimbledon.

A feature article in a British publication described them as 'masters of every stroke and every trick known to English players; graceful, good-looking and always well groomed ...' They had been educated at Westminster and Cambridge, where they had won their lawn tennis blues – 'and very pretty these light blue and white striped jackets are', added the article.

They both had dark wavy hair and, in repose, looked enough alike to be, well, brothers. But when standing, Reggie was nearly a head taller than his younger brother, which had produced the nicknames 'Big Do' and 'Little Do'. In the talk which had buzzed about the centre court during the week it was generally predicted that the challenging Americans would not be able to beat the Dohertys because of the latter's 'imperturbability and steadiness'.

Actually it was the second meeting for the two doubles teams. They had met at a pre-Wimbledon tune up at Beckenham three weeks earlier and the Dohertys had won two sets to love. But most observers realized that the Americans had been holding back, not using any of their normal stratagems. Once inside the gates of Wimbledon, however, the Americans had unveiled it all. The twist serves, the aggressive volleying, the high lobs, the eccentric court positions, all had been unleashed in the early round matches and all would be used again today.

The Americans won the first set 6-4. The Dohertys quickly adjusted, driving low returns to the man rushing the net and making sure their lobs went to Ward not Davis, and won the second set 6-0. Even when the rain started again, they played on, though Ward's serve, particularly, was affected by the soggy ground. The third set was tied at nine games all when the lowering heavens opened and a heavy downpour at last stopped play an hour and a half into the match. 'Rain Dohertys Wednesday,' cabled Holcombe Ward to his father back in New Jersey in terse cablese.

The young Americans had met the famous duo and were holding their own. Later that evening, at the dinner given in their honor by the All-England Club (and which, if there had not been rain, would have marked the end of the tournament) they had to feel hopeful about their chances. At the 11-course dinner (with eight wines) at the Café Royal on Regent Street, toasts to the King and 'our American visitors' were followed by a request from the master of ceremonies that the visitors explain in detail their twist serve. Davis included in his response allusions to certain Chinese and Boer leaders who had recently given Great Britain trouble, 'but somehow or other he quite forgot to explain the mysteries of the famous service', said one report of the jovial proceedings.

The following afternoon play resumed at 3.30 p.m., and the match started again from the beginning. On this day, reported one English newspaper, Davis was wearing 'a battered-looking drill hat above his round, good-humored face, looking quite incapable of the slaughtering smashes which, in the past week, Wimbledon players – and spectators – have come to know almost too well'.

Again there was the fixation on the visitors' footgear, those 'curious black leather shoes, like running shoes'. The appearance of the Americans contrasted strongly 'with the spotless whiteness from head to foot of the Dohertys', continued the newspaper, adding, tongue in cheek, that a 'truly unbiased lady in the crowd' was heard to say, 'I do hope they'll (the Dohertys) win; they look so clean.'

Just like the previous day the Americans took the first set 6-4. And the English team the second set, 6-2. This time, however, the Dohertys won the third set 6-3, to take the lead two sets to one. (Great applause from the crowd.) It appeared that both Davis and Reggie Doherty were the most affected by the postponement – in opposite ways. Davis would frequently shake his head in disgust as his hard overheads, so effective earlier, now went into the net or out of bounds. Reggie, on the other hand, seemed to be sharper.

In the fourth set the Americans were ahead 4-2, it was Ward's serve and it looked as if they could take the set and pull even. But after two deuce points Davis put a backhand into the net and misjudged a lob, hitting it out. Laurie won his serve to make it four games all; the window of opportunity for the Americans had slammed shut. In the 15th game Ward lost his serve and the defending champions went ahead to win 9-7. (In fact, the brothers would continue to hold the doubles title through 1905.)

As the galleries applauded enthusiastically Davis impetuously ran around the net to shake hands heartily with his opponents, 'beaming with a schoolboy smile', reported one newspaper account. 'It was a little touch, but it was typical of the thoroughly sportsmanlike spirit that the Americans have shown all through.'

Commented another English newspaper wryly: 'After all the American attack did not carry all before it. The knowledge is gratifying after the performances of the American jockeys, American runners, American jumpers, American rifle-shots, American steel, iron, tin and hardware kings; and Americans generally.'

Holcombe Ward's two-word telegram to his father that night said it all: 'Beaten close.'

Even before leaving England Davis and Ward were aware that a return match with the Dohertys as part of the International Challenge Trophy matches, was probably not to be, at least in 1901. In mid-July Dr. James Dwight was sent an official message from London that the British would not be able to send a team to challenge after all. It seemed that R. F. Doherty was still suffering from effects of sunstroke, which, some said, was the reason he had lost the singles championship at Wimbledon to Gore (though his condition had not apparently affected his play in doubles against the Americans). Gore was not coming since his new doubles partner, W. V. Eaves, was still suffering from a fever picked up serving in South Africa. The other two members of the previous year's team, Black and Barrett, were among a string of players who were prevented from making the trip by business or, in one case, marriage.

Davis, interviewed when he returned to the United States, said he was keenly disappointed, but that 'the Englishmen realised, after last year's experience, that it would be foolish to send any weak team over to meet our best men'.

'I can only hope that we may be able to send a representative team next year, (that is, if our challenge is accepted),' wrote the secretary of the Lawn Tennis Association in London. And though the LTA's official publication called the development 'one of the most unhappy chapters in the history of the game', no one on either side of the Atlantic seemed to be worrying, at least publicly, that competition for Dwight Davis's silver bowl might have ended before it had hardly begun.

CHAPTER 10

ROUND TWO

A cannon shot boomed forth into the evening sky of Brooklyn, New York, on Friday, 25 July 1902, and blotted out any residual disappointments at the cancellation of the 1901 matches for the International Challenge Trophy.

The British were coming, the British were coming – but not just any British. It was the Doherty brothers aboard the ship being welcomed by the Crescent Athletic Club as it steamed through the Narrows between Brooklyn and Staten Island and into Upper New York Bay. Also on board was William Collins, president of the English Lawn Tennis Association, team captain. The third member of the team, Dr. Joshua Pim, would be joining them later.

The next morning, with the ship at anchor off Bay Ridge, Brooklyn, flags were run up on the clubhouse on the shore, and the club's big cannon again fired a salute. At last the Doherty brothers had gritted their teeth and made the ocean crossing in order to challenge for Dwight Davis's silver bowl in the second internationals, as the competition was now frequently called. Playing for the Americans would be the country's top two ranked singles players, William Larned and Malcolm Whitman, and, in doubles, Ward and Davis, current US doubles champions. Whitman was team captain.

Ward's national ranking had moved up from seven in 1901 to four at the beginning of 1902. Davis, ranked number two in 1900 and three in 1901, was unranked for 1902. He had been back in St. Louis all winter attending his first year of law school at Washington University. Also, some said the knee injury he had sustained in a loss to Beals Wright during the previous fall's nationals at Newport was more than transitory. (Ward's and Davis's third win of the national doubles titles had occurred before the singles match.)

Since spring when the season opened, Davis and Ward had been practising hard to get back into competitive trim. Though they had not returned to Wimbledon this year, they had won three tournaments so far on the US summer circuit. However, there had been a serious setback a week earlier. Davis had gashed his foot badly while swimming at (sometimes rocky) Magnolia Beach and had even been on crutches for a few days. Though he could now walk about, he had been unable to practice. As a consequence, the match schedule had been rearranged and the doubles would be played on the final day instead of on the day between the singles as in 1900.

Also unlike 1900, the English team had given itself enough time to become acclimated and get in some practice before the matches. The Dohertys went first to Longwood, played briefly in the tournament there, then withdrew to concentrate on doubles and practice on the Crescent Athletic Club courts.

There may have been a bit more urgency than normal to their practice sessions. Earlier in the summer they had lost the doubles championship at Wimbledon to the Gloucestershire team of S. H. Smith and F. L. Riseley, though they would regain the title the following year and hold it through 1905.

The *Boston Herald*'s tennis reporter had got a look at the famous visitors while they were at Longwood and was impressed. R. F. had easily beaten Beals Wright. 'Both are magnificent volleyers and very accurate. Their method is to get opponents out of position and then pass them with a shot. They covered the ground easily and appeared to play easily, without strain, as compared to Americans.'

The Crescent AC in Bay Ridge was known as a 'muscular organisation' where members were interested in football and boxing as well as tennis and boating. The waters of the Narrows were just to the west of the two courts which had been laid out for the international matches.

Mindful of criticism from the visitors two years earlier, this time the turf had received special attention. Courts were described as 'smooth as velvet' and 'as green as a billiard table' after groundskeepers had gone over them on their hands and knees picking out small stones and hard bits of dirt.

The decision had been made to allow the public to attend the matches at no charge. Anyone could apply for tickets and receive them – free – as long as the supply lasted. Not surprisingly, this produced spectacular crowds.

At the end of the opening day, Wednesday, 6 August, the US was ahead in both singles matches (Larned over R. F. Doherty 6-2 , 6-3; Whitman over Pim 6-1, 6-1) when rain caused play to be discontinued until the next morning. Former champion Dr. Pim, 33, had been a sentimental rather than a strategic choice for the team. An Irishman, he had won the singles championship at Wimbledon nearly a decade earlier, in 1893 and 1894, and the doubles title twice during the same period. A robust man, he was considered a genius of early tennis. 'Although still very good,' one English commentator would write, 'Pim had no more than a shadow of his former skill, but alas a great deal more than the shadow of his former weight.'

Some said that because of concern about Laurie Doherty's endurance, the plan was for Pim to play singles, saving Laurie's strength for the doubles. Other American 'experts' claimed that the real reason Reggie and not Laurie was playing singles was because England did not want to risk having its current champion defeated on American courts, though team captain Collins implied that he chose the brother (Reggie) whose style of play would work better against the American attack.

The next day was a different story in the continuation of the Larned-Doherty match. The Englishman, having figured out over night how to keep Larned back from the net, took the next three sets and the match. On the adjacent court, after unaccountably losing the third set 1-6, Whitman polished off Pim in the fourth set 6-0. At the end of Thursday morning the two countries were tied 1 to 1.

The reverse singles followed in the afternoon, with the Larned-Pim match completed first, Larned winning 6-2, 6-3, 6-2. Loud cheers arose from the big crowd and bounced off the Staten Island hills across the Narrows. Then spectators streamed down from the stands and ran across the court to watch the conclusion of the Whitman-Doherty match, which Whitman won 6-1, 7-5, 6-4. With the US ahead 3-1, and the cup securely in American hands for another year, the final day's doubles match was now moot. This did not deter, however, the thousands who wanted to see a battle between the finest doubles teams from each country.

Weather for the final match on Friday was perfect. The excursion side-wheeler *General Slocum*, its three decks jammed with eager tennis spectators, left the Battery and the 12th Street pier in Manhattan and headed down the bay to the Crescent AC dock. Brooklyn streetcars bound for Bay Ridge were equally crowded. Though attendance the previous two days had been an impressive 4,000 and 5,000, by starting time Friday a crowd estimated at anywhere from 7,000 to 10,000 people was packed into the large amphitheatre. 'Surely such a gathering of spectators never before sat about a tennis court in this country,' said one New York paper.

All week it had been rumoured that President Theodore Roosevelt might show up; it was known for sure that several of his children, Kermit, Archie, and 15-year-old Ted Roosevelt Jr., were in attendance. (In another two decades Dwight Davis and Ted Roosevelt Jr., would move in the same Washington power circles as members of President Calvin Coolidge's cabinet.)

The American players, Ward and Davis, walked out onto the court and began warming up. The applause from the crowd was warm. Observers noted that Davis did not seem to be limping or otherwise show evidence of his recent injury. Then the Doherty brothers appeared, and this time the excited galleries erupted wildly. And no wonder. The two handsome, dark-haired men, one the shorter copy of the other, strode out to the court wearing matching broad-brimmed white hats and long flannel coats flaring open over their white duck suits. Never had mere mortals appeared more dazzling in tennis whites.

The Americans took the first set 6-3, their fabled twist serves and their dashes to the net behind serve disconcerting the Englishmen. Ominously for the home team, however, it appeared that Davis's go-for-broke style of tennis was, on this day, producing more losers than winners. At critical times his hard shots slammed into the net or, to the groans of the crowd, landed out beyond the white chalk lines. The Dohertys appeared cool and calm, observed one sports writer, while Ward and Davis were so keenly on edge they frequently appeared over-anxious.

The second set was the hardest fought, the first game going to the Dohertys and the next three to Ward and Davis. From time to time the Americans dazzled the crowd and their opponents with nervy, brilliant shots. But now, with greater regularity, the Dohertys' passing shots caught Ward and Davis ineffectually at the net. Back and forth went the lead until the two teams pulled even at 8 games all. Davis appeared to be tiring, and Ward was unable to carry the load alone. The Englishmen won the last two games to take the second set 10-8 and the third set 6-3. They led two sets to one, and the proceedings stopped for the home-court custom the British found so curious, the mid-match rest period.

Davis steadied a bit after the break and the Americans won the first game of the fourth set. Soon, however, he was hitting some shots – though not all – as erratically as earlier and Ward, who had desperately kept his thumb in the dike all afternoon, could do nothing. The galleries, realising the US champions were in danger of being beaten, cheered on the Americans, but it was over. The Doherty brothers took the last two games to win the final set 6-4, and the match 3-6, 10-8, 6-3, 6-4.

The *New York Times* called it 'the most remarkable tennis match every played on the courts of this country'. It was, said the newspaper, a case of 'the hare and the tortoise' – the sometimes spectacular Americans beaten by the steadiness and accuracy of 'plodding, painstaking players'.

Other comments in the article were more harsh – almost angry. 'That they (the Americans) did not win was in no way due to the superiority of the English team, but to an almost woeful exhibition of smashing by Davis,' said the article. 'Ward and Davis seldom play a mediocre game, for it is either brilliant or poor. But yesterday was a combination of brilliancy and poor playing which just fell short of winning.' And, insisted the article, just in case anyone should think that there might possibly be mitigating circumstances, 'in no part of the match did Davis show any ill effects of the injury he received … a week ago'.

The Davis Cup might be staying in the United States but its donor could not help but have been a bit disheartened by the results of this, the final match (as it would turn out) that he would ever play in its defence.

There was not much time to lick wounds, however. Ward and Davis plunged into preparations for one more meeting with the English team. This time the venue would be Newport and the prize would be the US National Doubles Championship.

On Thursday, 21 August, 13 days after defeating Ward and Davis at the Crescent Athletic Club, Reggie and Laurie Doherty walked out on to the court at the Casino with, as the *New York Times* put it, 'the scalps of all the American leading pairs' dangling from their belts. In recent days the Dohertys had quickly disposed of the other challenging doubles teams and now a record crowd had gathered for this, *the* match of the championships. Society's finest, including the Duchess of Marlborough, crowded into all available seats. The day had begun with sunshine but soon clouds gathered.

On the court the Dohertys were cool-headed and 'almost exasperatingly' accurate in winning the long, first two sets. In the third set, with the Dohertys leading 5 games to 2, Ward and Davis, showing some of their championship form, broke Reggie's serve and took the next game, to draw up to within one game of their opponents. However, the visitors won their final serve, the set, and the match, 11-9, 12-10, 6-4.

What a peculiar year for the English pair. They had lost their own national doubles title two months earlier, but now had claimed the American doubles title. It was the first US national tennis title to fall into foreign hands. (Reggie would make it to the finals in singles a few days later but Bill Larned, defending US champion, would defeat him, a reverse of their earlier match at the Crescent Athletic Club.)

Some newspaper writers, the day following the doubles match, thought that Ward had again been heroic and Davis off his game. Others claimed that in this match (unlike the earlier two meetings of the two teams) everyone had played his best. It was, therefore, a true test of ability and style of play and 'another triumph for the steady, safe game as against the brilliant, dashing, hard hitting game – the Ward and Davis method', said one writer. 'The game of force and angles is good and it wins, but it lacks the quality of steadiness, and when opposed by a team whose reliance is that very quality, it fails as it did today.'

The tortoise had won again.

In the fall, Davis returned to St. Louis and law school and Ward returned to New Jersey and his job with French & Ward, his father's woollen firm. In early December 1902 Dwight Davis wrote his long-time doubles partner with some thoughts about the future.

Dear Holc,

Have been trying to write you for some time but have been terribly busy. I rather agree with you (for a wonder) in some of your remarks about our tennis career and think that it would be just as well to quit halfway down the toboggan or just as we have mounted the freight train. Personally I doubt if I play next year as I do not expect to come East until later and it is impossible to get into shape here. I may also decide to go into the House of Delegates and fight our good boodler friends but doubt it. [Boodler was a slang term for corrupt politician.] If I did I would probably stay West most of the summer. How would you enjoy me as a 'boodler'! I do not expect to run, however, so do not worry that I will ask you to take the stump for me.

Life out here is one mad rush and I am about to pass away with fatigue. Why don't you come out here, you dog? We are waiting and watching for you and will do our best to give you a 'royal welcome ...'

Let me know what is doing with you occasionally and remember me to all the boys.

With love to family and best wishes to Ware & Ward, limited (very limited). If I can assist the new team by coaching or advice call on me.

Sincerely,
Dwight F. Davis

Davis, it appeared, had laid down his racquet and was considering turning his face into the winds of St. Louis politics. 'I regret that I must quit tennis,' he told a hometown newspaper interviewer six months later, 'but there are numerous reasons for my doing so. St. Louis is so far from the big eastern tournaments that I [would] have to undergo special preparations for them. What tennis I play this summer will be only for exercise.'

Davis's competitive tennis career had ended about as abruptly as it had begun seven years earlier. During that time, he had been ranked in the US Top Ten four times, including two years as the country's number two player. He had won the national Intercollegiate singles championship. He had held the US national doubles title for three years and had won the All-Comers and been runner-up for the lawn tennis doubles championship at Wimbledon. In US national singles at Newport he had a 16-6 match record and was twice runner-up in the All-Comers, including one year (without a challenge round) in which the All-Comers was, in fact, the championship final. He had a Davis Cup record of 1-0 in singles and 1-1 in doubles.

He apparently felt no compulsion to keep playing in order to go out a winner in either the national championships or the international competition for the trophy he had donated. As author William Faulkner would write many years later, 'It takes a brave man to quit while he's behind.'

In a magazine article eight years later about past American tennis greats, writer and former player Arthur Stanwood Pier would claim that an injury had 'practically terminated' Davis's tennis career, specifically the knee twist he received in the August 1901 second-round singles match against Beals Wright at Newport. This could explain his absence from the USNLTA's singles ranking in 1902. But there was no mention of any residual problems with the knee or the slashed foot in Davis's letter to Ward.

Malcolm Whitman also concluded his tennis career in 1902. He had graduated from law school and now joined his father in the family textile business. All through life Whitman would maintain an interest in poetry and other literary forms. After his wins in the second Davis Cup matches at Bay Ridge, Whitman had written a brief collection of maxims, which he titled 'A Reminder For My Son'. Here he applied the lessons of the world he was leaving – tennis – to the world he was entering – commerce:

In any serious game of accomplishment, whether in business or in sport, when you feel that you are winning, when your instinct tells you that you have the game well in hand, be all the more cautious, all the more painstaking, all the more careful. Make assurance doubly sure. Let the prospect of your success quicken and enliven you to renewed effort.

If you actually win, let it make you humble rather than proud. Never consider your crown of laurels, for too often it forms itself into a funeral wreath. The symbols of triumph can become the symbols of destruction in the twinkling of an eye.

Most of the Harvard hotshots who dominated US tennis at the turn of the century, however, continued to compete for several years after leaving Harvard. Holc Ward would win three more national doubles titles with Beals Wright as his partner (1904, 1905, 1906), the US singles title (1904) and play on two more US Davis Cup teams (1905, 1906). Beals Wright would win the US singles title in 1905, play Davis Cup in 1905, 1907, 1908 and 1911, as well as captain the team from 1906 to 1908. Bill Clothier, two years younger than Davis, would win the US championship in 1906 and make it to the finals in 1909, as well as play Davis Cup in 1905 and 1909.

Though Davis, unlike Whitman, had no father around to give him the biblical lecture about putting aside childish things and getting on with life, he may have gotten some variation of that message from his mother or two older brothers after he returned to St. Louis for law school. Davis, like the Doherty brothers, could easily have afforded to play tennis full time. But he had decided not to. Maybe it was the knee or advice from his family or a combination of the two. Or maybe it was a magazine article by Lincoln Steffens.

In October 1902, two months before Davis's letter to Ward, *McClure's Magazine,* a popular national monthly, began a series of articles by Steffens about corruption, greed, slums and despair in American cities. The first city so exposed by a new style of investigative journalism later known as 'muckraking' was – St. Louis. For some time, local St. Louis reporters had been writing about corrupt city officials. But now the St. Louis rock had been dramatically kicked over so that the whole country could see the vermin underneath.

Alarmed citizens and other local publications picked up the theme. There was talk of clean-up and reform, of bringing new blood into city government, of throwing out the 'boodlers', those crooked politicians and businessmen who were stealing the public's money. Possibly this was just the call to service that would appeal to an idealistic young law student. Dwight Davis's home town, it appeared, needed him.

In a review of the 1902 tennis year in *Spalding's Lawn Tennis Annual,* editor J. Parmly Paret (who, of course, had not only written about but played Davis) summarised – and gently criticised – the tennis style of the big left-hander. In an article advising young players to learn by comparing the styles of the experts (Larned, Whitman, Davis, Wrenn, etc.) Paret wrote, 'Davis is a thundering hard-hitter who takes wonderful risks, often unnecessary ones. Where one player might succeed at this style of play, a hundred would fail – yes, a thousand. Less strength in the stroke, a little less speed in smashing and fewer risks taken in placing ground-strokes into the furthermost corners of the court are likely to earn quite as many successes.'

Davis, later in life, would be described by many as affable but reserved, formal, earnest and possibly shy – hardly the daredevil. Nevertheless, as a young man he showed a taste for the dazzling, the brilliant and possibly the risky, in two important parts of his life – tennis and, as it turned out, romance. In both of these areas, he went for the corners.

CHAPTER 11

MEET ME IN
ST. LOU-IE

T hey had met, said the Boston newspapers in announcing the engagement of
Dwight Davis and Helen Brooks, at a Harvard class day, that sunny mélange
in and around Harvard Yard of proud graduates, lovely guests, solemn odes and
banjo music.

Helen Brooks was a local beauty – dark-haired, vivacious, beguiling. Her father,
Henry, was a retired hardware merchant from Newton, Massachusetts. Her
mother, Elizabeth Gill Brooks, had died a few years earlier. Some newspaper
accounts described the Brooks family as wealthy, but then some newspapers also
said that Dwight Davis was the *son* of the man who had founded the
international tennis cup series.

Their engagement was announced on 5 July 1904, Dwight Davis's 25th
birthday. He was four years out of Harvard and one year out of Washington
University Law School (where he had demonstrated a bit more academic
diligence, earning Junior honours, writing for the *Law Quarterly* and graduating
fourth in his class).

His bride-to-be was 27, the youngest of Henry and Lizzie Brooks' three
daughters who ranged, like stairsteps two years apart, from Helen, to Alice, to
Florence, the eldest. Both older sisters were married. It was a 'pretty little
romance', gushed one of the newspaper announcements, dating back five years
to Dwight Davis's undergraduate days. Probably it was more complicated than
that. In later years family lore had it that Helen had been deeply in love with
someone else, who had, instead, married one of her sisters. Helen collapsed and
was advised by her other sister, after a time, that she might as well marry the
attentive Dwight Davis, a good man.

The year 1904 was turning into a big year for Davis weddings. In July Dwight's
older brother Sam was marrying the girl next door, Emma Whitaker, whose family
had built a house at 13 Westmoreland. The Whitaker house – stone, square and

solid, with an air of impenetrability – looked a bit like a bank building, and, in fact, Emma's father, Edwards Whitaker, was president of a bank, Boatmen's, as well as president of a street car company.

Davis weddings, however interesting to a certain segment of St. Louis society, were not what was primarily on the mind of the rest of St. Louis in the summer of 1904. This was the summer of the St. Louis World's Fair – officially the Louisiana Purchase International Exposition. And also, in the back of the aggregate St. Louis mind, like a shadowy, half-remembered bad dream, were the ongoing political scandals of bribes and payoffs, that is, boodle. Civic leaders hoped the one (the Fair) would help rescue St. Louis's national reputation from the other (the boodle).

The exposition was to commemorate the centennial of the 1803 Louisiana Purchase, Thomas Jefferson's serendipitous acquisition from France of the land between the Mississippi River and the Rocky Mountains. The Fair was originally scheduled to open in 1903 but exhibitors, particularly foreign ones, could not meet the deadline, and it wasn't until 30 April 1904 that President Theodore Roosevelt, in the White House in Washington, pressed the button signalling the exposition's opening.

The nearly 1,300-acre fairgrounds was located in Forest Park, not far from the Davis's Westmoreland/Portland Place neighbourhood, with overflow west onto the new, but not yet occupied, campus of Washington University. Before the event ended seven months later, nearly 20 million people, warbling one of the year's hit songs, 'Meet Me In St. Lou-ie, Lou-ie', had ridden in the cars of the giant Ferris wheel; watched craft and technology demonstrations; wandered along lagoons and sunken gardens surrounded by spectacular (if temporary) ivory-coloured palaces; gawked at exotic strangers in the ethnology villages of the anthropology department; and sampled unfamiliar foods, including ice cream in thin, cookie-like 'cones'. Though the latter was deliciously popular, this was not the first time ice cream had been served this way, despite later myths about the Fair.

St. Louis civic committees had laboured for 15 years to produce the Fair. Dwight Davis's most public contribution was to pull his tennis racquet out of mothballs - for held in St. Louis, in conjunction with the Louisiana Purchase Exposition, was the 1904 Olympics.

This was the third Olympic games since France's Baron Pierre de Coubertin had, in 1896, resurrected the ancient sports competition. The second modern Olympics in Paris in 1900 also had been held in conjunction with a world's fair, the Paris Exposition, and in tennis the Doherty brothers had won the doubles and Laurie had won the singles.

Brought in to direct the St. Louis exposition's Department of Physical Culture, which administered the Olympic events, was James E. Sullivan. A long-time booster of athletics in the United States, Sullivan had been for some years secretary of the Amateur Athletic Union, the organisation which, in later years, would present an annual award named for him to the outstanding American amateur athlete. Among Sullivan's projects had been the establishment of playgrounds in New York City through the Outdoor Recreation League.

Developing public playgrounds was becoming a prime interest of Dwight Davis's as well. The playground movement was the fresh-air, run-and-play, happy-squealing-children pillar of the nation's expanding Progressive movement. It has been said that to understand a man, you must look at the world as it was when he was about 19 or 20 years old – the time when he becomes autonomous as a man and alert to life's possibilities.

For Dwight Davis this period was the late 1890s. Progressivism was in the air. One aspect of Progressivism was the City Beautiful movement which propounded the downright heretical idea that cities could do with some structured planning. In 1894 the first National Conference for Good City Government had been held in Philadelphia to discuss the problems of the cities and foster progressive and reform movements. Among those on hand was Harvard's president Charles Eliot. Out of this came the National Municipal League, an organisation in which Dwight Davis would become involved in future years. And in 1901 into the White House had moved Teddy Roosevelt, a trust-busting reformer who would even name his new third party, the Progressive Party.

The playground movement had started in 1885 with a supervised playground in Boston called the Sand Gardens. Cities were crowded. Children – if they were to develop into productive, responsible citizens – needed safe places to play. Playgrounds, the theory went, also could help convert the foreign born into Americans. One of the leaders of the playground movement in St. Louis was Charlotte Rumbold, a social reformer who had been educated at Columbia University and in Europe, and who, though much younger than Dwight Davis's mother (she was a contemporary of the older Davis brothers), probably would have known Maria Davis through their mutual membership in the influential Wednesday Club.

For it was the Wednesday Club and women's clubs elsewhere in the country that were converting the theory of beneficial playgrounds into swing-and-sandpile reality. Dwight Davis was recruited for the cause – possibly by his mother and her friends. In any event, he was named chairman of the St. Louis Civic League's Open Air Playgrounds Committee, and in 1903 he had organised a tennis tournament in St. Louis to raise funds for local playgrounds. (This using tennis to advance other societal goals was something Davis would do from time to time throughout his career in public service.)

The 1903 benefit tournament was on private club courts in Forest Park. Davis teamed with Walker McKittrick, another descendent of a St. Louis dry goods pioneer. They played (and beat) Joe Wear, who had played for Yale and was back in town setting up a dry goods commission firm, and Wear's partner, Ralph McKittrick, the St. Louis city champion in 1903 and 1904. (From 1928 to 1935 Joe Wear would serve as non-playing US Davis Cup captain and head the US Davis Cup committee from 1928 to 1930.)

For the 1904 Olympics, Dwight Davis and Ralph McKittrick put together a hometown team to play doubles. At these Olympics in tennis, as in other sports, different groups of events were held in St. Louis throughout the summer. Director James Sullivan considered them all Olympic events, though later records of the International Olympic Committee did not: some, as it turned out, were more Olympic than others.

The men's tennis events – unlike at Paris, there were no women's events or mixed doubles – were held on courts near the Washington University stadium. Davis won the Louisiana Purchase singles in May, beating a Kansas City player in two sets in the finals, and then joined with Ralph McKittrick to win the World's Fair doubles. The *World's Fair Bulletin* published during the exposition considered these all 'Olympic Games' winners.

Later IOC records, however, gave official status only to those who competed during 'Olympic Week', 29 August to 3 September. Davis's Boston friend, Beals Wright (ranked number four nationally), came out to participate during that week. Wright and Davis's ex-partner Holcombe Ward had teamed up a few weeks earlier to win the first of three national doubles championships at Newport. Also on hand for the Olympics were two other top ten players (Alphonzo Bell and Edgar Leonard) but not Holcombe Ward, Bill Clothier or Bill Larned (nationally ranked one, two and three in 1904).

Although athletes from about a dozen nations competed in other sports, only one non-American, a German, Hugo Hardy, competed in tennis. This, despite the fact that Davis had tried to recruit European participants for St. Louis and Newport while he was in Europe the previous winter. (If some players, particularly the British, had considered coming for a time, they well might have changed their minds when the executive committee of the USNLTA had made the surprising announcement in March that it would not be sending a team to England to challenge for the Davis Cup in 1904.)

Beals Wright won the 'Olympic' or 'World's Tennis Championship' singles and teamed with Leonard to win the doubles. Davis, no longer in competitive trim, easily won his first round singles match but defaulted to Bell in the second round. (A New York newspaper article a year earlier on Davis's retirement from national competition said the word was that Davis had put on a little weight. He looked slim enough, however, in World's Fair photos.) Davis and McKittrick lost in the doubles in the second round to Bell and Robert LeRoy.

No question about it, Davis's primary attention, by this time, had turned from the tennis court. Though he had been admitted to the Missouri Bar, he apparently had no intention of practising law. He was, however, increasingly involved with the committees springing up to combat St. Louis's urban problems and political scandals. And then there was his upcoming marriage.

On 15 November 1904, in Geneva, Switzerland, Dwight Davis and Helen Brooks were married. The wedding, a Protestant Episcopal service, was at noon on a Tuesday in the Chapel of the Macchabees, a small 15th-century medieval chapel off to the side of Cathedral St. Pierre in Geneva's old section. In the wood-panelled chapel, with light filtering down from high, jewel-bright stained-glass windows, the bridal couple said their vows. Family members on hand included Dwight's mother and Helen's father, her sister Alice and Alice's husband, Robert S. Gunn, who was best man.

The ceremony was performed by Geneva's 'American' pastor, who often performed weddings for Yankee expatriates. The newlyweds left in the afternoon for a tour through France which ended at Marseilles, where they embarked on an around-the-world honeymoon. The lengthy trip took them to Italy, Greece, Egypt, India, Burma, Ceylon, Straits Settlements (the British crown colony which included Singapore), Siam, China, Japan and the Philippine Islands.

In the Philippines the young couple paid a call on W. Cameron Forbes, an American official who knew Dwight's older brother, John. Forbes, currently serving as secretary of commerce and police, invited the young couple to his house and found them to be 'very delightful'. Helen Brooks Davis, Forbes noted in his journal, 'was very enthusiastic and pleasant, but somewhat used up by the heat'. Forbes tried to arrange a tennis game between Davis and the local English 'crack'. But the local star was sick 'and Davis indifferent'. A disappointed Forbes wrote that it would have done the Englishman 'much good to have got jolly well licked'.

The new Mr. and Mrs. Dwight Filley Davis returned to St. Louis early the following summer, and properly printed cards announced to their friends that they would be 'at home' after the first of June at 17 Westmoreland Place, the large pink granite mansion in which Davis's mother lived.

Like his brothers, Davis plunged into the life of the city, giving time to administering Davis Estate investments as well as serving on some of the more genteel organisational boards – those of the Public Library and the Museum of Fine Arts, for instance. Unlike John and Sam, however, the youngest Davis brother would display a more serious interest in public service and a willingness to take on public jobs with little glamour. There was, for instance, the chairmanship of the Public Baths Commission, a position to which Davis learned he had been appointed when he returned home from his honeymoon. No glamour job this, certainly, but public health concerns connected with the waves of immigrants crowding into St. Louis and other American cities made it a necessary one.

Davis's bath commission appointment had come from Mayor Rolla Wells, also a wealthy member of the St. Louis business elite. Though several years older than Davis, Wells had been elected in 1901 on the reform ticket within the Democratic party. Davis was nominally a Republican. However, reaction to corruption scandals involving politicians and St. Louis business leaders was blurring party lines.

Not only had St. Louis newspapers (particularly Joseph Pulitzer's *Post-Dispatch*) and national magazines continued to dig into municipal and corporate corruption, but in 1904 Lincoln Steffens again focused attention on St. Louis with the publication of his book *The Shame of the Cities*. This was a collection, in book form, of his earlier articles in *McClure's Magazine*. St. Louis was the subject of not one but two of these articles, though St. Louis, of course, was just one of the cities in which industrial growth at the end of the 19th century often had run roughshod over civic conscience.

In St. Louis, Steffens charged, business leaders hired political bosses to 'buy' permits, licenses and favourable laws from greedy 'riffraff' and 'illiterate' legislators, who had driven out the decent members of the Municipal Assembly. Everything the city owned was for sale by the officers elected by the people 'for a fraction of true value'.

Yet what seemed to disgust Steffens the most was that in election after election 'the people' put up with this arrangement, while business leaders – the suppliers of the 'boodle' – cynically supported the system's efficiency and profitability. 'St. Louis seems to me to be something new in the history of the government of the people, by the rascals, for the rich,' he had written in one article.

'Make politics a sport, as they do in England, or a profession, as they do in Germany,' he wrote in another article, 'and we'll have – well, something else than we have now ... But don't try to reform politics with the banker, the lawyer, the dry-goods merchant, for these are business men ... The commercial spirit is the spirit of profit, not patriotism; of credit, not honour; of individual gain, not national prosperity; of trade and dickering, not principle.'

Possibly this seemed to be hitting a bit close to home to the bankers, the lawyers and the dry-goods merchants reading in their wood-panelled studies on Westmoreland and Portland Places. Undoubtedly they had breathed a bit easier when only one neighbourhood resident, a Scots-Irish immigrant named James Campbell who had hit it big in railroads and utilities, was publicly named in the investigation conducted by crusading circuit attorney Joseph Folk. (Folk was later elected governor of Missouri.) However, Edwards Whitaker, Sam Davis's father-in-law, did happen to be president of the St. Louis Transit Co., a street railway company involved in one of the more spectacular bribe scandals Folk unravelled.

In 1907 Dwight Davis, at the age of 26, plunged into this cauldron of corruption and reform by doing what he had joked about doing in his 1902 letter to Holcombe Ward – running for a seat in the St. Louis House of Delegates. The House of Delegates, along with the City Council, the smaller upper body of members elected at-large, governed the city. This bicameral Municipal Assembly was a legislative body made up more of 'saloon keepers than society men', wrote one newspaper later. Davis ran as a Republican representative from the 28th ward, a silk-stocking west end district which included Westmoreland/Portland Place, and won the seat.

Election was one thing; power, however, was another. Davis was not a member of the majority 'combine' which ruled the House, though most of the time, apparently, he got along reasonably well with his fellow legislators. He was able, in 1908, to shepherd through the assembly bills authorising five small parks in the crowded tenement districts, as well as for a larger park on the site of the old Fair Grounds. On another occasion, however, he introduced a motion to get rid of a House employee who had been convicted of being an accessory to bribery. The motion was never voted upon because he could not get anyone to second it. Wryly, he would later describe himself as a 'would-be reformer in politics'. When his term was concluded in 1909, he did not run for re-election.

There was, by now, much in other areas of his life to occupy his time. Dwight and Helen had rented a modest (by neighbourhood standards) house at 38 Westmoreland Place, a block west of the Davis family home. They were living here when their son was born 31 July 1907. Young Dwight Filley Davis Jr. was joined a year and a half later by a sister, Alice Brooks, born 12 January 1909. The new baby girl was named for Helen's sister, Alice Gunn, who, with her husband, Robert, had died tragically in an automobile accident. In the winter of 1909, construction began at 16 Portland Place on a new house for the growing Davis family. The property backed up to that of the senior Mrs. Davis and was part of the original large plot bought by Dwight's late father.

Dwight and Helen Davis's new house was a graceful, three-storey Georgian Revival brick, a style increasingly favoured by several of the area's younger families, and aesthetically lighter than some of the neighbourhood's massive chateaux and mausoleums. The architect was James P. Jamieson, who would eventually design 14 houses in the neighbourhood. A generous-sized entry hall ran the depth of the house. On either side were a large library, a hall leading to the kitchen and, across the back, spacious panelled dining and living rooms. Along this south wall marched eight deep, arched windows and French doors, looking out onto a long terrace, rear lawn and garden. The door out onto this rear area was nearly as elegant as the front door. This produced a house which looked as if it had two 'fronts' – an English effect for which Jamieson was known.

On the second floor were four bedrooms, a nursery and a sewing room. On the third floor were smaller guest rooms, servants rooms, a trunk room and large playroom. In the north-west corner of the house was a carriage entrance and west of that, a separate brick carriage house/garage, with space for four automobiles and servants quarters. Topping this not unattractive outbuilding was a gracefully domed, copper roof with tall finial, something like a giant Prussian army helmet. With Dwight's two older brothers living in the neighbourhood – John and his wife Edith would soon build a house at 47 Portland Place – the area was, in effect, practically a Davis family compound.

Even without elective office, Dwight Davis had many public activities which took him away from the domesticity of his elegant new house with its rapidly filling nursery (another daughter, Cynthia, had been born 1 October 1910). He had ongoing business interests (Security Building Co., Davis Estate, directorships of State National Bank, Mortgage Trust Co., Mortgage Guarantee Co.), but it was progressive causes and municipal reform that claimed the bulk of his attention. (Though his brothers might be more interested in business and polo than the plight of the poor, there was no ignoring the fact that their tending of the family fortune and the steady and most ample income it provided, gave Davis the time and opportunity for public service.)

On the national level, he was now on the boards or executive committees of the National Municipal League, the Playground and Recreation Association of America and the United States National Lawn Tennis Association. In St. Louis he served on boards of the Tenement House Association and the Society for Prevention of Tuberculosis and was vice-president of the Board of Freeholders (which was rewriting the city's charter), as well as chairman of the City Plan Commission, another committee involved in municipal governance reform.

However, his most significant appointment came in the spring of 1911, when

Republican Mayor F. H. Kreismann named him commissioner of the St. Louis Park Department. Here it would all coalesce – his interests in public health, in recreation, in politics. In this job he would make his most notable contribution to his hometown.

St. Louis politics being what it was, the Davis nomination was at first turned down by the City Council. Word around City Hall was that a number of councilmen considered Davis 'too friendly' to the Terminal Railroad Association which might then gain undue influence on the Board of Public Improvements, and which was involved in the chronically incendiary 'free-bridge' issue. Also, at least one councilman was pushing his own candidate. (John Davis, a member of the Council, was excused from voting on his brother's appointment.)

At first Dwight Davis was noncommittal about his name being resubmitted. He told the mayor he would have to discuss it with his family. 'Davis is in no sense an applicant for Park Commissioner,' said Mayor Kreismann. 'I had to beg him, for several weeks, to get his consent to accept the appointment.' A day or two later the resubmitted nomination went through.

The St. Louis newspapers approved. The *St. Louis Republic* was jocularly extravagant in its praise of this new appointee: 'When a young man survives the double disaster of being born rich and being educated at Harvard, and comes out without being utterly self-sufficient or an insufferable snob, it is plain that he must have been rarely endowed with natural gifts.' The article explained that Davis had earlier ' brought out the surprising, astonishing and astounding fact that there was in St. Louis a rich young man who was willing to spend a few dollars on something [the Davis Cup] besides rye highballs, small beer and a plurality of wives.'

'He is a strapping, tall, kindly-looking young man,' continued the lengthy Sunday feature story. 'There is a bounding elasticity in his step, a firm grip in his hand ... But his best feature is the true kindly glint that comes into his eyes when he speaks of his work on the Playgrounds Commission and the work that he hopes to do as Park Commissioner ... the work he has chosen for himself – helping little children to be good men and women.' The paper also approved of the fact that the new commissioner was forgoing a summer vacation and sending his family off to cooler summer climes without him. 'The slum children need him too badly.'

In St. Louis parks, as in the carefully landscaped, verdant parks in many major American cities, stern KEEP OFF THE GRASS! signs traditionally poked up out of the ground along with the tulips and daffodils. Swooping down like a master gardener ever alert for weeds, Davis ordered them removed. This policy, dramatic and tangible, caught the city's attention and would, for years to come, be a philosophy proudly bragged about in discussions of the St. Louis parks.

The purpose of the parks was 'the raising of men or women rather than grass or trees', said the new commissioner. 'If we can't have the grass and the people in our parks, let's sacrifice the grass.' And later in the hot summer, as night brought no relief to stifling little bedrooms in the 'congested districts' (a common euphemism for slums and the later 'inner city'), Davis opened that grass for park sleepovers (proper clothing required; pyjamas acceptable).

In the winter, during an extreme cold spell, nearly 2,500 homeless men were given shelter in city bath houses (also under the jurisdiction of the park department), where they were provided with coffee and rolls, courtesy of the ever-helpful Wednesday Club. Reported Davis in the department's annual report, 'The good order and cleanly condition in which the bath houses were left, together with the desire expressed by many of the men for a bath in the morning, indicated that these men were not worthless loafers, but were temporarily submerged in pitiless industrial conditions.' (No record of how that last phrase might have struck some of his Westmoreland/Portland Place neighbours.)

The new park commissioner might value children and their development over grass, but that did not mean he could totally ignore traditional park horticulture. In his first years he and the department's consulting landscape architect, George E. Kessler, produced a master plan for the landscape and gardens in the park system. This included such things as planting hundreds of wildflowers and thousands of seedlings to continue the restoration of Forest Park's eponymous forest which had been cut down for the World's Fair. Kessler, who had trained in Germany, was particularly interested in building graceful, tree-lined boulevards which would connect the city's park areas.

Here also Davis reflected the influence of the progressive, 'City Beautiful' philosophy that flowers, trees and lush, green spaces were tools for achieving higher social goals. The new formal plantings of Lucas Garden, behind the public library, for instance, would 'bring a touch of nature to eyes tired by the labors and surroundings of an ugly and exacting industrial civilisation', wrote Davis in his first annual report.

This first annual report ran an energetic 15 pages, and, in places, ascended to earnest eloquence. 'Strangely enough,' he wrote in discussing potential new properties, 'there is now no public place in the city from which the magnitude and majestic beauty of the mighty Mississippi can be adequately seen.' In contrast, the previous year his predecessor's report had been a scant, four-page, bare bones recitation of roads oiled, roses planted and frost-bitten privet hedges resuscitated.

Always the question of adequate places for children to run and play as well as attractive open spaces for adults to escape the crowding of 20th-century cities continued to be uppermost in Davis's mind. He and Charlotte Rumbold (secretary of the Park Department's Public Recreation Commission) shared what later Forest Park historians Caroline Loughlin and Catherine Anderson would call the 'progressives' notion of improvement through recreation'.

Playgrounds. We need more playgrounds, was Davis's constant message. Of the 20 largest cities in the United States in 1909, St. Louis ranked fourth in population but 16th in playground expenditures. For St. Louis's 274,000 children, the available public playground space worked out to 2.20 square feet per child. The German government, Davis pointed out, insisted on 25 feet per child. Though new playgrounds had been added in the densely populated neighbourhoods, 'the streets are still crowded with children'.

Providing recreation facilities for those children had to come first before new tennis courts or a public golf course. 'A 10-cent bat and a 5-cent ball will give 20 boys infinite pleasure and valuable exercise. All they need from the city is a lot to play on.' Adults interested in golf or tennis could usually manage, argued Davis, 'but the little lads to whom a penny is riches can't do anything until the city does it for them'.

Nevertheless, public tennis and golf facilities had their own value, said Davis, particularly tennis, 'the most useful of games'. Though golf courses added beautified vistas to parks in addition to sport, they were expensive. In tennis, on the other hand, 'two make a game, and you can crowd forty tennis courts into the space needed for one baseball diamond and thus give a hundred and sixty people exercise where baseball gives exercise only to eighteen'. (As for himself, these days, he admitted, he played a great deal of golf, 'having given up tennis more or less'.)

One of his first acts was to add new tennis courts at Fairground Park to relieve congestion at O'Fallon and Carondelet parks, where St. Louis's first free, public park tennis courts had been installed under Davis's predecessor, Philip Scanlan. And for the recreation fields in Forest Park he proposed, in his first annual report, 24 tennis courts, six baseball fields and an 18-hole golf course.

In future years, when exactly who did what and when would become a bit murky, many would insist on crediting Dwight Davis with installing the first public tennis courts in St. Louis (and sometimes in the country) while he was park commissioner. (Davis, of course, never made this claim.) Though this was not the case, what is clear is that under Park Commissioner Davis all sports and recreation in St. Louis parks boomed.

By late spring 1913 there were tennis courts at four parks (including 32 new courts at Forest Park alone) and enthusiastic players were arriving as soon as it was light – sometimes as early as 4.30 a.m. There was the same crack-of-dawn enthusiasm for the new nine-hole Forest Park golf course, eventually to be 18 holes. Davis reported that a study of the players, who included 'bare-footed boys and men evidently in most moderate circumstances', proved that, at least on public links, golf 'is not a rich man's game'.

In later years, as Davis moved back into the national spotlight – and this time not on the sports pages – those who had worked for him at the Park Department would report that their boss had not taken his $3,000 annual salary as park commissioner. Rather, he had applied it – plus another $6,000 or so from his own pocket each year – to the financing of new park facilities and programs.

CHAPTER 12

TOURNAMENTS FOR ALL

T he attractive, dark-haired woman travelling by train east to Boston in May 1914, was obviously a lady – and obviously pregnant. There was easily time, Helen Davis had assumed, to make the annual summer trek from St. Louis to Cape Cod and get the family settled in before the baby arrived in July. Once she reached Boston, however, it became clear that this reasonable schedule had gone awry. The fourth Davis baby, another girl, arrived on 14 May 1914, two months early. She was named Helen Brooks Davis for her mother.

This, the fourth child in ten years of marriage had produced 'a batting average of .250 in the minor league', Dwight Davis told his classmates in the Harvard class report the following year, adding 'but have now retired from competition'.

There also had been another significant addition to the Davis household. Josephine Shaughnessy, was from Boston, an energetic, good-humoured Irish woman of nearly middle age. Miss Shaughnessy – soon 'Shon' to the whole family – had first arrived upon the scene to nurse Helen Davis and her newest baby. Afterwards, she had been prevailed upon to stay permanently as governess for the Davis children. Cheerfully dispensing maxims about good manners and good posture, she would function, through the years, as the family's domestic rock – when Helen Davis was ill, when Dwight Davis was absorbed by government duties.

The baseball analogy Davis had used in discussing the size of his family in his Harvard class report was not inappropriate for the park commissioner. At home, young Pete (as Dwight F. Davis Jr. was called) was becoming an enthusiastic baseball fan, particularly of the St. Louis Cardinals. In a few years he would regularly line up his younger sisters and insist they recite from memory the whole Cardinals' line-up. Pete's dog, a little terrier, was named Ty Cobb.

The park commissioner even occasionally took to the mound himself, for instance pitching an inning or two on opening day of the city's municipal softball league 'in a "form" worthy of Christy Mathewson', reported *Reedy's Mirror*, a weekly St. Louis literary journal covering politics and culture. (Mathewson was the famous right-handed pitcher for the New York Giants.)

William Marion Reedy, the *Mirror's* asp-tongued editor and publisher, normally delighted in stinging the broad rumps of the city's (and country's) political and power elite. But he respected reformers and he had become quite a booster of the park commissioner's. Davis was 'suave, diplomatic, approachable, and a man of action', wrote Reedy. Midst his activities in St. Louis, continued Reedy, Davis 'keeps a modestly affectionate eye on the Davis Cup, emblematic of the tennis championship of the world, over which every nation has fought for years'.

Davis, continued the *Mirror* article, 'is truly a remarkable triumph over the great American handicap of being a rich man's son, with the lure of ease and idle pleasure all around him ...' Which was not to say, of course, that Dwight Davis had become – or would ever become – a St. Francis (another son of a wealthy merchant, incidentally), forsaking wealth and the conveniences, opportunities and pleasures it provided.

He still played golf and polo at the St. Louis Country Club and sailed in races at Buzzards Bay during family vacations on Cape Cod. He played racquets, that hard, fast predecessor of squash and sport of blue-bloods, which required excellent eye-hand co-ordination and was the game which some consider the most difficult of all racquet sports. He played well enough that he and St. Louis friend Joe Wear went East and won the national racquets doubles championship in 1914.

And if such competitions were of value to Davis and his friends, they would be so as well to those whose private 'club' was the public park, he reasoned. Tennis courts, baseball diamonds and soccer fields alone were not enough. Municipal athletics too needed organised competition, decided the man who, more than a decade earlier, had helped spawn organised international tennis competition.

Davis, who would in later years be called the father of organised athletics in public parks, hired a director of athletics for the St. Louis Park Department. A municipal 'soccer football' league was organised first, followed by baseball leagues, with golf, tennis and basketball leagues to come.

'I believe that this Municipal League idea, when fully worked out, will be a great force not only for clean sport, but for good citizenship,' explained Davis. 'Just as "The battle of Waterloo was won on the playing fields of Eton", so the forces for the less spectacular but equally important battles of peace may be trained on our own playfields.

'Athletics, especially under proper supervision, benefit not only health, but also character. The boy who wishes to become a star athlete soon learns that he cannot loaf about in saloons and dance halls, or drink and smoke to excess ... Physical well-being in itself is a great incentive to moral well-being.' By spring 1915, the St. Louis Municipal Amateur Baseball League had played an inter-city series with Cleveland, and Davis had written to other cities suggesting a national organisation of municipal amateur leagues.

Meanwhile two other projects were absorbing great chunks of the park commissioner's time – or his park lands. One got his enthusiastic support, the other did not. The latter was the growing zoo in Forest Park. A small collection of animals had been housed in Forest Park since the early 1890s, augmented by animals and the spectacular, walk-through birdcage left in St. Louis when the 1904 World's Fair closed. In 1910, the year before Davis took office, the St. Louis Zoological Society was organised and more animals were collected.

Davis argued energetically against expansion of the zoo in the park, recommending instead that other ground be purchased, since 'park properties are already too limited'. And if there was to be a 'zoological collection on a large scale' – elsewhere, he hoped – why not try something new in the housing of the animals? Though seeing unfamiliar animals might be educational for children, admitted Davis, 'I have always felt that the sight of the monarchs of the forest and jungle cooped up in iron cages was also an education in man's inhumanity to dumb beasts. A glimpse of a herd of animals roaming apparently at will through natural surroundings is surely ... better ... than the sight of the same animals closely confined in a super-heated and super-odoriferous building.'

This time Davis lost. Forest Park was easy to get to, and the people of St. Louis desperately wanted elephants and lions, said the mayor, as he signed an ordinance in late 1913 setting aside some 70 acres of Forest Park for an expanded zoo.

Showing a pragmatic acceptance of reality that would later come in handy in Washington, Davis not only took a seat on the zoo's board of control but accepted its presidency. A special zoo tax passed in 1915 and school children donated pennies to help purchase an elephant to be named Jim in honour of the current school board president. On 5 April 1915 a parade of school children welcomed the arrival of the elephant – a female, as it turned out, who was quickly rechristened Miss Jim.

In later years, the innovations in some of the zoo's habitat – bear pits which looked like natural stone caves, a chain of small 'lakes' flowing into the seal basin – would bring visits and praise from outside zoo experts. Possibly some of these more natural and humane settings, said later historians, were a tribute to Davis's early arguments.

The project which Davis did wholeheartedly support was one spearheaded by

Charlotte Rumbold. An elaborate outdoor drama retelling St. Louis's colourful history would be an appropriate way to celebrate the city's 150th birthday, reasoned Rumbold and her fellow executive board members, including Davis. Other Progressive values could be served as well – democratisation, inclusiveness, pride in and improvement of the American city – not to mention the promotion of St. Louis to the rest of the country.

The Pageant and Masque, staged in a natural amphitheatre in Forest Park for four nights in early summer, 1914, involved more than 7,000 citizens and drew crowds of 100,000 a night. The eye-popping production included canoes in the water of the park's Grand Basin (representing the mighty Mississippi); an orchestra of 100 and chorus of 500; swirling clouds of dancers; actors portraying Marquette, La Salle, Lafayette, Saint Louis and Lewis and Clark, plus such symbolic characters as Pioneer, Cahokia (the site of ancient Indian mounds across the river from St. Louis), and the villains Gold, War and Poverty.

The pageant, with its 'easily-felt though invisible bond of spiritual feeling between those on and those off the stage', had produced all sorts of important by-products, wrote Davis in his next annual report. The new city charter had been adopted, free-bridge bonds voted in, and an ordinance passed authorising the City Plan Commission's Central Parkway. The Pageant Drama Association, concluded Davis, 'indirectly accomplished more for the welfare of the city than any movement since the World's Fair'.

Davis's main enthusiasm, however, remained organised athletics in the parks. In late March 1916 representatives of the park departments of 52 American cities streamed into St. Louis to organise the National Municipal Recreation Federation and to arrange inter-city contests in all major sports played in city parks. It was decided that the first of these would be tournaments in golf and tennis to be held in St. Louis in September 1916, following team eliminations by geographical section during the summer.

Further it was announced that a St. Louis insurance man interested in athletics was donating a perpetual trophy for the winning golf team and the United States National Lawn Tennis Association was donating a perpetual trophy for the winning tennis team. Possibly this was at Davis's suggestion. There was developing within USNLTA the realisation that one way to encourage and popularise the game was to support tennis beyond the private school and country club. 'In every new high school that is being built and in almost every recreation centre ... tennis courts are being introduced', the USNLTA's treasurer had pointed out at the organisation's February annual meeting. Yet, he added, 'the men who are responsible for these tennis courts probably never play tennis themselves'.

The USNLTA, it appeared, was in the happy situation of having a growing surplus of funds (a substantial chunk of which, appropriately enough, had come from revenues of Davis Cup matches). 'It seems to me that we are the custodians and we have really a responsibility resting on our shoulders that we have not had in years past,' added the treasurer as the organisation debated the advisability of funding basic publications or a field secretary to advise newcomers on tennis rules, skills and etiquette.

The Longwood Cricket Club, at its recent annual meeting, when electing Davis, Malcolm Whitman and Bob Wrenn honorary Longwood members, had specifically mentioned the work Davis and the USNLTA were doing to develop the game of tennis in public parks. And it probably did not hurt the cause of public parks tennis that American Davis Cup star Maurice McLoughlin, winner of the national singles championship at Newport in 1912 and 1913 and runner-up in 1914 and 1915, had got his start on public parks courts in California.

After attending the three-day meeting of the new Municipal Recreation Federation in St. Louis, the president of the New York City Park Board called the new movement 'a particularly healthy one'. It made competition possible for 'those people who could formerly indulge their natural keenness for sports only by standing as spectators'.

Before the meeting adjourned, the contentious issue had been settled of whether it was 'undemocratic' to bar from competition those who also belonged to private clubs 'which balloted for their membership'. Yes, it was, delegates decided, in an interesting twist on the concept of democratisation. All that was necessary was that a competitor's city be a member of the new federation.

Dwight Davis was elected president of the new federation, and Nelson Cunliff was named secretary-treasurer. Cunliff, Davis's park superintendent of construction, was now, in fact, park commissioner himself, for Davis had resigned in April 1915 at the end of his fourth year.

Earlier in 1915, when Davis's intention to leave the department was made public, the *St. Louis Republic* had said he planned a hunting trip to Alaska and then would be spending time with his family at a summer home in Maine. He was tired, said the article, of 'scraping for pennies' while trying to get adequate funding. For some years Davis had indicated frustration at being unable to convince voters and legislators that 'real progress in park development' could not be funded out of municipal revenue but needed a 'reasonably large' ($2.75 million) special bond issue.

Yet another factor surely was that Davis's attention, like that of many Americans, was increasingly focused overseas on the lengthening, dark shadows engulfing Europe.

CHAPTER 13

MEANWHILE, WITH THE CUP

The Pre-War Years

The Davis Cup made its first Atlantic crossing in the summer of 1903 in the arms of a British team, victorious at last. For a second year the Doherty brothers had swallowed their distaste for ocean voyages and had come to wrest the silver bowl from the Americans. This time they were determined to win. Irish veteran Harold S. Mahony might have been officially on the team but there was no way he was to be allowed to stick even a toe onto the courts at the Longwood Cricket Club. Even when Reggie Doherty was unable to play his first match against Bill Larned because of a strained shoulder, Britain's coach William Collins decided to default the match. According to the current rules, if Mahony had substituted, he would have been required to replace Reggie for all singles matches.

Collins' gamble that Reggie's shoulder would heal had paid off, helped by a rain delay of two days. Reggie and Laurie beat America's Wrenn brothers, Bob and George (the only time in a Davis Cup challenge round that brothers would play against brothers). The British defeated the US 4-1, and a new truth emerged about Davis Cup play which, in future decades, would give encouragement to countries no matter what their size or the sophistication of their tennis programs: with just two (albeit great) players, a country could win the cup.

With the Davis Cup in England, competing for it now became more affordable for several European countries. In 1904 Austria challenged but was unable to field a team. Belgium and France, however, met at Wimbledon and Belgium won the right to challenge England, the cup holder. England won again, but for the first time names of countries other than the British Isles or the United States were engraved on the cup's rounded surface.

The US had not challenged in 1904 and there were dissatisfied mutterings about 'the Boston crowd' which ran the USNLTA. America was back with a challenge in 1905 but the US team (Bill Larned, Bill Clothier, Holcombe Ward and

Beals Wright), after defeating France and newcomer Australasia, went down to defeat 5-0 before the British Isles in the challenge round.

It was a fortunate confluence of time and geography that had yoked together Australia and New Zealand as 'Australasia' at the time when each had one brilliant tennis player. In 1907, with Australasia challenging for a third time, the shrewd, wiry Australian Norman Brookes and the dashing, charismatic New Zealand native, Anthony Wilding, proved unstoppable. They defeated the British Isles team of Davis Cup veterans Arthur Gore and Roper Barrett 3-2. The cup was off on another voyage, this time halfway around the globe.

Australasia kept the cup for the next four years, and at first it resided nonchalantly on the sideboard in the dining room of Norman Brookes's home. His young bride, who had fretted that it overwhelmed all his other trophies and that nothing looked good 'alongside that darned bath', was relieved when it was sent off to a bank vault. One last time she decided to use it as a dinner party centrepiece. Decades later she would still remember the look of full, loose-petaled red peonies and candlelight reflected in the gleaming silver of the massive bowl.

Truly international tennis was proving to be a drain on the coffers of the world's tennis associations. In 1910, for the first time since 1901, no countries challenged for the cup, but the next year the US did send a team down to Christchurch, New Zealand – and was defeated. (Ironically, Tony Wilding stayed in England where he was living, and did not compete.) In 1912 two faces from the past appeared at Folkestone at England's first round match against France. Veteran competitors Roper Barrett and Arthur Gore helped defeat France 4-1, though younger players were substituted when the British team travelled to Melbourne and was finally successful in prying the cup away from Brookes & company.

Six nations challenged in 1914 for the right to meet the US, the current holder of the cup. In an emotional second-round match played in Pennsylvania, Australasia took on Germany just as radio broadcasts carried news of the outbreak of war in Europe. Australasia won and German players Otto Froitzheim and Oskar Kreuzer immediately sailed from New York for Germany. Three days after the matches concluded Britain declared war on Germany, and Froitzheim and Kreuzer were taken into custody at sea.

A month later, crowds of more than 11,000 jammed the West Side Tennis Club's new facility in Forest Hills, Long Island, to see Australasia's Brookes and Wilding take on America's Maurice McLoughlin, R. Norris Williams II and Thomas Bundy in the challenge round. McLoughlin, a hard-serving, red-haired Californian, won both his singles matches. His marathon first set with Norman

Brookes (which the American won 17-15) was to be judged one of the all time great Davis Cup matchups. Australasia, nevertheless, prevailed, winning back the cup. With Davis Cup competition suspended and safety on the high seas in doubt, tennis authorities decided that the cup should wait out the war in the vault of New York jewellers Black, Starr & Frost.

Tony Wilding, like many players, hurried to active duty. Serving as a captain in the Royal Marines, he was killed by a shell in France on 9 May 1915.

CHAPTER 14

WAR

On the first Friday in April 1917 at 3.15 in the morning, after a passionate debate which had begun 17 hours earlier, the United States House of Representatives, concurring with earlier action by the Senate, voted 373 to 50 to enter the war in Europe.

It was later reported by some present that tears ran down the faces of a few legislators who, nevertheless, voted aye. It is possible (though admittedly not likely) that someone among them recalled the words of John Bright in the British House of Commons 60 years earlier: 'It is a painful and terrible thing to think how easy it is to stir up a nation to war ... and you will find that wars are always supported by a class of arguments which, after the war is over, the people find were arguments they should not have listened to.'

President Woodrow Wilson had addressed an evening joint session of the two houses of Congress before the vote. 'The wrongs against which we now array ourselves are no common wrongs; they cut to the very roots of human life ...' said Wilson. 'The world must be made safe for democracy.'

Eight weeks earlier, the US had broken off relations with Germany, which had declared unrestricted submarine warfare in the Atlantic to break British control of the seas. And unrestricted it was: in the six-month period between April and October 1917, U-boats, hovering like tigers in the weeds off Hampton Roads, Virginia, New York City and other East Coast collection points for Allied convoys, would sink 56 Allied ships. America's neutrality, of course, already had been substantially shaken by the German sinking, in 1915, of the British Cunard Line passenger ship, *Lusitania*. Of the 1195 lives lost, 128 were American.

Dwight Davis was in London in February 1917 when US-German diplomatic ties were severed. He had gone to Europe in December for the Rockefeller Foundation's War Relief Commission, to monitor prisoner of war relief efforts in England, Norway, Sweden and Denmark. Now he headed home. With America entering the conflict, he would put into use the preparations he, personally, had been making for the past year and a half.

Eighteen months earlier the 36-year-old former college athlete had begun to get himself back into shape. His regimen of strenuous outdoor exercise included runs alongside the automobiles of his friends as they went for drives through the countryside or off to get provisions during outings at the Famous & Barr farm, a wooded resort area outside St. Louis for employees of the department store and friends. Davis was also one of 1,200 volunteers who bought their own uniforms and paid for their own meals to attended the first military training camp at Plattsburg, New York, established by General Leonard Wood to convert civilians into soldiers.

War mobilisation in America continued throughout the spring and summer of 1917. Back in St. Louis Davis enlisted in the Missouri National Guard which, in early August 1917, merged with the Kansas National Guard to become the new 35th Division, US Army. Dwight Davis was elected captain by the men of Company L, Fifth Missouri Infantry, one of 13 companies of men from St. Louis. The Fifth Missouri eventually became the 138th Regiment, one of four infantry regiments in the new 35th Division. With three field artillery units, three machine gun battalions, a trench mortar battery and various headquarters and support groups the 35th would eventually have a total strength of nearly 28,000 men.

During a hard winter of dust-in-your-mouth training at Camp Doniphan, on the Fort Sill military reservation in Oklahoma, the 35th's infantry units learned close order drill, musketry, trench and bayonet warfare. In February Davis, serving with Headquarters Company, was promoted to major and named assistant chief of staff.

By spring 1918 the men of the 35th were ready for France. And a good thing. Since mid-March the Germans had been openly bragging that they would soon be putting their feet under Paris tables. Off sailed the men of the 35th from New York-area ports aboard the *Karmala* and the *Khiva*, the *Shropshire* and the *Carpathia* and a dozen other ships with names that sounded equally exotic to more than a few Midwestern ears. Some units landed first in England, where boys from the Ozarks found they had to get used to tea for breakfast. Others went straight to France, and all converged at Eu, near the British front, for final training. By summer General John (Black Jack) Pershing (yet another Missourian) had assembled in Europe a total of almost one million men in his American Expeditionary Force (AEF).

In June the 35th's infantry units, with their Springfield and Eddystone rifles, moved down into the beautiful Vosges mountains in eastern France. Travelling by rail in '40 & 8s', the famous snug French boxcars which held 40 men or eight horses, the young soldiers could see, but not sample, Paris in the distance. On 6 July the 35th, supported by French guns while its own artillery units finished training in Brittany, met the enemy for the first time.

Then, in early September, came the battle for St. Mihiel on the eastern edge of the front. The 35th Division, now with its own three artillery batteries, moved into reserve position and helped the rest of the American First Army successfully recapture the pocket of German-occupied land which had protruded like an inflamed appendix down into France south of Verdun. Commanding Battery D of the Second Battalion of 129th Field Artillery, 35th Division, was a peppery little guy whose vision was so bad that he had brought along to France three or four spare sets of spectacles. (Captain Harry S. Truman had memorised the eye charts to pass his physical, said his brother later.) It is not recorded whether these two 35th Division officers – Major Davis, a 39-year-old Harvard patrician and future Republican leader, and Captain Truman, a 34-year-old western Missouri farm boy and future Democratic US president – ever held a sustained conversation.

By mid-September Major Dwight Davis had rejoined the division, having completed three months at the AEF's Army General Staff College in France. He was now adjutant of one of the division's three brigades, the 69th Infantry.

The 35th's biggest challenge was to come at the end of September 1918. It was here during the first five days of the war's final campaign – the fierce, 47-day Meuse-Argonne offensive – that the boys from Missouri and Kansas would show their mettle and their unquestioned bravery. But here also, some would later say, they showed raw combat inexperience and their incomplete training. They, like other American troops, for instance, had not been adequately schooled in the technique used by hardened British and French units of 'mopping up' the enemy from dugouts and trenches as infantry lines advanced. For the 35th, there also were strains resulting from regular Army officers being placed in command of National Guard units.

The American First Army, of which the 35th Division was a part, was to push forward to the railroad centre at Mézières and breach the German line as it extended from the Argonne Forest south-east down to the Meuse River. The French Fourth Army would be on the First Army's left, on the other side of the Argonne. The heights of the Meuse on the east and the rugged, high hills of the Argonne Forest had made the broad valley between ideal for German troops to defend. Battle lines in parts of the area had remained virtually unchanged for the past year.

The offensive, as envisioned by French and American commanders Foch, Pétain and Pershing, had several immediate objectives. The Germans were to be driven from the Argonne Forest, from the heights east of the Meuse River and from the high strategic areas such as Montfaucon and Romagne in the centre of the valley. The 35th was to push forward east of the Aire River, which ran along the edge of the Argonne Forest, and to protect the flank of the 91st Division on its right.

Through the centuries the Meuse and the Aire rivers had cut deep valleys through the countryside. Now fields and deep ravines and stands of thick woods bristled with dense German fortifications and curved lines of trenches. From Varenne west – the area to be penetrated by the 35th – the fearsome Hindenburg Line's stoutly reinforced concrete machine-gun emplacements hunkered down like snarling guard dogs. And in the Argonne Forest itself, once splendid trees, trunks now splintered, limbs broken and leafless, stood in the fog which frequently engulfed the area, like the remnants of some ghastly shattered army.

Here and there in the valleys were small villages filled with ravaged, shell-pitted buildings, formerly houses, shops and churches. Connecting these villages were narrow country roads, some dating back to the Romans. Soon these roads would be clogged with horse-drawn guns, trucks and lines of soldiers marching forward. And a bit later, ambulances would struggle against this throbbing tide, carrying the first wounded back to the rear.

In the cold predawn of Thursday, 26 September, the attack began. After three hours of artillery preparation, nine divisions, including the 35th, moved forward along the 24-mile front.

Fierce machine-gun fire and shells stalled 35th Division units as they attempted to move forward on the road to Cheppy. The once pleasant little village, now nearly in ruins, had been occupied by German forces long enough that vegetables had been planted and chickens raised. Anything still standing was fortified. Cheppy – like other villages – was not to be yielded easily. One company in the 35th, for instance, lost ten men in the first minute of action. Finally tanks appeared and cleared the road, and about noon American troops entered the town.

Throughout the early morning, movement had been hampered by a disorienting miasma of fog mixed with gas from artillery smoke screens and exploding shells. Leaders lost their men; units of various brigades and regiments became hopelessly mixed.

Compass in hand, Major Dwight Davis, the 69th Brigade's adjutant, moved forward through this obfuscating fog, leading a small headquarters detachment to its new location in the forward area. Shortly he became aware that he was leading but no one was following. The brigade commander and others had either lost sight of him in the fog or decided to strike out on a likelier compass heading. Alone, in an unknown field that obviously had been the scene of a recent battle,

Davis plunged on through the opaque swirls of mist towards the sound of firing.

Presently he came across a platoon of men by the side of the road. The platoon's commander was gone – the 138th was to lose an inordinate number of officers – and the young soldiers had no idea what their orders were. Fall in, Davis told them, and they all pressed forward.

Next a machine-gun company from the 91st Division, not only out of position but out of its sector, joined the group, as did other equally lost small groups of soldiers. Finally the fog lifted and there before Davis and his *ad hoc* fighting force was the village of Cheppy.

They did not know, however, that other elements of the 35th had already retaken the town. Davis's small force formed into a semblance of battle formation and began to approach the village. Suddenly one, then three, then more German soldiers, crying 'Kamerad', came stumbling out of dugouts to surrender. Soon, captured Germans outnumbered Davis's rump force. After sending the prisoners to the rear, Davis, realising the village was in American hands, marched in with his 'Free Rangers'. After sending the men back to their original units, Davis then 'returned to the business of adjutanting a brigade', later wrote a divisional historian. In all, some 300 German prisoners had been taken in the assault on Cheppy, some of whom were used to test captured stashes of beer for poison, before the liberating troops were given the spoils.

The morning of the second day the soldiers of the 35th again moved forward, protected by only a thin artillery barrage and this time facing reinforced numbers of German machine gunners. Late in the afternoon, with most of his units pinned down by blistering enemy fire, the 35th's Major General Peter Traub received an impatient message from General Pershing insisting that the division move forward.

Standing 'upon its feet amidst its dead', as a divisional historian put it, the 35th struggled forward, finally cracking the enemy's 'stiff crust'. Before the cold, wet, deadly night was over, two more villages, Charpentry and Baulny, had been seized.

The 69th Brigade and other units in the 35th Division took heavy losses. Many later blamed devastatingly poor communications which too often kept artillery units from learning the location of enemy guns raking infantry units. The colonel commanding the 69th had joined the brigade shortly before the battle and did not recognise the faces or know the names of many of his officers or the capabilities of their units. And because he insisted on keeping his headquarters constantly on the move from shell hole to shell hole, runners could not find it and there was never time to set up wireless communications. This, despite blunt objections from a lieutenant who was his aide and from Davis, his adjutant. Even carrier pigeons had proved to be useless messengers, possibly as confused as their human compatriots by the fog and din of battle.

By day three of the assault, many of the division's soldiers were hungry. The constant shelling, plus congested roads and a shortage of horses, mules and trucks, kept the rolling kitchens from reaching the advancing troops. As the exhausted soldiers finished off the two days worth of 'iron' rations which they had carried into battle, they searched through packs of fallen German soldiers for replacements or pragmatically took now unneeded rations from their own dead comrades – 'the dead man's last contribution to the cause'.

The division's two brigades were realigned in preparation for the next big push. Realigned in theory, that is. The reality was that the commander of the 69th Brigade could find only one battalion of one of his regiments and knew only that most of the surviving men in his other regiment were somewhere in the recently recaptured Montrebeau Wood.

Major General Traub went forward to see how his division was doing and was not pleased. 'I find that Brigade commanders know little about their brigades and the actual location of the units of their regiments,' he reported to his chief of staff. There was heavy shelling, he reported. 'Recommend reinforcements be sent at once to back up this Division. It has lost its punch [on] account of so many officer casualties resulting in disorganisation of units ...'

A divisional historian, having a trench-level view of events, later gave Traub's message his own response. 'The British say that the battle of Waterloo was won on the cricket lawns of Eton and Harrow,' he wrote. 'The 35th Division had lost its punch on the dancing floors of West Point, in the Efficiency Board rooms at Camp Doniphan, and in the United States Army system, which replaces National Guard officers, however competent, with Regular Army officers, however incompetent.' General Traub was a West Point man.

Davis, meanwhile, had obtained disturbing news. In the town of Baulny, one of the villages already captured by the 35th, a telephone centre and post of command had been set up underneath a shell-damaged church. Just to the north, at a place known as Chaudron Farm, a brigade headquarters and field hospital dressing station had been established. Now, with the division's troops withdrawing (as ordered) from the forward position of Exermont, the Chaudron Farm-Baulny area was in danger of being overrun by a strong counterattack. Infantry losses had been so heavy that even the division's regiment of engineers, who normally repaired roads and bridges, picked up rifles and gas masks and moved into trenches along Baulny Ridge as reserves.

Davis decided to round up any men he could find and go to the aid of the embattled area. He and his troops pushed forward to reinforce the line, and all through Monday, 30 September they helped hold off the Germans while the wounded were evacuated.

Said a citation issued two weeks later: Major Davis 'carried out the orders of his Brigade Commander in a manner utterly devoid of fear, under the most intense artillery and machine-gun fire. At Baulny, on September 30 and 29 he recklessly exposed himself to the enemy fire in order to obtain information of great value to his Brigade and Division Commanders'.

Four and a half years later Davis would be awarded the Distinguished Service Cross for:

> Extraordinary heroism in action between Baulny and Chaudron Farm, France, Sept. 29-30. After exposure to severe shelling and machine-gun fire for three days, during which time he displayed rare courage and devotion to duty, Major Davis, then Adjutant, 69th Infantry Brigade, voluntarily and in the face of intense enemy machine-gun and artillery fire proceeded to various points in his brigade sector, assisted in reorganising positions, and in replacing units of the brigade, this self-imposed duty necessitating continued exposure to concentrated enemy fire. Sept. 30, 1918, learning that a strong counterattack had been launched against Baulny Ridge and was progressing successfully, he voluntarily organised such special duty men as could be found and with them rushed forward to reinforce the line under attack, exposing himself with such coolness and great courage that his conduct inspired the troops in this crisis and enabled them to hold on in the face of vastly superior numbers.

Before dawn on Tuesday, the first day of October, shrouded in protective darkness, fresh troops from the First Division began arriving in the sector to relieve the 35th. Grimy with the mud of the Aire Valley and grey with fatigue, the men – boys no longer – from Missouri and Kansas limped to the rear.

Davis described his appearance in a letter home to Park Commissioner Nelson Cunliff: 'I fear the Park Department Association would have failed to recognise their first honorary president if they had seen him march out after sleeping six days in shell holes, without a wash or even taking off his boots, coat torn in shreds by barbed wire, haggard and tired. They say we were all sights and we certainly felt it. But it's good to have been in it and better to have come out.'

Many, of course, came out on stretchers or did not come out at all. In the Argonne campaign, the 35th had taken some 8,000 casualties, including more than 1,000 dead. Hillsides were dotted with the temporary cemeteries of battle – sad little clusters of rough, wooden crosses from which dangled round, metal identification tags, marking graves on which a helmet had sometimes been placed. Overall 120,000 Americans would be killed or wounded in the 47 days of the Meuse-Argonne campaign. And 11 years later F. Scott Fitzgerald would write about '... the country boys dying in the Argonne for a phrase that was empty before their bodies withered'.

The troops of the 35th had moved the front forward six and one-quarter exhaustive, blood-soaked miles, capturing along the way more than 1,000 German prisoners, four telephone systems, five howitzers, 15 field pieces and 85 machine guns. On 25 September, before the battle had begun, the division's artillery units had available 5,370 horses to move field guns and ammunition up to support infantry units. A count after the battle showed some 1,200 horses also had been lost – one reason for the often deadly delay in providing artillery cover for advancing soldiers.

By mid-October the 35th Division had settled into the quieter Sommedieue sector south of Verdun, and Davis, attached to division headquarters, had been named assistant chief of staff. On 3 November 1918, he was promoted to lieutenant colonel, infantry. His older brother Sam Davis, meanwhile, had also been in Europe working for the YMCA as business secretary of canteen services.

Even after the signing of the armistice on 11 November, the 35th Division had to spend five more cold, wet, miserable months in France training and drilling – months only occasionally sweetened by leaves to the Riviera and Paris or the excitement of a divisional review by General Pershing and the Prince of Wales.

Among the entertainments devised by the Army to keep the men occupied while they awaited transportation home was a big AEF tennis tournament in Cannes. Several hundred players came from all over Europe, though only a handful had ever competed at the international level. Among those who had were Colonel Bill Larned and Major Bob Wrenn, who teamed up in the doubles but lost in the semi-finals to Colonel Dwight Davis and his partner. In the finals, however, Davis and partner were beaten by a pair of captains – US top ten players R. Norris (Dick) Williams II, the 1916 US singles champion, and his partner, Watson Washburn (who would have much success as a doubles team after the war)

In March Davis went to Paris to join several hundred other American soldiers in forming a new veterans' organisation. It was important, decided initial planners Lieutenant Colonel Ted Roosevelt Jr. and others, that this new organisation be formed on French soil 'where the American Armies had fought so fiercely and victoriously'. Convening in Paris was also a pre-emptive move. The word was that sharpies and con men back home were ready to start their own veterans' 'societies' to pry dues out of returning doughboys.

For three days the caucus of 'citizen soldiers' met in an old Parisian playhouse, the *Cirque de Paris,* to argue, discuss and finally agree on the structure of this new group. But what to call it? 'Legion of the Great War' was the first choice of many, but finally 'American Legion' was adopted, 'although without enthusiasm at the time'. Dwight Davis and the others attending the Paris Caucus (as well as those attending the St. Louis Caucus two months later) would be considered founders of the organisation.

At last came word that the 35th Division was going home. In April and May 1919 units of the division began arriving back in St. Louis and Topeka and Kansas City. In smart formation they marched in massive homecoming parades through streets frothy with flags and wildly cheering homefolks.

'Give the credit to the doughboys,' said Davis in a newspaper interview after arriving back in St. Louis. 'The men did the real work and they deserve what credit there is.'

It is sometimes said of war that those who see the most action talk the least about it later. Her husband never talked about the war, or at least about the bad parts, said Helen Davis. Only sometimes in the night, locked in troubling dreams, he would get out of bed and wander around looking under the furniture. His words were always the same: 'I can't find the parade, I can't find the parade.'

In late 1918, while the division was still at Sommedieue, its commander, Major General Traub, had gathered the 21 officers of his staff together for a photograph. The beaming Traub, turned slightly sideways in the front row, would be relieved of his command before the division returned to the United States and eventually reduced in rank to colonel. He would be replaced by the major general who had originally trained the 35th at Camp Doniphan. Dwight Davis, the tall fellow on the back row, looking pleasant but reserved and slightly weary, would, seven years later, be named America's secretary of war.

CHAPTER 15

WASHINGTON CALLS

C aptain Harry Truman of the 35th Division came home from France and ran for (and was elected) eastern district judge of Jackson County, Missouri, a sort of county commissioner. Henry J. Allen, a Red Cross representative attached to the 35th Division, took off his uniform and ran for (and was elected) governor of Kansas. Lieutenant Colonel Dwight Davis too heard the seductive call of political office and in early 1920 announced that he would run in the Republican primary for the United States Senate.

Three candidates were running for the position, to be decided in the 3 August primary in which both Republican and Democratic parties would choose their candidates for the November election: Davis, James L. Minnis, a former solicitor general for the Wabash Railroad, and the incumbent Senator Selden P. Spencer, a former judge who had taken office in 1918 to fill out an unexpired term.

Davis formally opened his campaign in late March with speeches at rallies in Cape Girardeau and other towns in the south-eastern part of the state. He promised to visit all of Missouri's 114 counties. Those, the 'out state' or 'down state' regions, would be the challenge. St. Louis was lining up well. Mayor Henry W. Kiel, taking some heat for getting involved in the primary, had come out in support of Davis, his former park commissioner. Soon Davis's strong campaign committee had lined up most of the party leaders in St. Louis.

But could Davis carry his home town by enough votes to overcome his weaker support around the state, where Senator Spencer, in particular, was strong? And could Ozarks farmers and Jefferson City shopkeepers be convinced that their interests would be looked after by this big money, big city man, even if he was a war hero? In Kansas City and elsewhere clubs were organised of soldiers who had served in the 35th with 'Lieut.-Col.' Davis. His military title was used frequently in campaign literature and newspaper articles.

Through the spring and early summer Davis travelled the state explaining his platform. He was for: a businesslike, budget system for government departments; generous treatment for ex-soldiers; voters participating in primaries (whatever their party) rather than letting others select candidates for the fall elections; an end of wartime curbs on free speech and freedom of assembly; equal rights for women in matters of citizenship and in civil service opportunities (states were currently voting on whether to ratify the 19th amendment which would give women the vote); and entry into the League of Nations 'with proper reservations'.

He was against: waste and inefficiency in producing supplies during wartime; the excess profits tax; and 'autocracy', particularly on the part of the executive branch (the current president, of course, was a Democrat). But always what everyone wanted to know, whatever the candidate, whatever the party, was, Where do you stand on Prohibition?

The 18th amendment to the Constitution prohibited the sale, manufacture and transportation of alcoholic beverages in the United States. Its companion, the hated (in some circles) Volstead Act enforcing same, had gone into effect in January 1920. Senator Spencer had voted 'dry', though candidate Minnis accused him of being a 'pussyfooter' and 'straddler' when he came back to Missouri. Minnis, a moderate 'wet', had himself, at first, been vague about exactly where he stood. And no wonder. Sentiment in Missouri's big cities, including St. Louis with its large German population, was wet, but in many rural counties, dry. (In 1918 Missouri had voted dry by about 60,000 votes, despite a wet majority in St. Louis of about 80,000 votes.)

Even those opposed to Davis had to admit he was upfront about his position: he was unequivocally opposed to Prohibition – a 'moist', some called him. 'Although I recognise the evils of intemperance and of the saloon ... I am not in favour of the 18th amendment ...' he had announced early in the campaign.

In fact the Dwight Davises and the Harry Langenbergs (Dwight and Harry were first cousins) had given a fancy dress ball at the St. Louis Country Club shortly before the country went dry. 'The desert of tomorrow looms ahead', the invitations had read. The elegant couples swirling around the country club dance floor were also dancing on the grave of Davis's future chance for election, some would later claim.

As the campaign continued, Davis's photogenic family was put to use. In May the *Post* carried a candidate-at-home picture of Dwight and Helen seated on the back terrace at Portland Place, surrounded by their three daughters in charming, smocked dresses and young Pete, in jacket, tie and knickers, holding Ty Cobb, the family dog. Other pictures of Davis and the three girls and a separate, glamorous shot of Helen in pearls were included in a brochure, 50,000 copies of which were printed and mailed out by St. Louis businessmen to customers around the state.

Even Shon, the governess, did her part, taking to the hustings to hand out campaign literature. On through the summer went the campaign, through the

Republican state convention in May and the national convention (in Chicago) in June. But there were indications that it all might not be enough. A St. Louis expatriate living in New York (and friend of Dwight and Helen Davis's) wrote home that she had heard that Dwight Davis's chances for the Senate were 'not brilliant'.

On primary election day a small ad, a 'personal word' from Davis, appeared at the bottom of page two in the *Globe-Democrat*. 'I want your support ...,' it said. 'I have no ward organisation and believe the Courthouse ring and the boss-controlled vote will be against me ...'

A larger ad from Davis supporters appeared elsewhere in the paper. 'He gave St. Louis its wonderful system of free playgrounds, community centres, free baths and swimming pools for the children of the poor ...,' said the ad. 'He devoted 16 years to the human uplift in earnest, unselfish, constructive public service. He volunteered for war, helped organise and train a regiment, and was twice cited for gallantry in action ... His clean record – his fight for clean politics – his high standing as a citizen, humanitarian and volunteer soldier – commend him to every voter ...'

Said Spencer's campaign manager, 'Republican United States Senators are too scarce in Missouri for people to discard the only one they ever elected by direct vote.' Davis's campaign manager predicted Davis would carry St. Louis by 20,000 votes, plus 50 counties. Davis did carry St. Louis, as expected, but not by enough to counteract the larger totals Spencer racked up throughout the rest of the state. Some Republicans charged that the sweep by 'machine' candidates favoured by ward bosses 'reeked with fraud'. For whatever reason, Davis had lost. (Senator Spencer would go ahead and win re-election in the general election in the fall.)

In thank you letters sent to his supporters in coming months, Davis said that the efforts had not been wasted, since 'the campaign developed several side-issues of importance to good government', including 'the so-called "house-cleaners" movement'.

That was that. With the Senate campaign abruptly concluded, life at 16 Portland Place had returned, more or less, to normal. For the Davis children, neighbourhood playmates included cousins Alita and Sam Davis, the children of Dwight's brother Sam and Emma Davis. Alita was just two years older than Pete and four years older than Alice. Young Sam was a year younger than Cynthia. Alita was lively and fun. She also, in later years, had her own lighted, indoor tennis court built for her by her father, the scene of many tennis parties as she and her friends grew older. (Dwight's eldest brother, John, and his wife Edith had never had any children.)

And then there were all the Filley relatives, including the Langenbergers and the McPheeters. Westmoreland/Portland Place historian Julius Hunter would later calculate that the family with the largest representation in the neighbourhood over the years was that of Oliver Dwight Filley, Dwight Davis's maternal grandfather.

Maria Filley Davis still lived in the pink stone mansion on Westmoreland Place. To the youngest Davis girls and their friends, the house's spacious side lawn was like a park, marvellous for cartwheels, games and giggles. And the house's front entryway, with its three elegant arches, was perfect as a stage for the girls' summertime shows and ballet performances (admission: ten cents).

Not nearly as much fun were the dutiful visits inside (Shon insisted) to see their grandmother. They sat. She sat – now a dour old lady (it seemed to them) without the knack for talking to young people. More interesting was a visit to the gallery, a high-ceilinged room on the first floor. It was filled with exotic treasures from John and Maria's travels, such as the table-top, ivory model of the Taj Mahal and the giant, stuffed turtle on which a little girl could propel herself around the room.

The girls went to Mary Institute, the venerable school for girls associated, like Smith Academy, with Washington University. Pete, however, had not followed his father to Smith Academy (considered to be in its twilight years as St. Louis's prosperous families moved to western suburbs). His parents had enrolled him in the new Country Day School. Helen Davis served on the board.

Where Dwight was quiet and serious, Helen was lively and social – frivolous even, in the eyes of her stern mother-in-law. One young boy growing up in the neighbourhood, accustomed to his own perfectly fine but ordinary, plain-dressing, garden-digging mother, would remember years later his awe at the sight of the elegant Mrs. Davis, beautifully gowned, swathed in furs, climbing into a car to be whisked off to some glamorous event or other.

Shon was the one in charge of the minutia of the children's day to day lives, for these, like the children in many well-to-do families, were 'nursery children'. Their father was kindly yet busy and a bit remote. Their mother was beautiful and smelled good and would let them climb onto her lap for a bedtime story even if she was already dressed to go out for the evening. But it was Shon who made sure that dresses had buttons and the milk pudding got eaten at supper. It was Shon who ran her fingers down the spines of her young charges (and even visiting friends) at the dinner table to remind them to sit up straight.

And it was Shon who was there for the young Davis children on those mornings when they would awaken and find that their mother was gone – probably, they realised in later years, to a private clinic or sanatorium. Not only was her arthritis increasingly painful ('you couldn't even hug her,' her youngest daughter remembered decades later), but the grey mists of depression – or possibly what would later be called bipolar disorder – would sometimes engulf her.

Other times, however, she was her laughing, vivacious self. And not just young boys were dazzled. A few years later when Dwight Davis was named secretary of war by President Calvin Coolidge, Davis's photograph and that of his family appeared in the nation's newspapers. Harry Turner, editor of the sassy, smart-alec, gossipy St. Louis monthly, *Much Ado*, was incensed by the unflattering photos. 'And as for the picture of Helen (which I saw in a newspaper), for whom I have always had a remote, distant, respectful, er, er, what would you say (now that Dwight is Secretary of War) admiration, I tell you that I would not be even the wife of the Secretary of War and be so libelled,' he wrote in exaggerated indignation. 'The vivacious, the utterly charming, the pixie, sly, gay, insouciant, dangerous Helen Davis appears – well – appears no more like that than my own wife …'

'When one has a wife like Helen Davis,' he continued, 'and becomes Secretary of War on that account and then the newspapers print a picture of a woman who looks as much like her as I look like Babe Ruth after one of his five o'clock teas, well, were I Secretary of War there wouldn't be another newspaper in this Godforsaken country until they apologised in print and sent first-class photographs of my better half to everyone of their alleged subscribers.'

It was not President Calvin Coolidge, however, who originally called Dwight Davis to Washington, DC, but his predecessor, Warren G. Harding. In November 1920 Harding, a senator from Ohio, had been elected president. Out went Democrats, in came Republicans and with the changeover, opportunities for bright, ambitious, well-connected party supporters to serve in Washington. Davis focused on the new secretary of commerce, a wealthy mining engineer and hero of wartime Belgium food relief efforts, Herbert C. Hoover.

One of those talking and writing to Hoover in Davis's behalf was a fellow St. Louisan, Robert S. Brookings. Brookings, after making a fortune in manufacturing, real estate and other businesses, had retired at the age of 46 to turn his attention to public service. A powerful and effective booster of Washington University, he had been president of the board of trustees, where he had served with John T. Davis, Dwight's father. Brookings' Washington contacts were good. During the war he had served on the War Industries Board and, having become interested in how government and economic policies were developed, was currently board chairman of a five-year-old organisation called the Institute for Government Research.

'I have never known Dwight to undertake anything (except his recent Senatorial effort) which did not succeed,' wrote Brookings to Hoover. 'No man in St. Louis is more highly respected. He has never let his wealth or social affairs interfere in the most remote way with his duties.' In an earlier conversation with Hoover, Brookings had pondered aloud whether Davis had enough actual business experience to serve as assistant secretary of commerce. Now he sought to reassure Hoover on that point. 'While lacking in details of business experience, he is a man of wide information and sound judgement and I believe under your guidance would succeed at anything he would undertake. I gathered from our talk that you appreciate the personal equation – he has a strong, clean, earnest personality.'

Hoover wrote to Davis that what he needed from an assistant secretary was someone to handle the boring administrative desk work, 'unless I were myself to take over the daily grind of pure office detail'. Instead, he suggested Davis serve as part of the Commerce Department's informal 'cabinet', representing that department's interests on a board such as the War Finance Corporation. Dangling some figures before Davis as an indication of the board's importance, Hoover pointed out that the WFC 'was launching into the expenditure' of approximately $250 million, compared to the Commerce Department's expenditure of under $20 million. 'If you are willing, I will put this plan forward to the President at once ...'

Indeed Davis was willing. Almost immediately, on 22 March 1921, President Harding announced that he was nominating Dwight Davis of St. Louis as one of five directors of the War Finance Corporation. This board was responsible for making loans for financing exports, to aid in the 'rehabilitation of foreign commerce', as the *New York Times* put it. The goal was to help American farmers in particular, but also other industries, struggling to get on their feet again after the upheaval of the war, in short to boost foreign trade.

Not that the *Times* particularly approved (editorially) of the corporation. It was, in fact, controversial in several quarters. Created during the war, it had been dissolved in March 1920, revived by Congress, vetoed by President Woodrow Wilson, then saved again by the Republican Congress's override of his veto in January 1921. The selection of New York banker Eugene Meyer Jr. to again head the corporation as managing director, signalled vigorous future activity, predicted observers. (Meyer, the future owner of the *Washington Post*, indicated in later years that he thought it was also Davis's financial contributions in the election of 1920 that helped him snag the WFC job.) It was mentioned in national stories about Davis's nomination that he was 'director of a bank and several business concerns'.

At year's end the corporation reported to Congress that it had sent cotton and grain to Europe, freight cars and tobacco to China, as part of a total of $133 million in loans to exporters, agricultural co-ops, banks and other financial institutions. However, the corporation's most important contribution had been psychological, added the report. 'Its very existence has tended to inspire confidence ... The experience of the corporation has been that wherever it has lent, or agreed to lend a dollar, it has produced confidence to such an extent that others were willing to advance many dollars.' In spring 1922, Davis was nominated and confirmed by the Senate for a second term as a director of the corporation.

After coming to Washington Davis, always on the lookout for ways to get more exercise, had begun playing more tennis again. He had even talked his WFC boss Eugene Meyer into joining a tennis club, though as it turned out the heavy load which frequently stretched work days into evenings kept both of them from playing as much as they had expected. And on summer vacations at Dark Harbor, Maine, or on Cape Cod, Davis worked to pass along tennis skills to his children and any of their friends who might be visiting. Regularly each morning he would give each child a half-hour lesson, patiently tossing balls for them to hit.

When the Honourable Arthur J. Balfour, British Conservative statesman and former prime minister, arrived for the 1921-22 Washington Conference on Naval Armaments, his hosts discovered that he was also interested in playing a bit of tennis. Three other players were rounded up for a game of doubles at the Chevy Chase Club. Dwight Davis was paired with the distinguished visitor against the younger team of Vincent Astor and a major from the British embassy. Davis and Balfour won, even though Lord Balfour was in his mid-70s. Davis, at age 43, had apparently not lost the snap in his serve.

His game got a more serious test when he and Holcombe Ward decided to resurrect the doubles team of Ward and Davis for one last hurrah. In 1921 they played in the Seabright (New Jersey) Invitational, defeating the British Davis Cup doubles team of Woosnam and Turnbull, and a year later entered and won the first USLTA Veterans' Doubles tournament at Longwood. 'Their winning it did more good in stimulating Veterans' play than any one event that could have happened in the game,' said a tennis official later.

Tennis currently was absorbing more of Davis's time off court as well. In 1922 he was named vice-president of the United States Lawn Tennis Association, now more svelte – in name, at least – since the dropping of the 'National' from its title two years earlier. As expected, he ascended to the USLTA's presidency at the organisation's annual meeting at the Waldorf-Astoria in New York in early February 1923. There was much applause ('the heartiest demonstration of the meeting') as Mr. Davis 'of St. Louis' was escorted to the chair. (No matter that he currently lived in Washington. When you're an organisation frequently fighting charges of East Coast elitism, you flaunt your Midwesterners whenever you have them.) 'I will give to the association the best that is in me. I don't think any man can say more than that,' said the association's new president.

Davis lost no time in moving forward with the cause for which he had worked so enthusiastically back in St. Louis – public parks tennis. But this time his bully pulpit would be national. In a long newspaper interview the following day he announced that the USLTA would be arranging a tournament for a national championship in municipal tennis for 'regular' players in parks 'for whom private club privileges are not available'. And now he saw even more reason to spread the gospel of the value of athletics and exercise than he had a decade earlier when his principal concerned was 'the little lads' of the tenements. The recent war had uncovered the fact that great numbers of young American men were unfit physically, he told the reporter. It was the intention of the tennis association, he said, to do everything it could to correct that condition in the future.

Davis knew that supplying the all-important piece of silver would be no problem. The trophy would be (though he didn't discuss its origins publicly) the tall silver cup with graceful double handles which the USLTA had provided in 1916 for the earlier inter-city championship, stopped in its tracks by the war. It had been in St. Louis's keeping for the past seven years, and Davis was having the city send it east to New York jewellers Black, Starr & Frost where it would be refurbished.

Davis was not above using golf as a prod to develop support for public parks tennis. This new National Municipal Championship would be 'similar to the Public Links Championship which the golf association established last year', he told the USLTA executive committee. This cross-fertilisation – or competition – between the two sports was possibly one of the reasons golf had a new trophy as well. Two years earlier in 1921, an International Challenge Trophy for golf had been offered by George Herbert Walker, president of the United States Golf Association. The donor of what became known as the Walker Cup was a St. Louis native who had played polo there with Dwight Davis. He could not have been unaware of the success and prestige of the cup Davis had donated.

As USLTA president, Davis wrote an article for an upcoming issue of *American City Magazine*. In it he summarised the parks programs already available for 'lawn' tennis on courts with surfaces which included clay, dirt, gravel and asphalt in 75 cities around the country. Cities (like San Francisco) were lending balls and racquets and (like Pasadena) providing lights for play until midnight, he reported.

Davis had a full agenda of other matters that would need study and action during his year as president. Should the USLTA , which had just accepted an invitation to join the reorganised American Olympic Association, now join the International Lawn Tennis Federation? The official USLTA position after several years of 'friendly negotiation', was no, not until ILTF stopped insisting that now and forever the Wimbledon championships would be the 'world' championships.

What should be done about competition players (say, for instance, Bill Tilden) being paid for writing about their sport? About competition players working as salesmen for sporting goods firms? About competition players being paid by park departments for teaching the sport? ('The great sport-loving American public,' it was argued, 'would soon lose respect for and interest in the game, would soon be convinced that the leading players were making a living out of the game and would not regard them as amateurs ...')

There would even be an attempt to draw Davis into the developing controversy between the Dr. James Dwight/Nahant and Mary Outerbridge/Staten Island factions on who came first in American tennis.

But progress on this ambitious agenda was pulled up short just a few weeks after Davis took office. On the last day of February President Harding announced he was nominating Dwight F. Davis to be assistant secretary of war.

THUNDERBOLTS AND TENNIS BALLS

I n 1888, near the end of President Grover Cleveland's first term of office, construction was completed in Washington on a massive and spectacular office building with pillared porches, domed skylights and dramatic, high mansard roof. It towered over the low, simple White House to its east like some marvellously flamboyant *grande dame* looming over a small, elegant cat.

Soon gathered into the building's granite walls, rooms with 16-foot ceilings and nearly two miles of black and white marble tile corridors were the formerly scattered offices of three executive branch power centres: the Department of State, Department of the Navy and Department of War (which oversaw the Army).

Now, in early March 1923 in the War Department's offices which occupied the north and west wings of the State, War, Navy Building, the ceremony installing Dwight Davis as assistant secretary of war was drawing to a close. However, Secretary of War John Weeks had a surprise in store for his new number two. On to Davis's dark suit he pinned a bronze medal – a Greek cross topped by an eagle with wings outstretched, superimposed over a wreath of victory. The ribbon from which it hung was wide and blue, edged with hair-thin stripes of white and red. It was the Distinguished Service Cross, awarded for 'extraordinary heroism in action between Baulny and Chaudron Farm, France' in 1918.

Weeks was quick to point out that the award had been made by the War Department's Board of Awards *before* it was generally known that Davis had been appointed assistant secretary. This time lag in the presentation of decorations was not unique, and, in fact, a matter for which General Pershing was receiving some criticism, even though the Distinguished Service Cross and Distinguished Service Medal had been proudly instituted by him in the World War. Davis, for instance, was one of 259 to receive the DSC during the 1922-23 fiscal year. (More than 6,000 soldiers total would receive this honoured award for World War heroism, including 94 men in the 35th Division and the Unknown Soldier buried in Arlington.)

A few weeks later at a meeting of the USLTA executive committee in New York, Davis told the board that his new War Department responsibilities had given him perspective on a current sticky USLTA issue – whether it would be possible to honour one player each year with a proposed new award for good sportsmanship and conduct on court, without creating jealousy and hard feelings. 'While the secretary [of war] is away, I have to pass on the DSM (Distinguished Service Medal) awards,' said Davis. 'With the exception of this difficult proposition, the work of the War Department is a cinch. I suggest that no action on this point be taken ...' The motion to create such a tennis award was tabled.

Davis had announced that he was, 'with deep regret', resigning his USLTA presidency due to his recent government appointment. The executive committee, however, undoubtedly loath to give up such a high-profile officer, urged him to retain the title of president with the understanding that his duties would be taken over by other tennis officials.

Vice-president George Wightman of Boston said he was ready and willing to assume Davis's day-to-day tennis administrative chores. Davis's resignation was tabled. He did, in fact, keep his hand in, presiding over the fall executive committee meeting and missing the December meeting only because of his wife's illness. (George Wightman's wife, former national women's champion Hazel Hotchkiss Wightman, was in the process of organising a new inter-country team series for women players modelled, she said, on the Davis Cup. The series and the silver vase she donated as prize would be known as the Wightman Cup.)

Ted Roosevelt Jr. was currently assistant secretary of the navy (a position his father had held 24 years earlier). Both Herbert Hoover and Roosevelt would later claim credit for helping Davis land the position as assistant secretary of war. However, at the time, Roosevelt noted in his diary that even though Davis had called him to see if there was anything he (Davis) could do to 'raise his stock for assistant secretary of war', by the time he (Roosevelt) had had a chance to urge the president to appoint Davis, Harding had already made that decision. (The previous assistant secretary was resigning to run for Congress.) Davis, nevertheless, promptly sent Roosevelt a thank-you note, saying that he hoped 'some day I may have an opportunity to reciprocate'.

Roosevelt might make wickedly cutting comments about Davis's personality in his diary ('Dwight Davis ... is a dear, but as exciting as a plate of string beans'), but then Ted Roosevelt, much in the manner of his famously tart-tongued half sister, Alice Roosevelt Longworth, made wicked comments about most everyone.

Charles Evans Hughes was 'a bearded iceberg'. There was 'Ogden Reed, he of the polecat head', and 'Grace Vanderbilt ... who is a dear and very kind-hearted, but I never knew anyone who was so unutterable stupid of so many things ...' And these were the comments which made it past the later Bowdlerising scissors of his wife, Eleanor (the *other* Eleanor Roosevelt). 'I have cut out some of the personal items with frank statements about people, no historical value,' she later wrote in a neat, prim pencil note at the beginning of the diaries (whose pages, sure enough, are filled with gaping holes).

Davis and the young Roosevelt were among a group that frequently got together for dinner and bridge or poker, sometimes with their wives, sometimes without. In fact Davis and Roosevelt were among the half-dozen men who were playing poker at a Washington banker's house the night of Thursday, 2 August 1923. Shortly before midnight 'like a clap from the blue' came the news that President Harding, completing an exhausting trip through the Midwest and West, had suffered a heart attack and died in California.

Like most public officials Davis (acting on behalf of the absent Secretary Weeks) issued a statement. It was brief, if a bit fulsome, and called Harding 'as truly a martyr to duty as the brave boys who gave their all on the battlefields of France and Flanders'. Six days later Davis, in top hat and cutaway coat, marched at the head of a column of Army officers to the Capitol rotunda for the president's funeral. To his left marched Roosevelt leading a similar column of naval officers.

Around the country Harding was genuinely mourned. The skein of graft and corruption on the part of some of Harding's cronies and appointees had not yet significantly – or publicly – begun to unravel. Now, five months into his job, Davis found himself with a new commander in chief – the taciturn, largely unknown vice-president, John Calvin Coolidge, Vermont native and former governor of Massachusetts.

Much of the immediate communication between the secretary of war's office and the new president concerned veteran's affairs. This was not surprising since suspected chicanery in the letting of hospital contracts by the Veterans' Bureau was the first of the Harding-era scandals to be investigated by a Senate committee. The director of the bureau had resigned in February shortly before Davis's appointment. Boodlers, it seemed, were not just a municipal government phenomena.

But it was other matters within the war department that soon claimed a major share of the new assistant secretary's time. Amendments in 1920 to the National Defense Act of 1916 had given to the assistant secretary of war the responsibility for developing a plan to better mobilise American industry in case of another war. Most everyone agreed that matériel supply efforts in 1917-18 had been a disaster – American ammunition that never made it to the front, shortages of nearly everything, profiteering by unscrupulous middlemen. There was appalling inefficiency, waste and lack of co-ordination. Some of this Davis knew about first hand from his days in France, for instance the shortage of wire for communications, of trucks, of horses. Some of this he had talked about – at great length – in his Senate campaign, for example the problem of getting enough leather for soldiers' shoes.

That 1917 industrial mobilisation fiasco would not be repeated, insisted Davis, in the calendar-filling rounds of speeches he had begun making as assistant secretary. Next time 'business fitness' will be as important as physical power, he told a convention of American drug manufacturers in New York. 'Industrial generals will be as important as military generals in the national defense.'

Davis wrote to businessmen, such as Bernard Baruch, who had been involved with wartime procurement. What should be avoided next time 'to make our industrial effort in another war more harmonious and effective'? he asked. Baruch, a big man both physically and financially, was nine years older than Davis. He had made a fortune on Wall Street before taking on the role of advisor to American presidents starting with Wilson. (His influence would extend up through Kennedy in the 1960s and his unofficial office, journalists were fond of pointing out, often was a park bench in Lafayette Park across the street from the White House.)

During the 1917-18 war Baruch had been heavily involved in the attempt to mobilise American industry, first as a member, then as chairman of the War Industries Board. And now he saw himself as THE expert. Baruch had 'an instinct for power, publicity and prestige', said a later biographer. Davis, on the other hand, automatically assumed he had the first and the last and was not particularly interested in having the middle.

Baruch had quickly written to Davis at the time of his March appointment and seemed outwardly cordial to those in the War Department. But he absolutely did not want to see upper level control of industrial planning go to the Army rather than to business leaders. Davis and General Pershing, he wrote privately to associates, did not understand the industrial side of wartime mobilisation.

In a speech in Kansas City five months later, Davis reported that 'more than 700,000 industries have been catalogued by the War Department. We know what equipment they can manufacture, how much and how quickly. The profiteering of the last war will be eliminated'.

'Industry alone cannot win a war; but it can lose a war ...,' he wrote in a memorandum discussing the future mobilisation of America's chemical industry published in the *New York Times*.

However, in addition to the writings and speeches of almost revivalist fervour, in addition to the surveys and the cataloguing and the drafting of new model contracts, there was another important thrust to this industrial mobilisation overhaul.

Since the early 1920s a half-dozen or so officers – several who had been assigned at some point to the office of the assistant secretary of war – had been working on ideas for developing a trained cadre of military personnel who would be knowledgeable about procurement of supplies the next time around. A special Army-run school, an 'Industrial War College' was suggested. Davis was at first not enthusiastic – 'properly conservative', as one officer had put it. By August 1923 he had come around, after listening to arguments from the respected general who was chief of ordnance. Since those pushing the college had already convinced Secretary Weeks, the new institution was on its way.

Once on board Davis proved to be a valuable ally. For one thing, there was need to keep an eye on proponents of civilian control, like Baruch. ('I should like to have a little school or something of the kind ...,' Baruch said during the question and answer period following a lecture about industrial procurement at the Army War College in February 1924, when the plans for such a 'little school' were, in fact, well underway.)

In addition, within the Army itself there were those ready to swoop down and seize the new school as it hatched. The general staff, for instance, never a friend to the supply branches, felt that it, not the office of the assistant secretary of war, should be in charge of any such new project, since it supervised other general service schools.

An attempted *putsch* occurred in February, shortly before the new school was to open. The Army Industrial College's first class was to meet in available rooms in the Army's massive, three-storey Munitions Building on 20th Street and B (later Constitution Avenue). The official opening was scheduled for late Thursday afternoon, 21 February. Ten officers who had already begun studying military economics at the War Department would be moving in to complete their five-month course.

On Tuesday, 19 February, anticipating trouble, Davis had sent Weeks a memo suggesting that the secretary specifically place control of the new college with the office of the assistant secretary as part of that office's overall mobilisation planning mandate. Now, on Thursday, a general staff officer attempted to convince Weeks otherwise. He was a day late. Weeks had already endorsed the memo, approving the assistant secretary's suggestion. Davis's pre-emptive strike had saved the day. It was a move worthy of inclusion in a War College strategy lecture.

And in his address at the opening ceremonies, Davis subtly but unmistakably warned the general staff 'to stay off his turf', in the words of military historian Terrence J. Gough. The Army War College and Leavenworth Schools begun after the Spanish war had been most valuable in developing combat arms officers for higher command and staff, said Davis. But those institutions 'cover only the man-power problem ...and do not cover the problem of procurement of supplies. Nor is it believed they should be given such a mission. The character of the training, the experience and qualifications of the officers, the whole habit and trend of thoughts are, and properly should be, entirely different ... Their missions are distinctly dissimilar and should be kept so'.

A year later, in a long article in the *Nation's Business,* Davis told the public about the school and what previous mobilisation ills it was trying to cure. At many plants during the last war, he wrote, there had been nearly constant revision of specifications for armaments. Just when a plant 'would start to deliver guns or shells, along would come an officer with a new set of blueprints and all the work would have to be done over'. Those trained at the Army Industrial College would know better. 'The officers are studying and handling the problems from the attitude of business men ...'

In later years Davis would say that of all his official acts as assistant secretary and secretary of war, nothing ranked as high in importance as the establishment of the Army Industrial College.

In mid-March 1924, a year after Davis's installation as assistant secretary of war, in a ceremony on the south-west lawn of the White House, President Calvin Coolidge stuck his left arm deep into the bowl of the Davis Cup and pulled out a slip of paper.

The bowl and its new tray, gleaming in the winter sun, had been placed on a cloth atop a small table on the White House lawn. In the background were the high columns of the curved south portico. Overhead, a March breeze whipped the American flag flying from the roof of the White House. Standing in a half-circle around the president were more than a dozen ambassadors, ministers and other official representatives of the nations involved in the American Zone draw. Washington's diplomatic corps, of course, was ever ready for such occasions. Some were in morning dress with shiny top hats. A few sported bowlers. Here and there proper spats peeped out from under dark trousers.

Why yes, he'd be delighted to have the 1924 drawing at the White House, Coolidge had told Davis several weeks earlier. 'I will be glad to draw the first name as you have suggested, for I feel a real desire to testify my genuine interest in this notable international athletic competition.'

The Davis Cup competition, he wrote in the letter to Davis, is the occasion 'for establishing better acquaintance throughout the world and particularly for setting up fine standards of sport and giving them a universal significance. I am persuaded that the erection of such standards in the realm of sport is bound to afford a fine example in every other department of human activity'.

The Davis standing on the other side of the cup from the president on the White House lawn (dark Homburg, no spats) was a different Davis, certainly, from the tall, slightly gangly young man in rumpled tennis whites who had stood on the porch of the ramshackle Longwood clubhouse at the first draw 24 years earlier. The cup and its donor were both thriving. The reputation of each added to the reputation of the other.

Tennis officials, of course, were delighted to have the cup ride along on the coattails of an assistant cabinet secretary, as in the staging of the drawing at the White House. Bill Tilden's flashy tennis and victories for the US team were making cup matches extremely popular in the US. Beyond the US, more nations than ever wanted to participate. In 1924, 23 nations were challenging for the cup.

This excitement for tennis buffs of seeing foreign players who came to the US for Davis Cup matches and often stayed for the US Nationals was another reason the West Side Tennis Club needed its new stadium. Some of the funds had come from the USLTA. 'You have a profit in the Davis Cup matches as long as you retain the cup,' an official would point out at a USLTA executive board meeting.

As for Davis himself, in December 1924, Briton Hadden and Henry Luce decided to put him on the cover of *Time*, their brash, new 'Weekly News-Magazine'. Under a charcoal sketch of a grinning Davis casually dressed in a striped blazer, shirt collar open, no tie, was the line 'War's hypothecator'. (Hadden, ever on the lookout for unusual, forceful words, was said to edit with an annotated translation of the *Iliad* at his elbow.) The occasion, said a brief, accompanying article in *Time*'s 'Science' section, was his speech to the annual meeting of the American Society of Mechanical Engineers. In it he spoke of the money and lives that would have been saved if America had had a prearranged industrial plan before the World War. He spoke of how new commodities committees were working with Army supply branches and industry to plan commodity procurement in time of emergency.

'Thus spoke War's hypothecator,' wrote *Time*, 'pledging the nation's resources, in case of need, to war – preparing peaceful plans for future emergencies, enlisting scientists – peaceful scientists – in the interests of national defense. It was perhaps one of the last things one would have expected 25 years ago of the tall, good-looking young Missouri tennis-player, who, then at Harvard, offered the trophy afterwards to become famous as the Davis Cup ...'

One of the last things? Hardly. In fact the 'ideal tennis temperament' that writer Parmly Paret had spotted in the young Davis in 1898 could well be said to be a factor in Davis's political movement upward. To Paret that had meant having 'a variety of plays combined with the head to know when to use them'. Not bad qualities for someone working with fractious Army elements as well as Congress. And, of course, Davis had been a doubles player – one who believed in teamwork, that success, as he had written in that article on doubles for *Golf & Lawn Tennis* so many years earlier, depended upon encouraging and steadying your 'partner', not just keeping an eye out for the main chance for yourself. Just as he had as St. Louis park commissioner, in his annual reports for the War Department Davis praised others working in the department.

It was an intriguing combination for reporters, Davis's world of tennis and government. Subliminally, there was the juxtaposition of symbols – Mars, the god of war, thunderbolts jammed into one pocket and tennis balls in the other, grabbing a racket and hitting a solid, down-the-line backhand. Thwack. They liked to make connections, and he obliged them: 'Tennis tends to develop coolness and accuracy. A course in tennis is good for the coming diplomat,' he said on one occasion.

All in all, Davis seemed to be finding the Washington game satisfying. 'Things are very busy here and I suppose when Congress meets we will all be standing on our heads but it is still interesting and I am enjoying it, in spite of the troubles,' he wrote to a political supporter back in St. Louis. He was not specific about exactly what troubles.

Davis was obviously making an effort to stay in touch with his St. Louis political base, asking about and commenting on Coolidge's strength, cooling off supporters when they wanted to push him for various new jobs. And he had not sold his St. Louis home on Portland Place. The houses in which the family lived in Washington were rented.

Calvin Coolidge was nominated and elected to the presidency on his own in 1924. He kept much of the cabinet he had inherited from Harding a year and a half earlier, including Charles Evans Hughes as secretary of state, Herbert Hoover as secretary of commerce, Andrew Mellon as secretary of the treasury and Davis's boss, John Weeks, as secretary of war. Weeks' health, however, continued to fail. Increasingly, Davis functioned as acting secretary of war.

Which was why, on a Monday in late September 1925, it was Dwight Davis and not John Weeks in a chair in a hearing room preparing to testify on the riveting controversy that had captured the attention of the nation, the matter of Colonel William Mitchell.

To some, Billy Mitchell was an insubordinate, attention-seeking renegade. To others, including many of his fellow Army pilots, he was hero, prophet and brave protector of America's now and future air power. Brave he undoubtedly was. And, as events 25 years later would prove, amazingly right in many areas. (The value of strategic bombing was proven in World War II. The US, in 1947, did reorganise into a Department of Defense, as he recommended, encompassing the Army, Navy *and* an independent Air Force.) But tactful, perceptive and effective, he was not.

After the 1917-1918 war, Mitchell had been appointed assistant chief of the Army's Air Service, which gave him the rank of brigadier general. His dream, however, was for an independent unified air corps, combining the aviation wings of both the Army and Navy. Though always fractious and outspoken, Mitchell had, for some years, worked more or less within the system, attempting to convince his superiors of the rightness of this plan. He also had campaigned against what he saw as the nation's free-fall in post-war aviation strength and general preparedness.

But then his campaign went public. And where he had originally flailed away at the Navy Department, he now took on his own service, the War Department, as well. For months the ailing Secretary Weeks and Navy Secretary Curtis D. Wilbur had been embroiled with Mitchell in headline-grabbing charges and counter charges. In March 1925, Secretary Weeks (an Annapolis man, incidentally), wrote a lengthy letter to President Coolidge correcting, he said, some of the specifics in Mitchell's recent testimony to a House committee.

Concluded the letter, 'General Mitchell's whole course has been so lawless, so contrary to the building up of an efficient organisation, so lacking in reasonable team work, so indicative of a personal desire for publicity . . .' that Weeks did not recommend that Mitchell's position as assistant Air Service chief be renewed. 'I write this with great regret because he is a gallant officer with an excellent war record ...' With the loss of the Air Service position, Mitchell's rank reverted to colonel and he was assigned to a small base in San Antonio, Texas.

Coolidge, at this point, quietly contacted his old friend and Amherst classmate Dwight Morrow, the New York financier (and future father-in-law of aviation hero Charles Lindbergh). Coolidge asked him to be ready to organise and head a special presidential inquiry committee into Mitchell's charges if one were needed. (Many would later credit Dwight Davis with the idea of convening what would become known as the Morrow Board. Though Davis strongly supported the idea and conceivably could have suggested it to Coolidge, he apparently did not make the original contact with Morrow.)

In early September, a Navy PN-9 attempting the first flight from San Francisco to Hawaii was declared lost in the Pacific. (The crew was later rescued at sea.) Two days after the PN-9 disappeared, the *Shenandoah,* a navy dirigible, split apart and crashed

ABOVE. Heading west in the summer of 1899, to compete against Pacific Coast players, were (left to right) Dwight Davis, Beals Wright, his father (and American baseball great) George Wright, who accompanied the group, Holcombe Ward and Malcolm Whitman. The success of this series of inter-sectional matches helped give Dwight Davis the idea for the Davis Cup. (*George Wright*)

RIGHT. Dwight Davis's 'smash' was a formidable stroke. Davis 'kills lobs harder than anyone else who has ever played the game', wrote England's Doherty brothers in a 1903 book. (*Boston Globe*)

LEFT. The draw to see who would play whom at the first Davis Cup matches was held on the porch of the humble building which the Longwood Cricket Club used as a clubhouse. Holcombe Ward (centre) drew the names from hats held by the two team captains, Dwight Davis (left) and Arthur Gore. (*Boston Globe*)

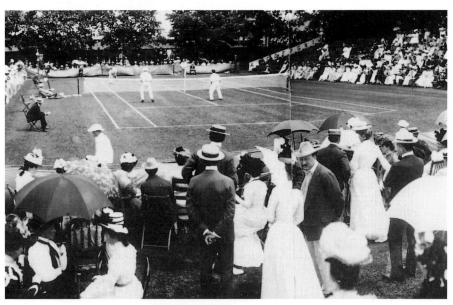

ABOVE. At Newport, Rhode Island, society's finest watched Dwight Davis and Holcombe Ward (foreground) win the second of three US national doubles titles in 1900, beating challengers Fred Alexander and Ray Little. (*Hare/Longwood Cricket Club*)

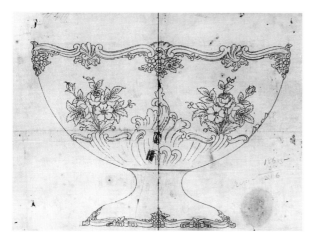

ABOVE. The designer of the Davis Cup was Rowland Rhodes, an English artist who came to the US to work for the Durgin Silver Co. in New Hampshire. Rhodes died in 1903 before seeing his trophy achieve international fame. (*Drawing, International Tennis Hall of Fame; Rhodes, Stanyan A. Lupien*)

ABOVE. The first American Davis Cup team consisted of three Harvard men: (left to right) Malcolm Whitman, Dwight Davis and Holcombe Ward, here with the new sterling silver International Lawn Tennis Challenge Trophy. (*USTA*)

ABOVE. America's reigning doubles champions, Davis (in hat at net) and Ward, competed at Wimbledon in 1901. After defeating Roper Barrett (rear, forecourt) and G. M. Simond to win the All Comers, the American pair lost in the challenge round to the Doherty brothers in four sets. (*Longwood Cricket Club*)

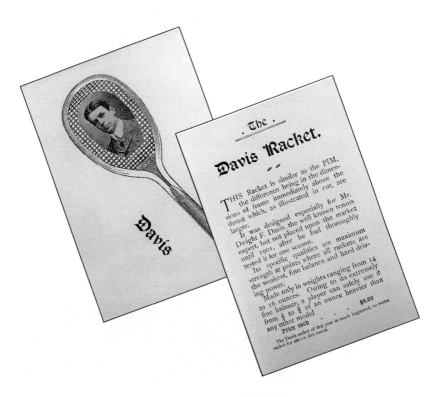

ABOVE. The Wright & Ditson sporting goods company included in its line of tennis rackets the *Davis*, available only in weights of 14 to 16 ounces. There was 'no better racket for use on dirt courts', claimed the company's 1904 catalogue.

RIGHT. While serving as St. Louis park commissioner, Dwight Davis grabbed an axe, took off his suit jacket and rolled up his trousers to lead a group of city notables on an expedition to cut Christmas trees for a civic festival. (*Western Historical Manuscript Collection, University of Missouri St. Louis*)

ABOVE. Helen Brooks of Boston and Dwight Davis of St. Louis were married in Geneva, Switzerland, in November 1904. She was beautiful, vivacious and frequently in poor health.

RIGHT. The palazzo-style home at 17 Westmoreland Place in St. Louis was built by Dwight Davis's parents in the 1890s, though his father died before it was completed. Dwight and his bride lived here briefly with Maria Davis before renting and then eventually building their own home nearby. (*Missouri Historical Society, St. Louis*)

ABOVE. Dwight and Helen Davis and their photogenic young family – left to right, Cynthia, Helen, Alice, Dwight Jr. (Pete) – posed on the terrace of their Portland Place home during Davis's campaign for the Republican nomination for US Senate in 1920. (*De Woskin & Yore/St. Louis Post-Dispatch*)

LEFT. John Singer Sargent's chalk portrait of Lieutenant Colonel Dwight Davis in uniform was done in 1923 after Davis received the Distinguished Service Cross. A Sargent portrait was highly sought after by government and social leaders on both side of the Atlantic. (*Private collection*)

ABOVE. With Dwight Davis serving in the US government, the White House lawn seemed an appropriate place for the 1924 Davis Cup draw ceremony. Here Davis (far left), representatives of Davis Cup nations and US tennis officials await President Calvin Coolidge who will reach into the bowl and draw the first country name. (*UPI/Corbis-Bettmann*)

RIGHT. Dwight Davis, his wife Helen and daughter Cynthia leave the White House after attending an annual New Year's Day reception. With the line often blurred between social and official Washington, top hats and fur coats could be considered work clothes. (*UPI/Corbis-Bettmann*)

TIME

The Weekly News-Magazine

DWIGHT F. DAVIS
War's Assistant Secretary
(See Page 20)

VOL. IV   NO. 24   DECEMBER 15, 1924

LEFT. Impressed with a speech of Dwight Davis's about military and industrial preparedness, the fledgling news magazine *Time* put the assistant secretary of war on its cover in late December 1924. (© *1924 Time Inc.*)

BELOW. Secretary of War Davis (arm on tire) and his War Department chief of staff and chief of ordinance (rear) were given a test ride in Potomac Park in 1926 of an Army vehicle modified to handle rough terrain. Davis would later play a role in nudging along the US development of a mechanised armoured force. (*UPI/Corbis-Bettmann*)

ABOVE. In September 1927 Davis (centre) briefly slipped away from official Washington duties to attend cup matches in Philadelphia. US players and officials (left to right) Julian Myrick (USLTA president), Frank Hunter, Dick Williams (US captain for the previous six years), Bill Johnston, Bill Tilden and Joe Garland (current captain) could not stop a determined French team which captured the silver trophy for the first time. (*UPI/Corbis-Bettmann*)

RIGHT. One of Davis's last official duties as secretary of war was to present the Distinguished Flying Cross to aviation pioneer Orville Wright and, posthumously, his brother Wilbur, who had died in 1912. Davis and Wright are pictured on the balcony outside the secretary's office in the State, War, Navy Building. (*UPI/Corbis-Bettmann*)

LEFT AND BELOW. Dwight Davis was appointed to serve as governor-general of the Philippines by his old cabinet colleague and the new US president, Herbert Hoover. Davis held the post from 1929 until early 1932. The Malacanang Palace (below), the governor-general's official residence, sits on the bank of the Pasig River and greeted Davis, his daughter Alice and niece Alita with a flooded first floor upon their arrival. (*National Archives*)

ABOVE. Helen, in school in the US, was met by her father upon arrival in Manila, when she and the indefatigable family factotum, Miss Shaughnessy, finally got their turn to visit the Philippines. (*UPI/Corbis-Bettmann*).

RIGHT. A caricature artist aboard the USS *Pittsburgh* unloosed his pencil on Davis and others in the governor-general's party during the 1931 goodwill tour of the East Indies. Cynthia, Pete and Philippines officials accompanied Davis on the 6,000-mile, six-week tour. (*Cruisin' Around*)

ABOVE. The first US Davis Cup team was reunited again in May 1932 at the North American Zone finals. From the left, Holcombe Ward, Dwight Davis and Malcolm Whitman, who died seven months later. (*AP/Wide World*)

LEFT. Alice Davis and Roger Makins, second secretary at the British Embassy, attended the fashionable Middleburg Hunt races outside Washington, DC, shortly before their marriage in the spring of 1934. (*UPI/Corbis-Bettmann*)

TOP AND ABOVE. After retiring from official governmental duties, Dwight Davis had time for duck and quail hunting at his Meridian Plantation in the upland game country of northern Florida and southern Georgia. Both hunter and dog could relax on the terrace after a day in the field. Davis also unsheathed his tennis racquet again for events such as the US Father and Son Championship in 1936. He and Pete (far right, below) took on former US singles champion Bill Clothier (far left) and his son in the finals, losing in straight sets. (*William J. Clothier II*)

LEFT. Dwight Davis went back
into uniform briefly during
World War II as director general
of the Army Specialist Corps.
Pete served as an Air Corps
officer.

BELOW. Pauline Sabin Davis,
Dwight Davis's second wife and
national director of the
American Red Cross, received a
Red Cross pin from President
Franklin D. Roosevelt to
promote the start of a 1943
wartime fund drive.
(*UPI/Corbis-Bettmann*)

ABOVE. A bronze bust of Dwight Davis was created for the Hall of Fame by another Davis son-in-law, artist Allen Hermes, who married Davis's youngest daughter Helen. (*International Tennis Hall of Fame*)

RIGHT. William McChesney Martin Jr., whom Cynthia Davis married during World War II, eventually not only served as chairman of the Federal Reserve Board for 19 years but was active in the organisation of the International Tennis Hall of Fame at the old Newport, Rhode Island, casino. His father-in-law, Dwight Davis, was inducted into the Hall of Fame posthumously during the second year of enshrinements, 1956. Martin received the same honour in 1982. (*Julia King/Washington Star*)

ABOVE. More than a century and a half after Samuel Craft Davis settled in St. Louis in the 1830s, his far-flung descendants (and spouses) began gathering for bi-annual summer reunions. Among those attending these "Tribal Rites" in St. Briac, Brittany, in 1995 were two surviving Davis daughters and two sons-in-law. Seated second row from top are Allen Hermes (husband of Helen); Cynthia Davis Martin (whose husband William McChesney Martin was ill and could not attend); Lord Sherfield, Roger Makins (husband of Alice Davis who died in 1985) and Helen Davis Hermes. Dwight Davis Jr. died in 1973, thoughs the Dwight Filley Davis name rolls on. Dwight III is in the top row, far right. His son, Dwight IV, is at Harvard.

RIGHT. An inevitable part of the Davis clan gathering is a tennis round-robin. In the chair, Lord Sherfield, with Helen Hermes and Cynthia Martin standing below.

in a storm over Ohio. Mitchell, asked by reporters for comments on the two disasters, released from San Antonio a fiery 6,000-word mimeographed statement blaming these tragedies on 'the incompetency, criminal negligence, and almost treasonable administration of the National Defense by the Navy and War Departments'.

That did it. The following week on Thursday Acting War Secretary Dwight Davis said there would be 'a full and impartial investigation' of Mitchell's charges. Davis believed, said the *New York Sun,* quoting him indirectly, that 'if there is to be a trial of Colonel Mitchell for insubordination because of his attacks on his superiors in violation of articles of war, it must be a free and open investigation, fair to Colonel Mitchell in every way'.

'That's bully,' said Mitchell from San Antonio. 'It's just the sort of investigation I've been fighting for.'

On Friday, however, Navy Secretary Wilbur announced that he thought an investigation was 'wholly unnecessary'. That evening Herbert Hoover, according to a report in the *New York Times,* did some arm-twisting to convince Secretary Wilbur to support the investigation 'as recommended by Acting Secretary Davis'. (It was not for nothing that Washington wags called Hoover the secretary of commerce and the assistant secretary of everything else.)

By Saturday afternoon Wilbur and Davis were reported to be presenting a joint letter to the president recommending that he, as commander in chief, appoint an inquiry board. At 6.30 p.m. that same evening Coolidge 'sprung a surprise', said the *Times,* apparently amazed at how quickly it was all falling into place. The president was announcing the names of the nine men he was asking to serve on such a committee – military men, engineers, businessmen (including, of course, Dwight Morrow), members of Congress – who would be 'selecting their own chairman'.

Davis, meanwhile, had slipped up to Philadelphia on Saturday to see another Bill (Tilden) do battle. The Germantown Cricket Club was hosting the Davis Cup challenge round and observance of the Davis Cup's 25th anniversary. A crowd of 10,000 had gathered at this, Tilden's home club, for the final day's matches between the United States and France, making its first appearance in the challenge round.

The size of the crowd was particularly amazing considering that the US, by winning the doubles the day before, was already assured of retaining the cup, which was sitting on a white cloth-covered table courtside. But then Bill Tilden was playing the new phenomenon, the 21-year-old Wimbledon champion René Lacoste. Tilden had been within a point of defeat four times in the third set.

Dumping pitchers of ice water on his head and even playing in his stocking feet, this Bill finally had won. For the other Bill, still down in Texas, the game was just beginning.

CHAPTER 17

AIR POWER, FIRE POWER, POLITICAL POWER

C olonel Dwight Davis (whose military title was sometimes still used by the president's office and the War Department) and Colonel William Mitchell (whose supporters and even the press sometimes still called him 'General') were born in the same year. Both came from affluent families. Both had been awarded the Distinguished Service Cross.

Both had been involved in the battles of St. Mihiel and the Meuse-Argonne campaign in France. Billy Mitchell, of course, was in the air, demonstrating the new concept of formation flying as he led his command of 200 planes which was supposed to provide observations and reports of enemy strength. Dwight Davis was on the ground with a division which cursed poor communications and promised scouting reports from the air which somehow never materialised.

One loved the limelight and controversy. The other was reserved, a team player who had, as one historian would later put it, 'progressed in power while blending inconspicuously into the background of his times'. Both believed in the coming importance of air power in both military and civilian life – one enthusiastically, almost (some would say) fanatically, the other cautiously. One believed in shaking things up to get important things accomplished. The other believed in the system and the fundamental primacy of military order and discipline.

Acting Secretary Dwight Davis was the first witness to testify as the President's Air Board began hearings on Monday, 21 September 1925, in the spacious Interstate Commerce hearing room in the House of Representatives Office Building. Reading from a prepared 4,500-word statement (which never mentioned Mitchell by name), he defended the quality of Air Service personnel and the general rightness of the Army's air program, as proved by the success of the recent, spectacular round-the-world flight, 'the outstanding aeronautical achievement of all time'.

If equipment was inadequate, Davis told Dwight Morrow and other board members, that was because of insufficient appropriations from Congress. He got in a plug for the War Department's extensive industrial war planning, particularly the 'very complex' aspect of it involving air power. He gave details of the ways in which the department supported commercial aviation development, while emphasising that for the Army 'the war mission must always govern'.

As to the primary question of a unified, independent air service, Davis told the board they would hear a variety of personal opinions during the day's testimony. The War Department's official position, said Davis, ever the good number two man, was the one presented to Congress earlier by Secretary Weeks. Weeks' lengthy statement, which Davis read into the record, concluded that the very importance of aviation meant that the Army could not acquiesce in any proposal 'making the air service anything other than a permanent and integral part of the Army, the same as the field artillery, infantry, coast artillery and other combatant arms'.

Said Davis, in concluding his testimony and with an implicit jibe at Mitchell, 'I can see no reason to be panicky about the condition of the Army Air Service.' This got a laugh from the room.

Davis's testimony was followed by that of two generals who supported the Weeks/Davis position. However, the day's third general, who headed the Air Service, while disagreeing with some of Mitchell's charges (whom he too did not name), said the Air Service had indeed been treated like a 'step-child'. He recommended its expansion, conversion into an autonomous air corps (with a relationship to the Army as that of the Marine Corps to the Navy) and the eventual (a key word) creation of a Ministry of Defense overseeing all military, including a unified air service.

Next the President's Air Board (or the Morrow Board, as it was often called) heard from the Navy. The following week it was Mitchell's turn. He arrived in Washington on a Friday night and was met at Union Station by a drum-and-bugle corps and a crush of cheering supporters (some observers put the number at 10,000), including members of two American Legion posts.

On Monday, 30 September, he began his testimony for the Morrow Board. It was not his finest hour, even by the reckoning of those generally supportive of Mitchell. On and on he droned, reading great chunks from his recent book, which many on the board had already read. Most of his charges they had heard before, though things got a bit livelier during direct questions the second day. Mitchell was applauded by many spectators in the hearing room when he finished his testimony.

A final report from the Morrow Air Board, which now moved on to study air routes and the commercial aviation industry, was not expected until early winter. Meantime the possibility was growing that the Army intended to court-martial Billy Mitchell. On 5 October Mitchell reported briefly to the War Department. In the inspector general's office he was given copies of charges that would be the basis of the court-martial 'contemplated' to discipline him because of his San Antonio statements a month earlier.

Secretary Weeks was feeling strong enough to travel to Washington in mid-October. In a meeting with the president he made official what many had been speculating about for some time. Because of his health he felt it necessary to resign. The next day, after Weeks attended his final cabinet meeting, the president's secretary announced that Dwight F. Davis had been selected as the new secretary of war. And the same day the War Department made it official – Colonel William Mitchell would stand trial for insubordination at a court-martial to convene at the end of the month.

The following day, 14 October, Supreme Court Chief Justice William Howard Taft administered the oath of office to Dwight Davis in a ceremony at the War Department. On hand were Helen Davis and two of the children, Alice and the youngest, Helen. (Pete and Cynthia were away at school.)

Davis, at the age of 46, had become the youngest member of the Coolidge cabinet and the 51st person to hold the title of secretary of war since Henry Knox in 1789. Back in St. Louis, Davis's appointment to the cabinet was given a page one banner headline. Not only was a local man spectacularly on the rise (the paper pointed out that Chief Justice Taft had been secretary of war before becoming president in 1909) but Missouri's and the West's hand was strengthened in the ever-present geographical scrambling for political power.

Press reaction elsewhere was also favourable. 'President Coolidge could not have made a better choice,' wrote the *New York Times*. 'As acting secretary, Davis has measured up to his responsibilities. In more than one emergency he has done the right thing when he might easily have blundered.' Wrote the *New York World*, 'Mr. Coolidge adds to his cabinet a man who on occasion has shown sound judgment and energy and gives promise of unusual capacity for the work to be done.'

The *Providence Journal* took a look at his Harvard/family fortune/public service background and insisted that obviously he was more truly of the New England than Middle Western 'type'. The *New York Telegram* said Washington old-timers wondered if this would revive the 'tennis cabinet' of President Theodore Roosevelt's administration. And proof that Davis was exactly the right man to provide *civilian* control of the department, said one Washington political column, was that, despite his agreeable personal characteristics, the Army had hoped someone else would be appointed.

For Davis, moving next door to the large, dark Victorian office of the secretary of war did not, however, mean much change in daily activity. There was still the matter of Billy Mitchell. The court-martial convened on 28 October before a board of 12 generals. Their number was reduced to nine after Mitchell exercised his challenges. (One who remained was Major General Douglas MacArthur, who struck reporters as being particularly debonair.)

The setting was an austere room in a one-storey brick building near the Capitol where the War Department stored records. Earlier some had suggested that the War Department rent the Interior Department's large auditorium or the House caucus room. 'This isn't a vaudeville show – or an advertising scheme,' said Davis. Mitchell and his supporters claimed later that Davis had chosen the small room with uncertain floor strength to limit the number of spectators.

Mitchell and his team had decided that he probably would, in fact, be found guilty of the actual charges, violation of Article 96 of war ('all disorders and neglects to the prejudice of good order and military discipline, all conduct of a nature to bring discredit upon the military service ...'). The trial, therefore, should be used to 'educate the American people about aviation', and to that end it should be kept constantly on the front pages of the country's newspapers.

For weeks the testimony continued. Early in the proceedings Mitchell's attorney threatened to call not only Secretary of War Davis to testify but also President Coolidge (actually his secretary). A compromise was reached. Neither the president's secretary nor any cabinet officers would be called if they would supply their records.

Newspaper accounts of the trial were followed by military personnel and civilians alike around the country. More than 200 aviation veterans attending an Armistice Day dinner in New York, hissed and booed the name of Secretary of War Dwight Davis after a telegram was read saying that because of the court-martial Colonel Mitchell could not leave Washington to be the evening's guest of honour. A correction in the paper the next day said Secretary Davis had been out of town and the telegram had actually been sent by the adjutant-general, also named Davis.

The new secretary of war got a much sunnier reception a week later when St. Louis celebrated 'Dwight F. Davis Day'. The city pulled out all the stops. In late morning motorcycles roared through the gates of Westmoreland Place, and the mayor and a reception committee, in automobiles trimmed with plumes and roses, picked up the guest of honour at his mother's home. As the civilian contingent of the parade moved downtown it was joined by the Sixth Infantry from Jefferson Barracks and an Army TC-7 dirigible circled overhead. At City Hall, a 17-gun secretarial salute was fired by Battery C, 14th Field Artillery.

That evening some 800 guests attended a civic reception and dinner at a downtown hotel 'tendered to the Hon. Dwight F. Davis, Secretary of War, by the Citizens of St. Louis'. Tied with red, white and blue ribbon, the evening's programs were embossed with a representation of the city's famous statue of Saint Louis, looking appropriately war-like. Davis, however, in his speech at the dinner, emphasised peace. 'I have often thought there is something of error about the designation of the great government department of which I am the civilian head as a Department of War. It is not the business of the War Department to prepare for war, but to prepare against war.'

In early December the Morrow board released its report. It 'ably dealt with the solid elements in Mitchell's position', a later military historian would write, ' [and] at once reassured the nation and also mobilised the support of Coolidge and the Congress for a series of legislative actions that added up to America's first broad aeronautical policy'. A more pro-Mitchell writer saw it differently: 'The Morrow board stole enough of Mitchell's thunder in its recommendations to lull the nation into a sense of security for another decade and more.'

After a trial that lasted more than six weeks, the court-martial panel released its verdict on 17 December. Colonel William Mitchell had been found guilty on all counts. He was given a five-year suspension with loss of pay and allowances. President Coolidge, acting, he said, upon the advice of Secretary of War Davis, restored to Mitchell all his allowances and half his base pay. 'I am moved to recommend such modification of the sentence,' Davis had written to Coolidge, 'because of the fact that the accused is married and has children dependent upon him ...' In early 1926 Mitchell submitted his resignation to the Army and Secretary Davis accepted it.

Mitchell's children (including a new baby born to Mitchell's second wife just two months before the start of the court-martial) might have touched the heart of Davis, the father of four, but he was firmly determined to let Mitchell's fate serve as warning to other restive officers in other Army branches. He knew that some were supremely unhappy with how their individual services within the Army were being affected by the Army's ongoing peacetime restructuring, he told a reporter for the Associated Press immediately following the verdict. Some were unhappy with 'settled' department or national policies sometimes connected with new international treaties.

Davis was particularly aware of this, said the article, having seen, as assistant secretary, the 'frictions' between branches involved with supply and industrial preparedness. It appeared he intended to use that 'inside information as a basis for settling internal rows as they come before him'. In his many speeches Davis had 'insistently preached team work as an essential army gospel ..., drawing on his experience both as an athlete and a combat officer ... to drive home his point'.

In March 1926 Davis approved (as a study) a report recommending an expanded Army air arm of 52 tactical squadrons, and asked that details be worked out as quickly as possible. Four months later President Coolidge signed the congressional act which, among other things, changed the name of the Air Service to Air Corps and provided for a new assistant secretary of war for aviation.

Named to this position was F. Trubee Davison, who found Secretary of War Davis ready to provide support 'but not overenthusiastic support. He [Davis] was always trying to balance the needs of the ground forces against the public demand for the development of the air forces'. Davis was 'a very fine man, quite on the dignified side, but a man you could absolutely trust', discovered Davison, though he didn't 'have an awful lot of zip and go to him'.

As in most of the world's capitals, all work in Washington was not done in hearing rooms or official offices. Dinner table diplomacy and social gatherings used to make contacts and take the measure of newcomers, historically had been part of the Washington power scene. Sometimes it seemed as if nobody stayed home in the evenings. Cabinet members were expected to entertain – one another, the president, important makers of opinion and law. Since everyone was seated according to rank 'pretty much every evening you'd sit next to the same lady you sat next to the night before', remembered one participant in the social rounds of the time. Possibly this was helpful to Davis. He had a poor memory for faces and had enrolled in a memory course. Though he studied diligently, it didn't help a bit.

This social side of Washington life the outgoing and effervescent Helen Davis enjoyed, at least when her fragile health permitted. She spent most of one summer in France consulting doctors. Another time when she and at least one of the children had accompanied Davis on a trip to inspect southern United States Army installations she took ill aboard the US Engineer Corps yacht (as also did the Davis child) and had to return to Washington. Her 'delicate health' had kept her out of the public eye, said one newspaper article in extolling her beauty and graciousness.

One of those in Washington whose friendship Helen Davis prized was Grace Coolidge, the slim, lovely first lady (who also happened to be married to a man of legendary reserve). Grace Coolidge was eager to learn how to ride and Dwight Davis, who had ridden since he was a young man, quietly helped her arrange to take riding lessons at nearby Ft. Myer. (Quietly, because the president was well known for disapproving of such frivolities.) Davis accompanied her to her first lesson. Somehow the newspapers learned about the lesson, and the president, who would not even allow his wife to dance in public, quickly put a stop to her new activity.

But the president could also be kind, learned the Davis children. One time when the Davises were hosting a dinner party in honour of President and Mrs. Coolidge, Alice, the second eldest of the Davis children, found herself called upon to substitute as hostess when her mother could not attend. Naturally, she was a bit nervous, a condition not helped at all by the prying questions of one of the women guests at the table. To her great relief, President Coolidge, sensing her discomfort, came to her rescue by launching into a discussion with her – about shooting craps.

At another Davis dinner party in their house on 18th Street (an impressive four-and-a-half-storey brick with long narrow windows), Cynthia and Helen, the youngest Davis girls, were in their upper storey playroom while the grown-ups dined downstairs. Suddenly a bat flew in the playroom window. The girls screamed in alarm and up the three flights of stairs ran dinner guests to the rescue, led by Herbert Hoover, wielding a tennis racquet and ready to battle unknown evil.

The girls were at school in the area – Alice at St. Louis College in Washington, Cynthia and Helen at private schools. At Holton Arms, Helen and her young classmates did military drills in their middy blouses, carrying wooden guns – great fun, they thought. The secretary of war's message about the importance of military preparedness even in peacetime was being heard everywhere, apparently.

Pete was at St. Mark's School in Massachusetts preparing for Harvard and playing lots of baseball ('game – St. Mark's' would occasionally be scribbled on the secretary of war's official appointment book). When he graduated in spring 1926, his father was one of the graduation day speakers. That summer Pete was enrolled for the summer at Plattsburg, the citizens military training camp in upstate New York that his father had attended the first year of its existence, 11 years earlier. Private Davis was to be shown no favours of any kind, announced his father.

In midsummer, when Secretary Davis visited the camp to give a speech, Pete was expected to attend the Sunday dinner given for his father. But no Pete appeared. Finally, and probably much to his father's chagrin, a corporal's guard had to be sent to round up the reluctant private. 'All the generals and colonels' that would be on hand had 'got his goat', grumbled the younger Davis. At the end of the summer session a bat signed by baseball great Babe Ruth was presented to the outstanding 'soldier athlete' – who turned out to be triple-threat boxer, runner, baseball player Dwight F. Davis Jr.

For Davis there was by now a familiar routine to affairs in the secretary of war's office, with its colourful military flags, its historical Army icons such as the folded flag that was fired on at Ft. Sumter, plus Davis's own additions – a favourite woodcut of Lincoln, etchings by Rembrandt and Whistler. The room had a fireplace mantel supported by huge winged griffins and walls panelled with mahogany and a popular material which imitated tooled Moroccan leather. The effect was substantial, solid and heavy – befitting the work that went on here, under the gaze of Mars, the god of war, depicted in the ornate frescoed ceiling. Doors on the west side of the large room opened out onto a balcony overlooking 17th Street.

Visitors streamed in – on some crowded days as often as every 15 minutes. Sometimes they were politicians from Puerto Rico or, particularly, the Philippine Islands, or the Philippines' governor-general. Both territories were administered by the War Department through its Bureau of Insular Affairs.

There were cabinet meetings next door at the White House (the secretary of war traditionally sat near the head of the table, though treasury secretary Andrew Mellon was said to be the real power in the cabinet). There were internal department scuffles to be settled, Congressional legislation to be pushed, receptions, racquet ball late in the afternoon, and speeches, always speeches. The country needed a stable policy concerning the need for and size of the Army, he told nearly 2,000 women who crowded into the ballroom of the Waldorf-Astoria for the largest luncheon ever held by the Women's National Republican Club in early 1927. The recently passed Military Defense Act, he told them, was the first comprehensive military policy ever adopted in this country based essentially on American principles of defence, not aggression and 'was the antithesis of militarism', he assured them. (There was a growing strain of pacifism in the country and criticism of a strong military.)

There were official trips to inspect flood control projects along the Mississippi River, the defences of Panama and the economy of Puerto Rico (on this trip he was accompanied by his cousin Harry Langenberg from St. Louis).

There were dedications of still more war memorials at Arlington and the Army's new aviation centre at Wright Field in Ohio, not far from the shed which once housed an airplane built by Orville and Wilbur Wright. America had an inferiority complex in aviation, the secretary of war said in his address, but there was no reason the country should not 'take its rightful place as the world leader in this great science'.

And there were official messages of congratulations to be sent to the country's newest crop of aviation heroes: Commander Richard Byrd, for instance, who, with three companions, had flown across the Atlantic Ocean, and, of course, the boyish Charles Lindbergh, who astonished the world by flying across the Atlantic alone.

Lindbergh's airplane, as the whole world knew, was named the *Spirit of St. Louis*, in honour of the city whose businessmen had financially backed his flight. What a happy coincidence that one of the country's highest ranking St. Louisans, Dwight Davis, also happened to be involved in much that was happening in American aviation. Davis found himself front and centre (literally) in the huge ceremonies honouring the aviator staged in Washington and later in St. Louis. And the Davis daughters were among those who got that most highly sought after perquisite of the Washington social season, a brief flight above the Potomac with the shy young hero.

It would also fall to Davis, some months later, to suggest tactfully to the prickly young pilot that he was too much of a national treasure to continue making risky – in the opinion of many in the country – flights about the globe. 'We had a chummy talk together,' Davis reported afterward. 'However, it is an inalienable fact that Lindbergh has a world of common sense and does not need much advice.'

On a Friday night early in July 1927 Dwight Davis, three days past his 52nd birthday, was in his stateroom aboard the White Star Liner *Olympic* preparing for bed. Early the following morning the ship would sail from its berth in New York City's Hudson River, bound for Cherbourg and Southampton. A knock sounded at the door and Davis found newspaper reporters in the corridor. Covering celebrities arriving and departing on steam ships was a staple of New York City journalism. If you could find them, you could usually get a brief interview. After all, where could they run?

For just this reason Davis's name and those of other notables had not been published on the ship's passenger list. The reporters were therefore very pleased with themselves for finding him. He agreed to talk to them briefly. No, he told them, there was no official significance to this trip to Europe. He had not had a vacation in five years, he said, and he was joining his family in the south of France (daughter Alice had been at school outside Paris since the previous September). They would all return in about two months.

This time Davis had good reason to keep a low profile. His boss, President Coolidge, had strongly urged the members of his cabinet to refrain from going to Europe during the summer. Affairs were delicate enough at the Geneva Naval Arms Limitation Conference without having miscellaneous high US officials roaming about Europe and likely to be quoted – or misquoted – about American positions. Davis had done some fast lobbying to convince Coolidge that concerns for his family necessitated the trip.

Not only had these plans been made much earlier, Davis explained to the president in a letter, but he, Davis, had no idea Coolidge disapproved, since 'Mr. Mellon [the treasury secretary] has been going for several years'. He would be in Paris only briefly before heading down to the south of France to check on his family, he assured Coolidge. 'No statement can be misconstrued as I do not intend to make any.'

His wife's health concerned him, he explained. Not only had she been forced to cancel a trip to England with daughter Alice, but 'she left Paris to take a cure while the other children were on their way abroad and thus was unable to meet them in Paris on their arrival ... For some reason, her foot has never healed properly since the operation last spring, and I am afraid there is some sort of infection in it'. He was able to write the president's secretary a month later that his wife was much better. 'I hope she will be stronger than ever next winter.'

Unofficial though his trip might be, Davis did visit American war cemeteries and, while in England on the way home, probably became aware of an event which, as it turned out, would be highly significant to the future of the US Army. In mid-August the British military staged extensive manoeuvres of a new Experimental Mechanised Force on Salisbury Plain, west of London. During the World War, the British, French and Americans had developed and used armoured vehicles which, because they had agricultural tractor-type tracks instead of wheels, could move over open ground and across trenches. 'Tanks' their wartime developers had called these new contraptions in order (according to legend) to convince the curious that these were just water or storage tanks they were building.

Some British officers were eager to see how much farther they could take the idea. For these summer 1927 manoeuvres they had put together a one-of-a-kind, experimental force of tanks and armoured cars. 'Crude and makeshift' as this new force was, the armoured vehicles repeatedly out-manoeuvred the old tried-and-true cavalry and formations of soldiers on foot.

London newspapers gave the manoeuvres lengthy coverage, and reporters who caught Davis at Waterloo Station as he was leaving for the US asked if he had been among the spectators. '"Busmen's holidays" do not give me any delight,' Davis responded (possibly remembering his promise to Coolidge) – and changed the subject to England's rain and roses. 'Secretary of War Davis sailed for home today on the *Berengaria* after a short visit in which he did not attend the manoeuvres of the new mechanised army,' the *New York Times* reporter cabled his paper.

But Davis knew enough about what had occurred to be impressed. The United States needed to develop a similar force he decided. When he got back to Washington he ordered his chief of staff, General Charles P. Summerall, to begin development of such a mechanised force, to be part of a military laboratory for experiment and development.

However, despite American field manoeuvres with dilapidated, left-over equipment the following summer and despite Secretary Davis's approval, in December 1928, of a move to create a permanent mechanised force, it would be many years for such a force truly to develop.

CHAPTER 18

MEANWHILE, WITH THE CUP

The 1920s

Through most of the 1920s the United States kept a tenacious hold on the Davis Cup. The US had not challenged in 1919 when the Davis Cup series resumed after the World War. It would not be sporting, the USNLTA had decided, since the US had suffered less than other countries in the war. But the following year the Americans were back and victorious, led by the quixotic and talented Bill Tilden. Tilden would eventually compete in more Davis Cup challenge rounds (11) than any other player.

Interest in the series was building in all parts of the world. Japan and India both had competed for the first time in 1921, the year the French tennis association announced that it would not, repeat not, name France's exuberant international tennis star Suzanne Lenglen to its Davis Cup team. Finally, in September, Japan's Ichiya Kumagae and Zenzo Shimizu, with their unorthodox Western grips and deft top spins, had led their country into the 1921 challenge round at Forest Hills. As the matches proceeded, it looked as if 'Shimmy' Shimizu would do the unthinkable, defeat US champion Tilden. Tilden, however, prevailed in five sets.

When Shimizu doffed his hat and rushed to the net to congratulate his opponent, the large crowd, nearly beside itself over the superb tennis and sportsmanship on both sides – not to mention Tilden's win – sailed seat cushions down onto the court, while players and officials good-naturedly ducked. Captain of the US team was Dick Williams, who won the doubles teamed with Watson Washburn. (The pair had been Dwight Davis's opponents in the armed services tournament at Cannes in 1919.)

Many things about Davis Cup were changing. By 1920 engravings recording the outcome of the first 14 challenge rounds had completely covered the outside of the silver bowl. Dwight Davis ordered a round, sterling silver tray more than two feet in diameter, at a cost of about $800, from New York's tony Fifth Avenue jewellers, Black, Starr & Frost.

Like the bowl, the tray was made by the Durgin Co. in New Hampshire. Rowland Rhodes' original design of swags, shells and flowers was duplicated around the edge of the heavy (300 troy ounces) tray. The recessed centre portion was left empty, a gleaming, blank silver slate on which the Davis Cup record could be continued. And two of these names to be engraved had changed as well. Since 1923 it had been Australia instead of Australasia. Since 1920 it had been United States instead of America – recognition of the fact that the American continents included, in fact, many countries, some of which had begun entering Davis Cup competition.

In late 1922, delegates from Davis Cup nations had met in London and decided to split the ballooning number of challengers into two geographical zones, European and American. A good thing, too. By 1927 a record 26 countries were challenging for the cup.

Like the three previous challenge rounds, the 1927 challenge round was held on Bill Tilden's home ground, the Germantown Cricket Club in Philadelphia. One of the courts, the one just east of the handsome Georgian brick clubhouse, was considered 'Tilden's court'. The roof of the Tilden family home could be glimpsed off to the north, just beyond a wall.

For a second year France was the challenger, with a team of four stalwarts whom sportswriters would dub The Four Musketeers: René Lacoste, Henri Cochet, Jean Borotra and Jacques Brugnon. At the end of the first day the matches were even, 'Big Bill' Tilden beating Cochet, 'Little Bill' Johnston losing to Lacoste. After a doubles win, the US was ahead 2-1. On the third day 34-year old Tilden lost to the 23-year-old Lacoste, and Cochet beat Johnston. The US's seven-year string of victories had ended. France had won the cup, 3-2.

Back in France, sports fans were jubilant. Their country had become only the fourth nation to win possession of the famous trophy. (Among the blizzard of newspaper stories about the event was one on page two of the *Concord Daily Monitor & New Hampshire Patriot*. It was headlined proudly, 'Davis Cup Is Local Product, Made At Durgin's'.)

In midtown New York six days later, members of the French team escorted the large silver bowl and its tray from the Fifth Avenue sales offices of Black, Starr & Frost to four cars flying French flags waiting at the curb. Loud cheers erupted from the crowds lining the street and filling the windows of nearby office buildings. The pieces of silver, gleaming in the bright autumn noonday sun, were placed on a platform in the car in which Lacoste and team captain Pierre Gillou were riding and police guards climbed onto the car's running boards. Preceded by motorcycles with sirens wailing, the procession of cars moved majestically down Fifth Avenue and then crosstown to the docks. At the top of the gangplank of the ocean liner *France*, the ship's captain received the trophy, now officially on French 'soil'.

That evening at a banquet aboard the ship, American Secretary of War Dwight F. Davis bid farewell to his trophy. Even though the cup was going to the European continent for the first time, he said, its loss to the United States was not the blow it might seem. After all, the cup was given with the hope that it would foster friendly competition among tennis nations of the world and this it had done. In fact, said Davis, its best work might lie ahead of it while it was in the custody of France.

A week later the cup arrived in Le Havre where a customs agent insisted that, according to France's new tariffs, 60 percent of the value of these rather nice pieces of silver (or 42,000 francs) be paid before they would be allowed into the country. *Mon Dieu!* Into the safe of the Custodian House went the cup. Two days later the director of customs waived the duty and the trophy at last was on its way to Paris for display before the French people.

CHAPTER 19

HOOVER TAKES CHARGE

D wight Davis's rosy bon voyage sentiments about the Davis Cup fostering friendly relations between countries was soon put to the test. The fuss was initially between United States Lawn Tennis Association officials and its gifted, if perennially difficult Davis Cup star, Bill Tilden.

The association ruled in the summer of 1928 that by filing dispatches from Wimbledon, Tilden had violated the player-writer rule which controlled the amount of writing (for pay) that players (amateurs, of course) could do. Tilden was off the team, announced the USLTA from America just before the US and Italy played in the inter-zone Davis Cup final in Paris. In Europe with the team were Joe Wear, the non-playing US team captain (and good friend of Dwight Davis's dating back to their St. Louis boyhood) and Samuel Collom, president of USLTA. Wear fumed that such a last minute decision made the US look ridiculous. The US defeated Italy and was now due to face France in the challenge round.

Though Tilden was, of course, not happy with this development, it was the French who were really furious. They had just completed a brand new red clay tennis temple, Stade Roland Garros, for worshipping and, it was hoped, successfully defending *Le Coupe*, the beautiful silver bowl which they had won a year earlier. 'Beeg Bill' was immensely popular in France and French officials were counting on him to help fill the new stadium.

The French Tennis Association not only cabled its objections to the USLTA back in New York but contacted the American ambassador to France for help. He, in turn (some say) contacted President Coolidge to see if it was all right to get involved in this burgeoning international crisis. Go ahead, the president apparently responded.

The rally continued. The Ambassador contacted Collom requesting 'further consideration' of the suspension. Two days before the challenge round was to begin Collom announced that he was taking personal responsibility for reinstating Tilden 'in the interest of international good feeling'. The incident had 'created a most unfavorable impression among the French', said Collum with considerable understatement, in a cable to the USLTA telling them what he intended to do. Responded the USLTA, 'Inasmuch as our Ambassador to France is the personal representative of the President of the United States, to have refused his request would have been an ungracious act.'Point over.

Tilden won his first singles match but lost his doubles and second singles matches. The French retained the cup 4-1. 'A tempest in a tennis court,' a *New York Times* editorial called it.

Davis, at least publicly, kept his head down and out of the line of fire about all of this. Reporters tracked him down in Denver, however, while he was on his way with two of the children to Hawaii to represent the government at the gala celebration of the 150th anniversary of Captain Cook's discovery of the islands. Tilden 'probably is guilty of professionalism and should be barred from amateur competition, from what information I have at present ...', said Davis. It had been, of course, during the Davis-Wightman USLTA presidency that development of the player-writer rule had begun.

Dwight Davis's attention undoubtedly was focused on off-court matters. The year 1928 was, after all, an election year. A year earlier, in August 1927, from his vacation headquarters in the Black Hills of South Dakota, Coolidge had made his surprise and cryptic announcement: 'I do not choose to run for President in 1928.' Immediately all kinds of people began to eye the White House. Apparently one of them was Dwight Davis.

Davis had been in France visiting his family at the time of Coolidge's announcement, and after he returned to Washington he had lunched with William R. Castle, of the State Department. Castle, a somewhat cynical observer of the Washington scene, kept a gossipy diary. 'Dwight Davis, just returned from Europe ... is badly bitten, I think, with presidential aspirations,' he noted in an August entry. 'Perhaps he will get the complimentary vote of the Missouri delegation, but I doubt whether he goes any further. It really would be absurd if he did.' Castle made sure to pass on the news to Hoover the next day.

In early November a newspaper in St. Louis carried news of a 'Favorite Son Boom' boosting Davis for president. Several Davis proponents were travelling the state assessing his support among the Republican party faithful. One supporter reported that he thought it would be easy to build the foundation for a candidacy for Davis in Missouri. Said another, 'it would be a fine thing to send a delegation instructed for Davis to the convention'.

But elsewhere in the country Herbert Hoover was picking up support, though some thought Coolidge might accept a draft from the convention. In late November Hoover told Castle that Davis was taking his [Davis's] candidacy seriously enough that he was thinking of resigning from the cabinet to formally announce as a candidate. Hoover and Castle both found this amusing. 'Of course the ways of politics are dark but Dwight's chances certainly seem none at all,' wrote Castle in his diary.

Meanwhile, Missouri was having a 'free-for-all', according to one political analyst, 'with candidates for high office, even the Presidency of the nation, hanging from almost every limb of the political tree'. The Dwight Davis boom was finally brought to a halt by the announcement from Missouri's governor that he intended to be a candidate for the Republican vice-presidency. This, of course, meant that a Missouri favourite son could not also be pushed for the top spot on the ticket.

By February 1928 Washington insiders, like Alice Roosevelt Longworth, were putting their money on Hoover, and sure enough, at the Republican convention in June 1928 he was nominated. Davis offered his congratulations and his help during the campaign, and on his way to Hawaii paid a call on Hoover at his California home to report on the issues that were of concern to voters in the country's midlands.

In November Hoover was elected president of the United States, the first president born west of the Mississippi River. Now the question Davis and others were pondering was, how would he reshuffle his cabinet. Who would go and who would stay?

But that was in the future. The secretary of war still had duties to perform for the current administration, which was why Dwight Davis found himself, in mid-December 1928, bouncing along over rough, unfinished corduroy roads, through piney woods and swamp bogs in a caravan of more than 50 automobiles heading for a narrow, wind-raked, sandy spit of land off the coast of North Carolina. It was here at Kill Devil Hills near Kitty Hawk on 17 December 1903, that two self-taught engineers from Ohio had first demonstrated that man could fly in a powered, heavier-than-air machine.

Now, on the 25th anniversary of Wilbur and Orville Wright's momentous, world-changing achievement, a historic marker and a cornerstone for a future memorial were to be unveiled and dedicated. Not only Washington officialdom had made the laborious trip by boat, bus and finally car. Also in the party were representatives of foreign governments and some 200 delegates to an International Civil Aeronautical Conference in Washington. And, of course, 57-year-old Orville Wright. (Elder brother Wilbur had died in 1912 at the age of 45.)

This had not been Dwight Davis's normal smooth, first-cabin travel experience.

A dangerous Potomac River fog had kept the steamer from departing from Washington until 2 a.m. on the first leg of the trek. Then came the bone-rattling overland crossing and next a ferry ride across to Kitty Hawk, during which a guest from Kansas fell overboard into the icy waters of Currituck Sound. Fortunately, just as the hapless man's heavy overcoat seemed sure to sink him permanently, a quick-thinking sailor got a hook under his collar and pulled him back on board.

Little had changed on the desolate Outer Banks since the Wright brothers had first set up camp there with their gliders and their original 'flying machine' with its two propellers, approximately 12 horsepower engine and fragile, long, drooping wings. In fact, not a whole lot had changed since the late 1500s when the first English settlement in America had been established on nearby Roanoke Island. The wailing winds still bent the sea grass and the clumps of stubborn trees. The sand dunes still moved slowly, inexorably. In fact, Big Kill Devil Hill from which the first flights had been launched was said to have moved hundreds of feet since then – and 30 feet in just the past six weeks. Shrubs and grass had recently been planted around its base in hopes that it would stay put now that it was to be the site of an official government monument.

After the good ladies of Dare County (named for Virginia Dare, the first baby of English parents born in the New World) fed the visitors a lunch of ham, turkey and barbecued pork, it was time for speeches. The crowd, now swollen to about 3,000, gathered near a temporary platform decorated with pine boughs, which had been built atop the dune. Several retired Coast Guardsmen who had been in attendance 25 years earlier were introduced to the crowd and shook hands with their old friend Orville.

Politicians were introduced and spoke. Finally it was Secretary of War Davis's turn. 'Just as we today lay the foundation for this monument, so the aviation of today is laying a foundation for the future, a great structure that will vastly further the ends of peace, civilization and prosperity throughout the world,' said Davis. His words, like those of the other speakers, were whipped away over the sands by a howling, 35-mile-an-hour wind. The cornerstone was lowered into place. Wright made no speech and, in fact, observed one newspaper reporter, seemed a bit restless, staring off at the horizon.

Davis, other officials and the crowd now moved 600 feet to the north where a large piece of granite, cut to resemble a boulder, had been placed to mark (as best as anyone could actually determine) the actual take-off spot. Aviation's rising female star, Amelia Earhart, stood next to Orville Wright as the white parachute covering this marker was pulled away and 15 carrier pigeons, released into the air, spiralled up into the winter sky and headed north.

And still the drama was not over. Some of the local drivers had left the ceremonies to get warm, and their passengers, having missed the ferry for the return trip, were given a ride back to the mainland in a decrepit government boat normally used to chase rumrunners, which not only leaked but got lost. Meanwhile aboard the ferry, Dwight Davis stood talking to a real estate developer from New Jersey who was one of the donors of the land for the memorials. Suddenly the man keeled over. Fellow passengers rushed to his aid, but he was dead before he could be lifted from the deck. Back on land one of the cars carrying the visitors was sideswiped by another car, though injuries didn't amount to more than cuts on the face of a congressman from New York. All in all, wrote *New Yorker* reporter Eric Hodgins, the return to Washington bore a resemblance to Napoleon's retreat from Moscow.

In early January 1929 Dwight Davis paid a call on Herbert Hoover in the incoming president's temporary offices at the Mayflower Hotel. Afterwards Davis was non-committal to reporters. His talk with Hoover had been of a general nature, he said. The press continued to predict that Davis was in a 'receptive frame of mind' to stay on as head of the War Department, as did a private memo about cabinet possibilities sent Hoover by one of his Republican party advisors.

The selection process for the cabinet and diplomatic posts proceeded slowly, and the steady parade to the Mayflower Hotel of politicians, their supporters and the GOP faithful from all corners of the country continued. Hoover probably would not announce his selections until the March inauguration said insiders, and Washington seemed agog that Hoover – who would be the first US president with a telephone on his desk – would be doing much of that notification by telephone.

For Davis the phone did not ring. Davis, like all cabinet officials, had submitted a pro-forma letter of resignation. In mid-February Hoover, in Miami, wrote Davis to acknowledge its receipt and say that, as a matter of fact, he had other plans for the secretary of war position. 'It is due an old friend to know as early as possible that I shall want to make some other arrangement about the office you hold. I would be happy if at some future time there should be some other opportunity where you can serve if you desire to continue to devote yourself to public interest, although such opportunities are not likely to develop for some little time yet.' James W. Good, a leader of the Hoover campaign committee and a former congressman from Hoover's home state of Iowa, would be named the new secretary of war.

Davis, according to Washington gossip, was possibly interested in a diplomatic post in Europe. Supporters wrote to suggest him for Paris; earlier speculation had him going to London. In April Hoover named Charles G. Dawes, Coolidge's vice-president, ambassador to England. As it turned out, Davis had never even been on the short list for the post.

However, there was one of Hoover's lists on which Davis's name had surfaced in early February, even before Hoover had written him that he would not be reappointed as secretary of war. It was the list of a half-dozen possibilities for governor-general of the Philippines, a prickly post requiring someone acceptable to the Filipinos yet with 'established reputation and confidence at this end', as Hoover put it. Back and forth went the cables between Hoover and the current governor-general, Henry L. Stimson, on his way home from Manila to join Hoover's new cabinet as secretary of state. ('I virtually had to select the new governor-general for the Islands,' Stimson would claim in his diary.)

One by one names were eliminated. Hoover's first choice was former Assistant Attorney General William J. Donovan, who insisted on being attorney general or nothing and turned down what newspapers were calling 'this plum' and 'springboard to higher office'. 'Finally I reached the conclusion,' wrote Stimson (Hoover might have been surprised at the choice of pronoun), 'that ex-secretary Davis by temperament and departmental experience with the Philippines was the best available man. He was friendly, broad-minded, tactful and I became convinced would treat the Filipinos with the necessary consideration and tact.' With an annual salary of $18,000, the position was the highest paid of any administration official under the president.

In May, Davis's 'phone call' (actually a telegram) came. At lunch at the White House on Monday, 13 May, Hoover offered Davis the post of governor-general. Davis, it seemed, was particularly well-suited for the job. His former cabinet position had kept him intimately in touch with Filipino affairs. He was a civilian, which mollified those determined to have a civilian in charge, yet a military hero and former Army boss, which appeased those just as determined to have military control.

Davis headed home to St. Louis to confer with his brothers and other advisers. Among the factors being considered, said reports, was whether the health of his wife was compatible with the climate of the islands. After hours of discussion, the decision was made, and from St. Louis Davis made a phone call to the president. On Thursday Hoover announced that Dwight Davis had accepted the appointment as governor-general of the Philippines.

CHAPTER 20

SHARING THE SIDEWALK

The man on the bridge of the SS *President Taft* – tall, hair mostly grey, a bit of fullness now about the jaw, white trousers, white shoes, dark jacket, straw hat – raised his hand and waved to the large crowd of the curious waiting at Manila's Pier 7. After the gangplank was in position, Dwight Davis walked down onto Philippine soil for the first time since his honeymoon 25 years earlier.

Helen Davis had not made the trip this time. Instead, the new governor-general was accompanied by his eldest daughter Alice and her cousin from St. Louis, Alita Davis, Sam's daughter. A heavy rain had been falling sporadically all morning, a remnant of the typhoon which had narrowly missed the *Taft* as it steamed across the China Sea. But that hadn't dampened the welcome. Sirens sounded and small boats bearing signs of welcome had buzzed about the steamship after it passed Corregidor and moved into Manila Bay. A general holiday had been declared and the celebratory crowd on the docks cheered loudly at first sight of the person who now embodied the power of far away America.

The broadly smiling Davis and his party and their official hosts climbed into cars and, preceded by mounted cavalry, passed through the old walls of the handsome Spanish colonial city to Marble Hall. Cheers from people along the streets accompanied the procession like outriders of sound.

At the inaugural ceremony Davis delivered the brief address on which he had laboured on the ship coming out. It was a reworking of the draft of suggested remarks handed him before he sailed by the efficient staff of the Bureau of Insular Affairs. Stacks of books borrowed from the Congressional Library, reports and position papers on Filipino affairs had also been provided for his shipboard reading. Davis, ever the team player, had sent back enroute several passages touching upon such sensitive matters as sugar quotas and Philippine independence to the War and State Departments in Washington for comment.

From there the party moved on to lunch at Malacañang, the 18th-century palace on the Pasig River which would be the Davis family's official residence, and where the staff had been frantically mopping up the rain-swollen Pasig which was overflowing into the palace's ground floor. (For representatives of a republic supposedly steeped in Jeffersonian disdain for 'tinsel aristocracy', the day so far had come rather close to the colonial pomp for which the US sometimes smugly criticised its European brethren.)

In the afternoon Davis went to his office, where the elaborate, high-backed 'crested chair' at the desk awaited its new occupant. He conferred at length with the Vice-Governor Eugene A. Gilmore (at least one Manila newspaper had expressed disappointment that Gilmore had not been named the new governor-general rather than Davis) and held his first meeting with the press. Manila had both English and Spanish language newspapers as well as correspondents from stateside papers and wire services. The ground rules, he told reporters, were that there was to be no direct quoting unless he released statements in writing – possibly the practice he had used at the War Department.

Next a meeting with the Malacañang staff, back to the office for more work and, that evening, the inaugural ball for some 2,000 guests. The next day Davis would meet with his cabinet and receive the governors of the various Philippine provinces who were currently in Manila. A fairly typical, if very full, schedule for a newly arrived official. But apparently not exactly what the Manila press had expected. 'He did not engage in any sports on the day of his arrival,' commented the *Manila Bulletin* solemnly at the end of a long article, possibly disappointed that he had not come dashing down the gangplank swinging a tennis racquet.

Tennis, however, was again proving to be a useful diplomatic tool for Davis. During the voyage from the United States, he had stopped over in Japan to show the girls the ancient temples and other places of beauty that he and Helen had visited 25 years earlier (a visit which Davis had said helped develop his lifetime interest in Japanese art). As part of the official Japanese welcome, a tennis exhibition was staged between former Davis Cup players Kumagai and Fukuda. Said officials, 'the name known to young people of Japan by its association with tennis's most famous trophy gave his welcome today a popular note which is usually missing.'

An event several months later had even more benefits. Davis, looking for a way to get exercise, invited three good young Filipino players to join him for a game on the court at the palace. (The Philippines had competed in Davis Cup for the first time three years earlier.) The event caused an immediate sensation. Pictures of Davis and his tennis companions appeared in local newspapers as well as those back in the United States.

Davis realised he had stumbled upon something that had 'a good effect far beyond its importance', he reported later in a personal letter to the new American secretary of war, Patrick Hurley. (James Good had died after only a few months in office.) The Filipino public as well as political leaders 'like the idea that I have not limited my recreational companions to Americans, although I originally did it largely because the Filipinos were the best players'.

'The Filipino mentality is entirely different from ours and they react differently from us,' wrote Davis. 'They are an exceedingly sensitive people, and many think that this is due to a sort of inferiority complex. The fact remains that the way a thing is done is often more important to them than the thing itself.'

Davis reported that he had learned at least one new reason why relations had deteriorated between an earlier governor-general, Leonard Wood, and the Filipinos. Wood insisted on having another person in the room anytime he conferred with a Filipino politician. He wanted a witness, they surmised. They had noticed immediately that Davis operated differently.

If the political leader telling him this 'knew that he was being trusted', said Davis, 'he would lean over backwards not to break the trust', but if he was 'being suspected of double-dealing he would not be hesitant to double cross the other man to the best of his ability, which is considerable'.

Davis was particularly concerned that leaders in Washington be aware of these insights in dealing with the Philippine mission in Washington, particularly the country's up and coming younger leaders like Manuel Roxas and Sergio Osmeña. 'I realise from my own experience as secretary of war how little we know in Washington of these psychological factors and the underlying motives behind things that go on here,' he wrote Hurley in another private letter. Davis said he was learning that it was most effective to accomplish everything behind the scene, 'letting the secretaries of departments and others get the public credit for any policy which I may want them to carry out, and thereby I get their cordial co-operation in matters which otherwise they might carry out only passively or even indirectly oppose...

'I believe that this method of handling a situation is far wiser than the British method in the past of wielding the big stick, kicking the natives off the sidewalks, etc., as they are now reaping the whirlwind of racial hatred.' Davis, it seemed, was ready to share the sidewalk.

Before leaving Washington, Alice had been carefully coached by ex-Governor-General Stimson and his wife on her role as official Malacañang hostess. But she would receive her own lesson in the sensitivity of native peoples during a stopover in the Philippine Moro province of Davao (a current trouble spot) on a trip which she and Cynthia were making to Java. Supposedly the American girls had snubbed local officials, refusing to accept an invitation to a formal reception.

At a meeting the next day the offended Filipinos announced they were reciprocating – by boycotting American cigarettes.

An exaggeration or misunderstanding, possibly, for the 21-year-old 'first lady' was a particularly effective representative of her father's administration. To a tea given in her honour she wore (and was, of course, photographed in) a traditional Philippine dress, a graceful, puff-sleeved *balintawak*.

'Alice Davis Has Islands' Heart', said a gushy, lengthy feature article in Manila's *American Chamber of Commerce Journal*. Alice talked with enthusiasm of visiting more than 40 of the Philippine provinces, as well as elsewhere in the Orient. 'The country is beautiful and the people with their different habits, customs and beliefs fascinate me.' She even liked the weather. 'I revel in hot weather and sunshine. The hottest day in Manila or the provinces doesn't bother me a bit.' She would be leaving soon for France, she said, and hoped to bring her mother back with her, though 'everything depends entirely on her condition when I get there'.

Concluded the article, 'No one who has ever seen Governor Davis's face light up with a reviving smile after a wearisome afternoon in his office at the sight of a pair of lithesome figures slipping by beneath his window will forget the sight. The two figures that provoke that smile are Alice and Cynthia Davis or Alice and someone else – at least always Alice; who hath done virtuously, who excellest them all.'

With their father in the Far East and their mother in and out of hospitals in the United States or off to consult doctors in France or Switzerland, life for the four Davis children sometimes was one long, complicated travel itinerary. At the vortex of this maelstrom of reservations and arrangements was Shon and the infinitely patient General Francis Parker, chief of the Bureau of Insular Affairs. The girls, as proper young women of their class, were always carefully chaperoned when they travelled. Even Alice, who had been functioning very capably as official Malacañang hostess. Shon travelled to Seattle to meet her boat and accompany her to Washington. Another time she sailed with Alice to Europe so that she could join her mother, then turned around and came back to the United States.

On one occasion, when it was Cynthia's turn to visit her father and Shon apparently could not be spared ('little Helen' was still in school near Washington), Helen Davis, *mere,* asked to see the passenger lists (particularly including War Department personnel) of three steamers leaving the West Coast at about the same time. 'It is quite likely that the family of the governor-general will know some one booked for these steamers,' the Bureau had explained to the steamship company. Sure enough, there was General Hull sailing on the *President*

Lincoln (he happened to be going out to the Philippines to serve as Davis's legal adviser). He and his wife agreed to take Cynthia under their wing. 'I am thrilled to have her with me,' Davis said in a message to his wife after Cynthia's safe arrival.

Helen, the youngest Davis daughter, and Shon finally got their turn to visit the Philippines during one summer vacation. 'Can't wait to get out there. We start tomorrow,' wrote young Helen to her father in a schoolgirl's round hand, with a schoolgirl's bright enthusiasm. 'Thanks loads and loads for presents. Loads of love.'

There were visitors other than family, of course. Former Australian tennis star Norman Brookes and his wife Mabel came to visit and were taken to Mansion House, the governor-general's mountain summer residence in Baguio. It, like the Malacañang Palace, was being remodelled during Davis's term of office. Another guest was W. Cameron Forbes, who had been Dwight and Helen Davis's host during their brief 1905 visit.

Forbes, now American ambassador to Japan, frequently provided hospitality to the Davis children on their stops in Japan during travels to and from the mainland. As a former Philippines governor-general himself, he was eager to give Davis advice. The suggestions were unfailingly politely responded to by Davis – even if ignored. After visiting in March 1931, Forbes reported to Secretary of War Stimson that he found 'an era of good feeling, and I hand it to Governor Davis. Following your [Stimson's] lead, he has cultivated and maintained a spirit of friendliness which seems to be manifest on all sides.'

One group of visitors proved to be a disaster, however. In an attempt to encourage tourism to the islands, Davis was persuaded to hold receptions at Malacañang for American passengers on tour boats. On one occasion visitors took Christmas cards which were for Davis's own personal use from a table in the library – and complained that there were no stamps. Another time, several women were discovered pawing through dresses hanging in Alice's bedroom, which they said they assumed were for sale. The receptions stopped.

Davis's mandate had been to continue the policy of 'co-operation' established by Stimson, his predecessor. In practical terms this meant a continuing adjustment in the balance of power compared to that in administrations of some earlier governor-generals – a bit less for the Americans, a bit more for the Filipinos. This did not always sit well with Manila's American business community. Many originally had been publicly critical of Davis's appointment, but gradually he was winning over most of them.

Rooting out political corruption had become a hallmark of Davis's administration. 'Dishonesty among public servants must be fearlessly suppressed,' he had stated in his inaugural address, and words condemning the public official who betrays the public trust made it into most of his public speeches. It was not just talk. 'He accomplished the unprecedented feat of removing a provincial governor because he was a grafter, and cleaned out a dozen ranking officials from Manila's top-heavy bureaucracy,' wrote Frederick Marquardt, an associate editor of the *Philippines Free Press,* in a later book. Shades of the St. Louis boodlers.

Discussing Davis's crackdown on corruption, another Philippine editor, H. Ford Wilkens, writing in the journal *Current History,* made the point that Davis never overlooked an opportunity to take his crusade to the public. 'He knows that the real root of the graft evil is in the attitude of the people themselves, not in the actions of errant officials,' wrote Wilkens. Lincoln Steffens had made the same point about St. Louis voters 30 years earlier.

On the always inflammatory question of Philippine independence, Davis placidly pointed out that this was not within his jurisdiction but a matter for the US Congress. What was important, he insisted, was to strengthen the country's economic foundations so that it would be ready when independence came. Like his predecessors, he continually pushed legislators to invest more time and energy on economic matters and less on politics.

Privately, Davis told Washington that some Filipino politicians (despite what they might be saying publicly) 'for the first time in all the years of agitation' were beginning to understand the practical implications of independence, 'particularly if combined with the loss of free trade privileges'. Davis insisted, however, that it would be a great benefit to both countries if a specific timetable were announced, particularly because of 'the unrest and the desire to throw off foreign domination – which seems to be gaining ground throughout all the Far East'.

Davis was doing much of the work of his administration by what management gurus a half century later would call 'management by walking around'. His lifetime willingness to pick up and go had manifested itself in a peripatetic travel schedule – inspection trips to a record 42 out of the country's 49 provinces in just his first year. Though he sometimes used the government-owned yacht *Apo* (for which he bought a Cris-Craft motor boat to facilitate landings), other trips were sometimes fairly rugged.

This had amazed and converted some of his early critics, such as Walter Robb of the American Chamber of Commerce in Manila. Wrote Robb, in the Chamber's *Journal,* 'Governor Davis whiled away the month of August traversing Davao and Agusan from the mouth of the Tagum on Davao gulf on the south, up to Saag to the Divide and the headwaters of the Agusan, and down the Agusan to Butuan, the provincial capital and metropolis at the mouth of the Agusan ...

'Minor incidents of the excursion were ten hours on a wilderness trail one sweltering day, and four hours up the bed of a stream, the only trail available, another day. In fact, Governor Davis made a pioneer trip – especially for a Philippine executive.' What really seemed to impress Robb, however, was the extent to which Davis carefully and systematically followed up on some of the grievous conditions these trips uncovered as Davis hiked through the Davao-Agusan wilderness, 'holding nightly pow-wows with the tribes'. With him on this excursion was Pete, who was also to make a later trip which had a much different tone.

The 26-year-old cruiser, the USS *Pittsburgh*, was about to be retired as flagship of the Asiatic fleet. A ship with a proud history, she was the last of the 'armoured cruiser squadron' and in her lifetime, said Navy sources, 'had probably visited more places throughout the world and steamed more miles than any ship we ever had'. Before she headed back to the United States to be scrapped, the Navy agreed to let Davis use the ship for a goodwill tour through the East Indies to make friends for the Philippines (and, of course, America), study trade and the colonial administrations of the Dutch, French and British.

Accompanying the governor-general on the six-week goodwill mission were three members of the Philippine cabinet: the ministers of agriculture, of commerce, and the cabinet financial adviser. Also going along were Pete and his younger sister Cynthia. Pete, as tall as his father now, was a great favourite of the young, party-going social set in Manila. He had graduated the previous spring from Harvard.

Cynthia, 20, had inherited her mother's good looks. Brown-eyed, with the stylishly short brunette bob of a flapper, she had completed her year at Mlle. Boisser's school in France. A fellow classmate had been her close friend from St. Louis, Mary Taussig who had gone on to Bryn Mawr, while Cynthia had come out to the Philippines to replace Alice as *doyenne* of the governor-general's household. The Davises, like many of their time and social stratum, believed in educating their son but 'finishing' their daughters.

The goodwill ambassadors played tennis with the French Indo-China champions in Saigon (the Davis father and son team won 'a corking fast match', while Cynthia lost in mixed doubles, though 'she played a grand game'). They saw Cambodian dancers perform in bright moonlight at Angkor Wat and the historic Bondo-bovo dance, with its thrust-and-parry, fencing movements, in Java. They travelled overland by car and ferry to Phnom-Penh, by special train to Bangkok and by airplane to the mountain city of Bandoeng. They witnessed an eye-popping spectacular night-time illumination of the palace of the Indo-China governor-general and an ear-popping 17-gun salute in Singapore Harbour.

They donned tropical pith helmets and spiffy, short white mess-jackets and all the decorations an American citizen could be expected to lay hands on and attended state dinners, balls and other on-shore extravaganzas. They reciprocated with daytime luncheons on deck for as many as 70, where the exotic fare of turkey and cranberry sauce delighted guests, and evening receptions with the old warship's decks illuminated by the soft light of swaying Chinese lanterns.

The ships officers and men were also entertained on shore, and at some stops the crew challenged on-shore military units to baseball games. The whole ship, of course, was involved on 24 March, when, on the passage between Sumatra and Java, 'Neptune Rex' held court before dunking the some 600 'polliwogs' who had never before crossed the equator. This included Pete and Cynthia, but a gallant Dwight Davis was given permission to substitute for his daughter in the time-honoured watery initiation ritual.

Amidst the frivolity and the elaborate, pasha-like entertainments, Davis and his ministers pursued more serious matters. They looked at rice mills and visited rubber plantations and tin mines. They asked questions about agriculture, post office operations and education. They discussed with their hosts the effects of the world wide depression on trade throughout the area. Davis told the *Malay Mail* in Kuala Lumpur that he 'believed in personal contact as a way of obtaining information ... I find you can get more by the personal touch than you can by the ordinary official letter'.

Back in the United States *Time* printed a lengthy detailed article on the trip complete with informal, illustrated map captioned 'Governor-General Davis Does the East Indies'. Said the article, 'To millions of brown and yellow natives, to thousands of white residents in the East Indies, the visit of the Big White Governor & children was news, fun, sufficient excuse for brief but lavish festivities.'

And expensive, grumbled others back in penny-pinching, purse-lipped America, where the stock market had crashed and Depression panic was growing. 'The junket de luxe cost the government $200,000 on transportation alone,' complained the *Milwaukee Journal*, figuring three months of the ship's annual cost of $1.2 million.

For his part Davis was already putting to use the stacks of statistics and reports he and cabinet officials had gathered on the trip. He spoke sternly to Philippine legislators about how poorly their country compared in many economic areas to some of its neighbours. For instance, sugar yield per hectare in Java was nearly three times that of the Philippines. Rice yields in Java, Siam and Cochin China were nearly two and a half times better. On the other hand, the Philippines, he noted, spent an admirable 28 percent of its budget on education, compared to an average six percent in the countries he had visited.

Earlier in the year there had been bloody riots by rice tenant farmers in an area north of Manila, which a later historian of the Philippines, Lewis Gleeck, said Davis was 'ill equipped by experience and social origins to understand'. Nevertheless, said Gleeck, Davis spoke 'eloquently' about the land in his July 1931 message to the legislature after returning from the goodwill mission: 'Every effort should be made to build up a sturdy body of independent farmers, owning their own lands, with good title, free from the burden of debt, their own masters. An independent middle class is the greatest bulwark of any country, an oppressed peasantry the greatest danger.'

Much about this, Davis's third annual address to the opening session of the Philippine national assembly, had displeased legislators. This time, there was no applause. For one thing, he again emphasised that they needed to concentrate on economic matters not politics at a time when, for various reasons, 'politics', that is talk of independence, was heating up, having seized the public's fancy.

Another irritant was the governor-general's proposed new economic plan which would substitute long-range, systematic expenditures for the current 'pork-barrel' approach which was, of course, a boon to the power of the majority party. Such revamping had already been submitted by Davis's goodwill-tour companions, the secretaries of agriculture and natural resources, and commerce and communications. 'Pork is an unsound foundation for roads,' said Davis.

Davis 'was serene in the face of threats of legislative non-co-operation', reported a cable to the *New York Herald Tribune* a week later. 'Agitation among the masses is diminishing, and the governor-general's position is concededly the strongest it has been since he assumed office.'

As it happened, something new was developing which was agitating both 'the masses', officials and the Philippine press. Rumours were surfacing with increased frequency that Dwight Davis was soon to resign. One official said he knew this because Davis had said, at a recent cabinet meeting, 'I do not want to leave a treasury deficit behind me', – and pounded the table for emphasis.

Davis in a table-pounding mood meant something was up. The governor-general found himself in an awkward position. Helen's health had not improved and he needed to rejoin her in Europe. He explained his need to resign to Washington, yet premature public announcement, everyone realised, would imperil the work he was doing in the Philippines. Despite their recent pique, Philippine politicians were again enthusiastic in their praise of Davis. One extreme nationalist newspaper quoted leader Manuel Quezon as saying 'We should be happy if Governor Davis were to remain in office indefinitely'. Senator Sergio Osmeña, acting head of the Philippine legislature, suggested that instead of resigning, Davis take a long leave of absence to visit his family in Paris.

And that, as it turned out, was how his impending departure in November at the end of the current legislative session, was officially described. Even if they knew better, this gave Filipinos the faint wisp of hope that their tall, genial, respected governor-general would return.

Ripples of anxiety about Davis's exact status and intentions reached across the globe to Puerto Rico, where Ted Roosevelt was serving as governor. If Davis were to resign as governor-general, Roosevelt wanted his job. Throughout the fall of 1931, Davis in Manila publicly carried on with business as usual, and privately began packing up. Meanwhile Ted, in Puerto Rico, plotted strategy by letter and cable with his wife Eleanor, in New York, and mother Edith, while apparently 'Sister' (Alice) sent in plays from the sidelines and made occasional intemperate public statements. President Hoover, according to Ted, had said in the spring that he intended to send him (Roosevelt) to the Philippines in January 1932. Yet nothing official had happened.

Should Ted resign his Puerto Rico post and risk being thought 'petulant'? Should Davis be contacted after he returned to Washington but before he talked to the president and Secretary of War Hurley? Roosevelt was feeling ill-used. 'I see no reason why I should be the churn-dog or goat of Hurley, Dwight Davis, or anyone else,' he wrote to Eleanor. 'By the way, isn't it the irony of fate?' he wrote her two days later. 'If you recall, the people who really started Dwight Davis were Sister and me when we took the matter of his being made assistant secretary of war up with Harding ...'

The problem was that there were objections to the sometimes mercurial Roosevelt both from Hurley and Secretary of State Stimson, as well as from the Philippines. 'By all means, if we must have a Roosevelt, let it be Alice,' wise-cracked the independent weekly, the *Philippines Free Press*. As it turned out, Roosevelt would eventually get the appointment from President Hoover, 'who has had his leg pulled by Alice and Eleanor', claimed Stimson. Davis apparently did his part. 'He [Davis] did reciprocate in 1931,' noted Eleanor later.

At an emotional banquet in Manila on 20 November 1931, attended by more than 1000 people, a Filipino in the costume of a poor labourer presented Davis with a handsome humidor 'in behalf of the masses'. The crowd cheered at every opportunity and the Philippine constabulary band played 'Auld Lang Syne'.

Davis, deeply moved, spoke of the progress made in the Philippines during the last 30 years under American control, particularly in such things as infant mortality, sanitation and education. 'If this be tyranny, I'm proud to be a tyrant,' he said. New prolonged waves of applause arose from both Americans and Filipinos.

If he had not, as some claimed, done enough to curb overproduction of sugar, he had begun cleaning up the chaotic land title situation. If he had not fully understood the problems of farmers, he had dealt firmly with graft and corruption, modernised banking and encouraged concrete action to produce an economically developed Philippines.

Reported the Manila correspondent for the *New York Times*, 'The extent to which the entire country has become vocal, demanding the Governor's return, is almost inconceivable.'

The next day, in a tropical rain mirroring the weather that had greeted him 28 months earlier, Davis, accompanied by daughter Cynthia, sailed slowly away from Manila and the cheering thousands standing on the pier. 'Davis was in several respects the most successful governor-general,' historian Lewis E. Gleeck Jr. would write many years later in his study of the Philippines' 13 governors-general and high commissioners from 1901 to 1942.

An editorial in the often unsympathetic Filipino newspaper, the *Philippine Herald*, rendered a more immediate judgement on the day before Davis left. 'What the Filipinos want first is independence. After that they want Dwight Davis.'

CHAPTER 21

FAMILY MATTERS

D wight Davis returned, in late 1931, to a country bruised and bewildered by the growing economic Depression. At its height – or depth – 16 million Americans would be unemployed, about one-third of the labour force.

Yet the Davis family's fortune, like that of many of the country's truly wealthy, had not been ravaged. Shrewd decisions to get out of the market before the October 1929 crash, plus continuing readjustment of holdings, had protected Dwight Davis from the economic climate, just as the fur-lined overcoat which the efficient Miss Shaughnessy arranged to have delivered to him onboard the *President Jefferson* protected him from the shock of winter weather when the ship reached North America.

'The pessimism at home seems to be lightening a little and some people are beginning to feel that the world is not coming to an end after all,' Davis reported to Ted Roosevelt, now in the Philippines, later in the spring of 1932. 'Conditions have not improved much but the sentiment is better so that will help.'

For some time the usual political rumours concerning Davis's future had been swirling about. Some had been polished and proudly pushed forward by the Philippine press, which seemed touchingly eager to believe that great new political opportunities awaited their highly regarded governor-general. Davis was going to run for the Senate from Missouri. Davis was going to be named to the Court of St. James to replace the departing Dawes (actually Hoover used this opening to move Andrew Mellon out of the cabinet). Davis would be a member of the US delegation to the Geneva disarmament conference. Davis was going to be named ambassador to France or be on the ticket as vice-president – or even be a dark horse candidate for president himself. Davis laughed and issued denials: 'I believe strongly that the Republican party should renominate my chief, President Hoover.'

Though the presidential rumour might be duly reported on the *New York Times* news pages, the *New York Times* editorial page was not about to play the game. Here was a new way for Republicans to get publicity, said a *Times* editorial, mentioning the dispatch from Manila, 'D.F. Davis Won't Run'.

'Won't run for what? This is the question in the mind of the average reader of that headline. For governor or senator from Missouri? Not at all. It is the Republican presidential nomination for which the governor-general has refused to file ...' The editorial was not ready, however, to blame Davis personally for this throw-it-up-bat-it-down ploy. 'His [Davis's] own good faith in the premises is beyond question. The ex-secretary of war has not been considered a foolish man.'

All Davis had to say publicly was 'I am ready for a rest'. Whether or not he was ready for a permanent rest from political appointment, this, nevertheless, was what he would get. Davis, at 52, had completed what would turn out to be his last major public assignment. The Depression, it seemed, would affect Davis's political fortune, if not his financial one.

An anguished Herbert Hoover, unable to convince voters that he was on the right track in solving the country's economic woes, would be unable to win re-election in 1932. Into the White House would go the Democratic Roosevelt, Ted's distant cousin Franklin. And with Democratic power, of course, would come Democratic prerogatives for naming cabinet officials and ambassadors.

Returning to Washington after spending the Christmas holidays in St. Louis, Davis officially tendered his resignation as governor-general on 9 January 1932, as expected. He then left for Europe to check on Helen's condition, stopping in Boston to see her father on the way. What he found in France was not encouraging, he reported in a letter to friends. 'Helen is not at all well, unhappily, and cannot be moved until June, so I expect to go home and return then.'

While he was in France, Davis was invited to attend the elaborate Davis Cup draw ceremonies at the Elysèe Palace. The cup, which the French had held since 1927, was beginning to seem as permanent a fixture in Paris as the Arc de Triomphe. Before the ceremony, Davis was ushered into the private apartments of French President Doumer where he was named a Commander of the French Legion of Honour, and given its insignia and cravat, in honour of his wartime service in France.

Among his commitments back in the United States was an historic reunion with his fellow team-mates from the first American Davis Cup team. The occasion was the third round Davis Cup match between the US and Australia in Philadelphia. (The United States team won and now would challenge France for the cup later in the year.) Malcolm Whitman, looking handsome and confident in blazer and bow tie, had come down from New York where he was practising law. Holcombe Ward was living in New Jersey and still in the textile business, though in 1937 he would begin a ten-year reign as USLTA president.

It was the last time the three would be together. Whitman, it subsequently developed, suffered from intermittent bouts of schizophrenia and at the end of 1932 would kill himself by jumping from the terrace of his New York City apartment. His interest in writing had continued through the years. A small collection of verses included one entitled 'The Reason':

Before I die
I want to paint upon my evening sky
Some glorious and wished for
Metropolis of cloud.

And as no painter's touch
to me belongs,
I sing my glorious city
In these songs.

On his return trip to Europe in the summer of 1932 Davis stopped in London from whose tennis scene he had been absent during his years in the Orient. Tennis writer and historian A. Wallis Myers set up an 'ordinary, friendly game' at Queen's Club, pairing Davis with 25-year old Henry W. (Bunny) Austin, current British Davis Cup star.

Davis was also feted at a luncheon given in his honour by Sir Samuel Hoare, president of England's Lawn Tennis Association. Along with the toasts came some humorous but good advice from Sam Hoare: don't be surprised, he cautioned the guest of honour, if, despite your reputation as a statesman, people only want to talk to you about the world-famous tennis trophy you have donated. There appear to be only two ways public men can keep their memories alive, he said. They could have a popular dish named for them – Peach Melba (for the opera singer) or Sole Colbert (for the famous 18th-century finance minister). Or they could be associated with a world which was much more important than politics – the world of athletics.

Though Davis was one of the most distinguished public men in the United States, continued Sir Samuel, his name would chiefly go down to fame – and he was to be congratulated on the fact – identified with one of the greatest athletic contests of the modern world.

Undoubtedly there was much convivial laughter. But there was a solid core of good sense to the remarks, and particularly useful for Davis to hear. He was becoming a bit ambivalent about his famous silver progeny. Naturally, he was proud of the cup's fame and contribution to tennis's booming popularity, as well as to international good-fellowship. That pride had been evident in the chapter he had written for the USLTA's 1931 commemorative book, *Fifty Years of Lawn Tennis in the United States.*

'A common understanding, a broad tolerance of others' viewpoints, mutual goodwill are essential if people are to live together in the great family of nations,' he had written. 'Modern science, the developments in transportation and communications, progress in civilisation are slowly bringing peoples more closely together physically,' he continued. 'Any element which assists in bringing them closer spiritually performs a valuable service to mankind. A love of sport seems to be such an element. So the ultimate influence of the Cup may well be more far-reaching than the mere winning of a world's championship in one field of athletics.'

And yet, and yet ...

Take the incident in Paris, for instance. Davis was interested in seeing the Chamber of Deputies in session, and Ambassador Walter Edge made the arrangements. Davis found himself seated behind a pillar. His companion went to see if he could arrange a different seat for this recently retired governor-general of the Philippines. *Mais non,* said a French official. But this gentleman has served in the American president's cabinet as secretary of war, continued the companion. The official was still not impressed. But this is the Monsieur Davis who donated the *Le Coupe Davis,* said his companion. Ah, that's different, said the official. And an excellent seat for Davis was immediately found down front. In later years Davis retold the story to a son-in-law. 'Now you know what's important in life,' he added.

And sometimes being the Davis of Davis Cup – even *at* Davis Cup events – was no guarantee. In late July with America playing France in the Davis Cup challenge round, Davis was invited to sit with the French president and US Ambassador Edge. After ending up by mistake at the Tribune of Honour section where there were no empty seats, he introduced himself as Davis. 'What of it,' someone replied, according to the story. Another version had Davis then trying the team bench where he was also turned away. Not surprisingly, he left. The next morning, according to this version, Jean Borotra and team captain Pierre Gillou called on Davis and offered apologies. And on this day when he arrived at the stadium he was introduced to the crowd by Borotra and greeted with great applause.

Davis was disgruntled by the 1932 matches for other reasons as well. Just before the third day's matches the slow red clay of the Roland Garros stadium court had been thoroughly soaked, which made it even slower. This, feared Americans, could affect the fast-court game of Ellsworth Vines, though French officials insisted it was just a groundskeeper's mistake. In the day's crucial first game, with France ahead 2-1, victory was snatched out of American Wilmer Allison's hands at match point. A serve of Borotra's, which some observers thought was out by at least six inches, was instead called good. An astonished Allison never recovered. France won 3-2, and Dwight Davis was heard to grumble that he wished he had never even donated the cup. The ensuing squabble made one American newspaper question whether international sports events were really good for international relations after all. (At the following year's annual meeting of the Davis Cup nations, rules were tightened governing the treatment of court surfaces before a match.)

Earlier in the summer, Helen Davis, rather than being ready to return to the United States as her husband had anticipated, had moved on to try the mud bath cure at Pisek, a spa south of Prague. It was young Helen's turn to be 'on duty' as a companion to her mother, who was now nearly bedridden. Actually the youngest of the Davis children, now 18, would always treasure this leisurely, languid Czechoslovakian summer spent with her mother. In the fall she too, like her older sisters, would go to France for the season to buff up her American upbringing with some Old World polish.

She might still be 'little Helen' to the family, but her nickname sometimes in France was '*le Coupe*' – the Cup – which she found not at all flattering. On one occasion her connection with her father's famous silver bowl was even more direct. At the first-round matches between Austria and Czechoslovakia in Prague, she, as a representative of the Davis family, was asked to hit the first ball out onto the court. She did so with gusto – right into the stomach of a very fat gentleman sitting near the net.

In the fall young Helen went off to live with a French family, and her mother, accompanied now by Alice and Cynthia, sought treatment in a Berlin clinic specialising in arthritis. It was there that she died on 10 October 1932. Davis had recently returned from Europe and was travelling on business in the southern United States when he received word. He hurried back to St. Louis to be there when his two eldest daughters returned to America.

Five days after her death, Helen Brooks Davis's will was filed for probate. Her husband was named executor and trustee of her estate, valued at just under $230,000. A trust was established with income to go to her father during his lifetime, the principal of the trust eventually to go to her children. A string of pearls went to Alice to pass down to her eldest daughter; jewellery went to the other children. And a gift of $40,000 was left in trust for 'my dear friend' Miss Josephine Shaughnessy.

The visitor in the guest room at Meridian Plantation carefully opened her eyes a crack. There in the misty grey light of a Florida morning a boy, a young black boy (though probably at the time she would have used the term Negro), was quietly building a fire in the room's fireplace. He finished and left as silently as he had come. To her northern, Bryn Mawr mind, it was a surprising, even exotic, start to the day. The visitor was Mary Taussig, a friend of Cynthia Davis's from school days in St. Louis and France.

Since 1929 Dwight Davis had been leasing land near Tallahassee, Florida, primarily for hunting. Duck and upland game birds – dove, quail, woodcock – proliferated in the rolling hills and open fields of the Georgia-Florida border country. Now Davis decided to buy the place. The house on Meridian Plantation, reached by a drive lined with towering live oaks and vivid pink camellias, was a one-storey English brick cottage, situated on a high bluff overlooking one of several lakes on the grounds. There were stables and a tennis court, and near the house Davis had begun some serious landscaping, terracing the slope and adding dogwood, Japanese magnolia and other flowering trees to the native pines.

Friends often came down for the hunting from Washington and St. Louis. And some, like Cynthia's friend Mary, were rather inexperienced sportsmen. On the first morning the young visitor appeared dressed all in khaki which she thought would be appropriate for hunting. 'No, Mary,' said Dwight Davis, 'go put on a red hat or red vest so the other hunters can see you and you don't get shot.' A day or two later she appeared wearing the requisite red item. 'No, Mary,' said Davis, 'go back and take off the red or the ducks will see you down on the ground.'

The younger Davises were not necessarily as enthusiastic about hunting as their father. Helen, in a duck blind, would take a shot at the birds flying overhead and mutter, 'I hope, I hope, I hope I miss.'

One visitor to Meridian Plantation was a proper young Englishman named Roger Makins, an attaché in the British Embassy in Washington. He had come down to see more of Alice Davis's family and was met at the train station in Tallahassee by ice-cream-cone-eating Davis girls, who laughed at his astonishment as an ice-cream cone was pushed into his hand as well.

In April 1934, Alice and Roger Makins were married at Meridian Plantation, and shortly thereafter left for Oslo, Norway, where Makins had been posted. Later the rising young diplomat would become assistant and then deputy under secretary of state in the Foreign Office, concentrating on economic affairs. His relationship through the years with his American father-in-law would be a warm and admiring one. Unlike many who considered Davis taciturn and reserved almost to a fault, Makins would find him jovial and easy to talk to. They had, of course, many areas of common interest – political affairs, the challenges of governmental service, military history (Makins' father, a brigadier general, had been a hero of the Boer War).

Two weeks following Alice's marriage, Pete also was wed in a lavish, New York City ceremony which news services called 'an important spring wedding'. His bride, Dorothea Gay, was a pretty, brunette socialite of New York and Southampton, whose family had previously lived in Boston. They had been engaged since the previous December. The following summer of 1935 Dwight Davis acquired his first grandchildren – three in less than one month. Dwight F. Davis III was born to Pete and Dottie on 17 June, and in England Alice had twin daughters, Molly and Cynthia, born 15 July. Pete, with his insatiable love for baseball, had told his wife that he wanted to name the new baby 'Dizzy' after St. Louis baseball star, Dizzy Dean. Only her copious tears (as he would later tell the story) got the baby a reprieve – but his nickname would forever be Dizzie (and his younger brother John would be called 'Daffy' for another Cardinals star).

Meanwhile, Cynthia was seeing, from time to time, a friend from St. Louis days, Bill Martin, more formally William McChesney Martin Jr., who was also now living on the East Coast and a partner in a brokerage firm. Occasionally she would join Martin, who was publishing a quarterly newsletter, *Economic Forum*, and a small group of friends who gathered regularly at the New School for Social Research in New York's Greenwich Village to earnestly discuss the country's economic problems. (She was there, in fact, that critical day in 1933 when, all over America, the banks closed.)

Sometimes she and Shon would travel up from Washington to see the latest Broadway shows with Martin, who was enthusiastic about the theatre. Actually, he was enthusiastic about many things, for instance tennis. He had played at Yale and been good enough to play in the US championships at Forest Hills in 1932, 1933 and 1934, though never moving past the second round, where he had the misfortune to run up against John Van Ryn one year and Gene Mako, another.

Helen, the family rebel, at least politically, had gone to work for the National Recovery Administration, the NRA, one of the alphabet agencies of the New Deal and part of the distasteful (from her father's stalwart Republican point of view) Franklin D. Roosevelt administration. He never mentioned any disapproval to her, however. One New Year's Eve when Helen happened to be down at the plantation in Florida, one of her father's hunting guests, a particularly vehement Roosevelt foe, raised his glass in what was intended to be a wickedly humorous toast.

It was extreme, like much Republican, anti-New Deal, Roosevelt-hating rhetoric heard in board rooms and country clubs all over the country. 'Bad health to the president,' he said. Young Helen slammed down her glass of champagne –

hard. So hard, in fact, that it broke and pieces of glass and champagne went flying, much to the astonishment of the others in the room. Even though she had not originally thought of breaking the glass, it was a moment of which she would always be proud.

As a widower, Dwight Davis's name was now occasionally linked with various eligible women, even Grace Coolidge. President Coolidge had died 5 January 1933, at the age of 60, and there had been later newspaper speculation that Davis and the former first lady were about to become engaged.

In 1935 the women's magazine *Good Housekeeping* ran a four-month series called 'The Real Calvin Coolidge'. Dwight Davis was one of the former cabinet members among many Coolidge associates asked to contribute a brief remembrance. Though the president had a reputation for being reticent, wrote Davis, 'when he was talking to some one in his confidence, or when he had something definite he wished to say, he would talk very freely'. (Interesting that Davis had picked this topic.) 'As a result, when he did "choose" to talk, people listened attentively …'

Davis described a time when the two were talking alone just after someone had embarrassed the administration by talking too much. '"You know, Mr. Secretary,"' Davis remembered the president saying, '"I have found in the course of a long public life that the things I did not say never hurt me."'

But it was not Grace Coolidge but the glamorous, politically active widow of a wealthy New York banker who would become Dwight Davis's second wife. The *New York Evening Journal*'s society columnist 'Mme. Flutterbye' made the announcement breathlessly on 4 March 1936 in a page one copyrighted article. 'One of the most surprising and altogether exciting marriages of the year is scheduled to take place most unostentatiously sometime in the early Spring,' said the article. 'The bride-to-be is no less a person than the very charming and amazingly efficient Mrs. Charles H. Sabin, and her future husband is to be Dwight F. Davis, who is so well known both in political and sporting circles.'

Pauline Morton Smith Sabin was attractive, smart, strong-willed and politically well-connected. She was also perceived by some as manipulative, selfish and extravagant. This latter group included Davis's children who never would get on well with their father's second wife.

Pauline Sabin's grandfather had been secretary of agriculture under President Grover Cleveland and her father had been secretary of the navy under President Teddy Roosevelt. 'Polly' Sabin, 'charming as ever', popped up frequently in Ted Roosevelt Jr.'s diaries, playing bridge or poker or giving him her assessment of the New York state political situation. She and Charlie Sabin had known the Davises politically and socially and had been dinner guests at their Washington home.

Her first marriage to J. Hopkins Smith (whom she divorced in 1916) left her with two sons. Her second marriage to Charles Sabin (who died in 1933) left her with nearly $3 million and Bayberry Land, a 300-acre seaside Southampton estate with a 28-room, grey stucco English manor house.

After successfully organising the Women's National Republican Club in the early 1920s and becoming the first woman named to the Republican National Committee, she had refocused her energies on repeal of the 18th amendment prohibiting the sale and use of alcohol. Prohibition, she said in one address, 'has led to more violation of and contempt for law, both by private individuals and public officials, and to more hypocrisy, than anything else in our national life'.

When Herbert Hoover remained a committed dry, Pauline Sabin, the 'Wets' Joan of Arc', as one headline called her, resigned from the Republican National Committee and switched her support to the Democrats. By 1932 her Women's Organisation for National Prohibition Reform had more than a million members, and the Democrats had put a plank in their 1932 platform calling for repeal.

Such a woman was not to be deterred by a frosty reception from the grown children of her intended. Pauline Sabin and Dwight Davis were married by the Reverend Harry Emerson Fosdick in a late afternoon ceremony before family members, in the chapel of Riverside Church in New York City, on 8 May 1936.

MEANWHILE, WITH THE CUP

The Early 1930s

B y 1933 the Davis Cup's large tray was full. Names of challenge-round winners and losers (as well as of all countries competing each year) had filled all available space. The problem was solved by adding a base to the trophy, a large disk of wood, a 'plinth'. Around the edge of the plinth were silver plaques on which the engraved Davis Cup record could be continued. Between the plaques were decorative, blossom-like silver cartouches.

The continued victories, on-court antics and charismatic personalities of the fabled four Frenchmen – Lacoste, Borotra, Cochet, Brugnon – had filled newspaper pages and helped push interest in Davis Cup to a new high. More and more countries were fielding Davis Cup teams – 29 in 1932 and a record 31 in 1933. Another zone had been added in 1931 when the American Zone was split into North and South sections.

Also in 1931, another measure of the Davis Cup's importance had been demonstrated at the lawn tennis championships at Wimbledon. Francis X. Shields, a tall handsome New Yorker with a devastating smash, was to play another American, Sidney Wood Jr., in the final. Frank Shields, however, had injured his leg in an semi-final match against Borotra. The US Davis Cup non-playing captain, Sam Hardy, decided that Shields should default in order to save himself for the upcoming Davis Cup inter-zone finals. Shields did, giving Wood the Wimbledon title by default.

The leg had healed sufficiently by the time the US faced Great Britain, but the US still lost 2-3 to England's rising new Davis Cup power combination of Fred Perry and Henry (Bunny) Austin. For the first time since the war, the United States had lost before getting into the challenge round. France, with Lacoste now serving as non-playing captain, had beaten Great Britain to win the cup for a fifth year.

The results were reversed two years later in 1933 when Perry and Austin, along with doubles specialist Pat Hughes, at last claimed the trophy for Britain. The year was also notable as the time when bare male knees had first appeared in a challenge round. Bunny Austin (the nickname was a holdover from Repton schooldays) had begun the sartorial revolution the previous year at Forest Hills during a particularly hot, muggy American summer.

On the third day of the 1933 challenge round, after Fred Perry had won the fifth and deciding match, the crowd of more than 13,000 Frenchmen stood as the silver trophy was carried to the centre of the court of the stadium, built by and for the Davis Cup. The cup had been in France's possession for six years. Now it was presented to the British captain, none other than Herbert Roper Barrett who had competed for England in the very first Davis Cup matches. A 'talking machine' played the *Marseilles* and *God Save The King* (who, from back in England, had dispatched messages of congratulations to the team). Barrett hugged the bowl 'tightly as though it were a baby', reported the Associated Press, 'while the fans, with lumps in their throats, bade it godspeed'.

In the evening, after the traditional banquet, players from the two teams celebrated by taking the big silver bowl on a tour of Paris night-clubs. Teetotaller Fred Perry – *Monsieur Limonade* to the French – even joined in these champagne toasts. Britain would successfully hang on to the cup for the next three years.

CHAPTER 23

BROOKINGS

T he timepiece was small, a pocket watch. A carefully crafted symbol in metal – gold and platinum – to express gratitude for another symbol in metal – sterling silver. On this Monday morning in late July 1936 at London's Savoy Hotel, Dwight Davis was being presented with the repeater watch and chronograph (No. 11170, maker: Messrs. Jules Jürgensen and Co.). It was an exhibition piece with a mechanism so precise that it was guaranteed to vary less than one-hundredth of a second for each degree of rise or fall in temperature.

On one side of the case, a three-quarter-inch-high, meticulously detailed replica of the Davis Cup in platinum, was inlaid in the gold. Underneath was the Latin inscription 'D.F.D. DEDIT A.D. MCM'. On the reverse side, also in platinum and inlaid, was Davis's monogram. Curving around the lid inside were the words 'Presented In The Year 1936 By The Lawn Tennis Associations Of The World To Dwight F. Davis Founder of the International Lawn Tennis Championship'.

The occasion was the annual meeting of the Davis Cup nations taking place during the challenge round being played at the All England Club between Australia and Great Britain. (The British team had won the cup for a fourth straight year.) Sir Samuel Hoare, president of the host tennis association, made the presentation of the watch. Davis responded that actually those seated around the table deserved the credit. 'You made the cup stand for what it is today, not myself who happened by fortune to be the donor.' If other statesman of the world would meet together in the same spirit as those before him, he added, the world would be far happier.

Davis these days had more time for such tennis occasions, and even for tennis. After he and Pauline returned to the US from their wedding trip, he and Pete entered and reached the finals of the USLTA's Grass Court Father and Son Doubles, played each year at Longwood at the time of the National Doubles tournament. There they took on Davis's Harvard friend Bill Clothier and his son Bill II, who was currently playing the summer grass circuit.

The historic, big, left-handed Dwight Davis serve still had some bite to it, discovered Bill Clothier II, though it was Pete who mainly concerned him. Pete's game could be wild. But if Pete was on his game he was pretty effective, knew the younger Clothier, who had been beaten by him in a tournament a few years earlier. On this day, however, the Clothiers won in straight sets, taking the Father and Son title for the second straight year.

Dwight Davis and the senior Clothier (a former national champion) had decided to enter the Veterans Doubles. Their opponents were a couple of striplings just past the entry age of 45. The two former national stars, Davis, 57, and Clothier, 55 – hair a bit lighter, middles a bit broader than during their Harvard playing days – walked out onto the court. Who *are* these old guys who think they can come out and play, the youngsters – one of them a bit arrogant – obviously were thinking.

The game was on an outside court, and when the main doubles match had concluded the crowd streamed over to watch the end of this match which had gone into a third set. Taking the last set 10-8, Davis and Clothier won, to the astonishment and chagrin of their younger opponents.

Davis's opinion was still sought on affairs of the day. After returning from one European trip he lamented in a newspaper interview the state of America's military preparedness, particularly the lack of progress in motorised warfare, an area of his particular interest while secretary of war. He also voiced displeasure at the general drift of the Roosevelt administration, predicting that the country wanted to get back to sound principles, such as 'balancing the budget'. Voters, he said, are finally beginning 'to fear the burden of taxation our trial-and-error government is rolling up against the future'. (This was before the 1936 election and Davis thought there was at least the chance of Republican victory. He was wrong. Roosevelt won in a landslide, carrying every state except Maine and Vermont.) In England, said Davis, 'they believe as many of us know over here that if the federal finger were not caught in the wheel of national industry it would turn more quickly'.

Another of Davis's long-time beliefs – the value of athletics in preparing fit, healthy young people – was the subject of his remarks as one of the speakers at an annual *New York Tribune* Forum. (Another tennis celebrity appearing on the Forum was Helen Wills Moody.) Having just returned from abroad, Davis was impressed, he said, with what other nations were doing to develop youth through athletics, though he was careful to add that he did not approve of the regimented, dictatorial context in which these programs existed.

Nevertheless, he said, 'we cannot deny the remarkable improvement in the health and strength of their coming generation. It constitutes a challenge to our democracies to get the same results through democratic rather than autocratic methods'.

The focus of much of Dwight Davis's attention these days was the Brookings Institution in Washington, the private policy research organisation with offices on Jackson Place a half block away from Davis's old War Department offices in the State, War, Navy Building. Robert Brookings, the St. Louis businessman and philanthropist who had helped Davis land his first Washington appointment, had continued his work in public policy. In 1927, he combined several earlier organisations into a research institution bearing his name. It was the first of what later generations would call 'think-tanks'.

Brookings had died in 1932, but interest in and support of the institution had been continued by his wife Isabel, whom the wealthy, life-long bachelor had married in 1927 at the age of 77. In 1935 Davis joined the Brookings board of trustees. The Brookings championing of traditional laissez-faire economic policies with minimal government intrusion meant inevitable collision with the policies of the New Deal. Frederic A. Delano, who had succeeded Robert Brookings as chairman of the Brookings board of trustees, advocated more co-operation with the Roosevelt administration. Harold G. Moulton, Brookings' president, strongly opposed such wandering away from the institution's fundamental philosophies. The trustees backed Moulton, and on 17 May 1937, Delano resigned. Four days later, Dwight Davis was named chairman of the board.

Moulton and Davis worked well together, the earnest, former University of Chicago economics professor and the seasoned statesman with top drawer contacts. They shared an internationalist outlook not always found currently in men of their economic and philosophical stripe. 'Rah! Rah! Davis Cup!' wrote Moulton with shy, *bonhomie* in the postscript of an otherwise routine letter mailed to Davis after the 1937 US victory.

Though Moulton would, from time to time, flatteringly ask his board chairman for comments about Brookings' publications, Davis's primary contribution fell into four areas: determination of policies, advice on investment of the Brookings' portfolio, input into the selection of new trustees and fund raising for the institution's endowment.

Davis, who had an office at Brookings, would pass along his own thinking on specific investments (sometimes even turning thumbs down on something like Radio-Keith-Orpheum as 'too speculative'), as well as golf-course and club-dining-room tips on specific stocks. And later, as World War II drew to a close, he outlined for Moulton the criteria for evaluating companies for their post-war strength being developed by his own investment councillors at Morgan & Co.

Davis, like other board members (Marshall Field, Clarence Phelps Dodge, Harry Brookings Wallace) concentrated on raising funds for the institution's endowment from those who might be interested in the organisation's program of research and publishing. In his opinion, said Davis, 'the Brookings Institution is doing some of the most constructive research along broad economic lines that is being done in this country'.

Sometimes the calls and letters were directly to friends, at other times to those whose name and support of Brookings would influence others. Men, for instance, like former President Hoover whom Davis went to see at his apartment in the Waldorf- Astoria in October 1937. The meeting went well and Hoover offered to help, though he could not, he said, do any active solicitation. He suggested being given a list of likely prospects around the country, and when he was in those cities talking to those people, he would bring up the work of Brookings.

The next day Davis sent him a letter with the names of 21 possibilities from Wall Street (Morgan, Shearson) and corporate America (Pew, Ball, Fisher, Wrigley). The relationship between Hoover and Davis was still relatively formal – 'My dear Mr. Hoover', 'My dear Davis', – though this would warm up by the early 1940s into 'Dear Dwight', and 'Dear Herbert'.

Cynthia's friend Bill Martin was continuing to make his own mark in the financial world. After impressing his elders with his efficient and honourable work in reorganising the New York Stock Exchange, the former St. Louisan was selected as the first paid president of the Exchange, at the breathtakingly young age of 31.

In Washington, Davis, who had been leasing an estate on Foxhall Road, a few miles outside of town, in 1938 finally bought his first house in the nation's capital. The massive brick house on Decatur Place loomed above everything else in the charming neighbourhood of narrow streets and over-arching trees, in the area known as Kalorama. It was another in a long line of spectacular Davis dwellings. Behind iron gates was a brick-paved forecourt, flanked by two one-storey wings topped with terraces. The house had its own impressive pedigree. Built in 1907, it had been designed by the influential architect Ogden Codman for his cousin, Martha Codman, a Boston shipping heiress. Thirty-one years later she sold the house to Davis.

Ogden Codman had co-authored, with novelist Edith Wharton, the classic book, *The Decoration of Houses*. The Codman connection undoubtedly appealed to Pauline, who, at one time, was said to have had her own sub rosa (women of her position of course did not work professionally) interior decoration firm in New York City. Her commercial clients were said to include the Waldorf-Astoria hotel.

Living with Davis and Pauline were three of her grandchildren, the children of her son, Morton Smith. To them Davis was kindly 'Uncle Dwight' who was an approving, supportive male presence at their horse shows and other activities. (Even Davis family members who did not get along with Pauline would, in future years, speak admiringly of the job she did in raising her grandchildren.)

Meanwhile, Alice, of course, was in England with her husband and now three babies, which worried her father as talk increased of the unthinkable – imminent invasion of England by Germany. In the summer of 1939 he decided to bring them to the United States. Making his apologies to Davis Cup officials who had expected him in Philadelphia for the draw at Merion, he headed for Europe to scoop up his family. Roger Makins received a telegram from his father-in-law telling him that arrangements had been made for Alice and the three children to sail for the US with dependents from the American Embassy. It was not presented as a suggestion or a choice. 'That was an order and I treated it as such,' said his English son-in-law with a laugh some years later.

Now Davis had five grandchildren in the US – Pete's two boys, Alice's three girls. But there were sad markers as well to the passing years. Davis's eldest brother, John, who had been an invalid for several years, died in 1937 at his summer home in Maine. With no children of his own, he left his estate in trust to be divided, after his wife's death, between the children of his two younger brothers. Sam died three years later in St. Louis, following a brief illness.

CHAPTER 24

MEANWHILE, WITH THE CUP

The Late 1930s

The two men – one, a lanky, freckled Californian with a shock of red hair, the other a handsome blonde European aristocrat – stood at the arch leading from the changing rooms to the Wimbledon Centre Court. Accompanying them was Ted Tinling, who served as sort of a sergeant at arms for important matches at the All England Club. With the score tied 2-2, America's Don Budge and Germany's Baron Gottfried von Cramm were ready to play the fifth and deciding match in the 1937 inter-zone finals. The winner would challenge, and probably defeat, the current cup holder, Great Britain, now minus its star Fred Perry who had turned professional.

A telephone in the locker room rang – or didn't ring – according to which version of the story is later believed. In the yes-it-rang version, a locker room attendant called von Cramm to the phone, while Budge and Tinling waited impatiently. *'Ja, mein Führer,'* said von Cramm several times and hung up. It was Hitler calling to wish him good luck, said von Cramm impassively (he was well-known to be no supporter of the Nazis). The two players walked out onto the court, bowed to the Royal Box and play began.

Whether such an event did occur (as Budge would always maintain) or was *Land der Mär*, a fairy tale, as von Cramm will later tell questioners, about one thing there would always be agreement: the spectacular quality of the tennis in the ensuing singles match, which some will call the greatest ever Davis Cup match. Just to add more drama to the proceedings, Bill Tilden, sitting in the stands, had been working as coach – of the German team.

Budge started slowly and was soon down two sets. Von Cramm was playing brilliantly. Budge pulled even. The shots from both side were dazzling. Points were won, not lost on errors. In the fifth set von Cramm was ahead 4-1, but Budge told Walter Pate on a cross-over, 'Don't worry, Captain. I won't let the team down'. It's 4-all, then 6-all. Both men were tiring.

Budge was leading 7-6 and serving. The lead switched back and forth through a long series of ads. Three times von Cramm held on at match-point. Again it was Budge's ad, and again he served. The return of serve came deep to his forehand. He bent low and hit a spectacular, down-the-line forehand. Von Cramm, rushing in, lunged, but the ball landed safely behind him, just inside the line. Without looking back, von Cramm, always the impeccable sportsman, got up and came around the net to congratulate Budge. 'No need to look back,' wrote *New York Herald Tribune* tennis reporter Al Laney. 'He knew and we all knew the moment the ball was struck that it was a winner and the wonderful match was over.'

The challenge round, which started three days later, was perfunctory as expected. Bunny Austin defeated Frank Parker in the first match but after that it was a clean US sweep. On the final day, with the cup already locked up for the US, Budge and Austin decided to give the crowd some laughs in the fifth game. After the first three sets of straight tennis, with Budge leading 2-1, Budge suggested to Austin that they exchange racquets. This left the diminutive Britisher flailing away with a racquet which felt as if it weighed 'about 15 stone' (about 200 pounds), much to the crowd's amusement.

Back in the United States, an elated Dwight Davis, who had not been in England for the matches, said that it was high time the trophy came back home. 'I like to see it rotate from country to country, but ten years is a trifle too long for it to stay away.'

In early August, as the 71st Regiment Band played *The Star-Spangled Banner*, America's newest sports heroes, enveloped in clouds of cheers and confetti, walked down the gangplank of the USS *Manhattan*, bringing the silver bowl back to American soil. Budge, Frank Parker, Gene Mako, team captain Walter Pate and Bryan 'Bitsy' Grant (who had played in the inter-zone match) then climbed aboard a Fifth Avenue double-decker bus and waved to crowds from the open, top deck as the parade moved through the streets of New York. Riding in a front seat so that all might see it was the famous cup.

At a later hotel ceremony, the elegant silver trophy – like a glamorous star who takes off her diamonds, dons an apron and slips into the kitchen to fix dinner – now assumed its other role as 12-quart punchbowl. Dwight Davis was among those offering champagne toasts as the cup was officially turned over to USLTA president Holcombe Ward, Davis's old Davis Cup teammate.

In 1938 the US fended off an Australian challenge, but the following year was a different story. Don Budge had turned pro after a spectacular 1938 in which he became, by careful strategy, the first player, man or woman, to win in one year the championships of Australia, France, Wimbledon and the US – the Big Four, as Budge called it. (Interestingly, Budge picked these as the four most important championships because they represented the four nations who had won the Davis Cup.) Reporter Allison Danzig, in his story the day following Budge's win at Forest Hills, referred to 'a grand slam', using a term from the wildly popular card game, bridge. The achievement had not yet been publicized and capitalized into Grand Slam.

The experienced Australians John Bromwich and Adrian Quist defeated the Americans Frank Parker, Bobby Riggs and the young doubles team of Jack Kramer and Joe Hunt to reclaim the cup for Australia. Most of the rest of the world was focused on other events, however. German tanks had rolled into Poland. It was an eerie repetition of 1914 when Norman Brookes (on hand in Pennsylvania to see this 1939 Australian triumph) and Tony Wilding took possession of the Davis Cup just as another war was beginning.

If the cup had to go, said an editorial in the *New York Times,* 'there is no custody in which we would be happier to see it than in that of the Australians ... It is probable that the Davis Cup will be withdrawn from competition for the duration of the present war. It is in excellent hands.'

CHAPTER 25

TAPS

I n December 1941, with the attack on Pearl Harbor, America again went to war. The two youngest Davis girls, like young women everywhere, arranged hurried weddings and then sent their new husbands off to be soldiers. In April 1942 Cynthia married Bill Martin, who had been drafted and was serving as a private. ('You were lucky to be drafted because you obviously would have starved to death on the outside,' a drill sergeant, exasperated at his ineptitude on the training field, told the former president of the New York Stock Exchange.) And the following December Helen married a young artist, Allen Hermes, from Connecticut, whom she had met at a party in New York given by Pauline's sister.

Pete had joined the Army Air Corps where, as a lieutenant in his 30s, he was called 'Grandpa' by the young fighter pilots. Pauline, who had returned to the Republican fold before the 1936 election, also returned to public life in 1940 as national director of volunteer forces of the American Red Cross. Often photographed in Red Cross uniform with snappy billed hat, she had already flown to England for a three-week inspection trip of volunteer services there (she was later decorated by the British Order of Dame of St. John). She continued to oversee development of expanded programs for the Red Cross's some three million volunteers, with a roster of assistant directors which read like a Washington *Who's Who* (Mrs. Walter Lippmann, Mrs. Archibald MacLeish, Mrs. Richard Bissell).

Davis, too, at the age of 62 went back into uniform – briefly. His old friend and colleague from the Coolidge and Hoover administrations, the Republican Henry Stimson, had been named secretary of war by Roosevelt to cloak the war effort in bi-partisanship. Stimson asked Davis to head something called the Army Specialist Corps.

This new corps was a response to a problem about which Stimson had strong feelings, as did, presumably, Davis. Stimson thought that regular Army commissions (and regular uniforms) should not go to those scientists, lawyers, production specialists and civilian technicians who were overage or could not meet Army physical standards – that is, who were not doing the fighting.

On the other hand, their technical expertise was often badly needed. The solution, decided Stimson, was this new group, with its own slightly different uniform and its own special ranks. In February 1942, Davis was sworn in as director general of the Army Specialist Corps. 'Brains, not physiques, will be our test,' said Davis. A tentative pamphlet of regulations listed 37 different job categories from which specialists might be needed – ranging from statistics to ship loading and including 12 different kinds of engineering.

At first Davis was given the special rank of lieutenant general. By May, however, he had decided he could work more efficiently as a civilian head. But to others the uniform, the rank did matter. Staying a civilian or being some sort of specialist – a 'chocolate soldier' with ASC on your collar and 'non-combatant' on your left sleeve – just wouldn't do. Too many wanted the cachet of being regular Army – at least a colonel, possibly a brigadier general. 'Some thought it was infra dig to start in just as a colonel,' Harvey H. Bundy, who worked on the corps idea with Stimson, would say later. Without regular commissions the Army wasn't getting the men it wanted to come to Washington.

'Army commanders who needed high-class men for specialist civilian duty, and needed them in a hurry, found it so much easier to get them by pandering to the itch to wear the Army uniform that they threw their influence against the Specialist Corps and failed to support the effort to preserve the dignity of their own uniform,' a disgusted Stimson would later write.

At the end of October 1942, the War Department announced that the Specialist Corps was being abolished and that the more than 1,300 specialists already selected would be folded into the regular officer procurement process. Davis would continue as advisor with a relative rank of major general. It had been, wrote Stimson, 'an experiment noble in purpose'.

Davis's name had been lent to another noble cause a year earlier. Tennis champion Helen Hull Jacobs enlisted Davis, Don Budge and other tennis luminaries to be part of a lawn tennis committee she had organised to raise funds for the borough of Wimbledon, as part of the British War Relief Society. A German bomb had first fallen on a corner of the All England Club's famed centre court in October 1940, one of 16 bombs that would fall on the facility before the war was over. Club parking lots had been ploughed up for vegetable plots and pens installed for raising pigs, geese and chickens. Other areas were used by drilling troops. 'The people who used to line up 12 hours before the matches to give us their support are lining up now to seek shelter from bombs ...,' said Jacobs in her public appeal.

The mayor of Wimbledon cabled thanks to Jacobs and her colleagues for their offer of aid. 'Distress caused here by bombing is great, but spirits are high and we shall see this struggle to victory. With your help victory will come soon. Roll on the day when you play tennis here again.'

Wartime or not, lives continued. Three more Davis grandchildren arrived: Christopher Makins in the summer of 1942 and two baby girls, both named for their mothers, in 1944 – Cynthia Martin, in June, and Helen Hermes, in October. Pete was now an Air Corps captain. Draftee William McChesney Martin had worked his way up into the officer ranks (he would finish the war a colonel) and was stationed at the Army War College and in the services of supply. (His postwar career would be capped by 19 years as chairman of the Federal Reserve, serving under five presidents from Truman to Nixon.)

Roger Makins was serving in the Mediterranean as assistant to the resident British minister at the Allied Force Headquarters. (His contact there with General Dwight D. Eisenhower would be particularly useful in the 1950s when Eisenhower was president and Makins, as Sir Roger Makins, returned to the US as British Ambassador. Coming to Washington with the Makinses would be their one-year-old son Dwight Makins. He was named, of course, for Alice's father, but those in the Washington diplomatic corps would often marvel at how clever, not to mention prescient, Roger and Alice Makins had been to name their son for the American president. Eventually, Roger Makins would become the first Baron Sherfield.)

Pauline's son James Hopkins Smith Jr. (Jimmy) was a Navy carrier pilot in the Pacific. (He would be named assistant secretary of the navy (air) during the Eisenhower administration.)

Pauline had resigned from her Red Cross position in 1943 because of poor health. Davis's health too had begun to fail. The problems were nothing exotic – hypertension, general and coronary arteriosclerosis – but no less serious because of their ordinariness. In May 1945 Davis had a heart attack. Throughout the summer he rallied, however, and was well enough to travel out to Southampton and Bayberry Land where he could sit in the sun in the walled rose garden and, as he had written in an earlier letter, 'get in the way of the gardener'. In July Dr. Moulton of Brookings wrote that he had heard that Davis had been spotted 'in good fettle' at Southampton sporting events. 'We are all delighted to have this good news.'

Returning to Washington in the fall, Davis had a caller from the past. Australian Davis Cup star Norman Brookes – now Sir Norman – and his wife were passing through town. While she went to a cocktail party in the Decatur Place neighbourhood, Norman went to see his old friend. The two, 'both reserved men', sat and talked by the fire, 'of past days, of the Davis Cup's national significance, of golf matches ... of the interests and pleasures of men whose lives had been ruled by the code of the sports they had loved ...' wrote Dame Mable Brookes later.

'Dwight was dying, and knew it ... "Don't keep the cup too long, Norman,"' she quoted Davis as saying. '" It is meant to travel, its appearance in any country brings a flock of exterior implications very beneficial to sporting unity in the tennis world ... If I had known of its coming significance, it would have been cast in gold."'

(Even if it were unlikely that Davis used – or Norman Brookes exactly remembered – such phrases as 'flock of exterior implications', this is undoubtedly close enough to the conversation Brookes later recounted to his wife.)

When it was time for Brookes to leave, Davis with difficulty walked him to the door and watched as his car drove away. 'That's the last time I shall see Dwight,' said Brookes to his wife.

In November 1945 Davis's condition worsened. A concerned Moulton sent a message to Pauline, enclosing a note for Davis: 'Since our telephone conversation I have had no further word as to his condition,' he wrote, leaving it up to her as to whether Davis could be given his note. A week later, with Davis in a coma, all four of his children gathered in the house on Decatur Place. Robert, his driver since St. Louis days, was there, of course. On Tuesday night, Helen, the youngest, went off to a boxing match with Pete and Robert, to whom she had always been very close. 'I hated boxing but I wanted to spend time with Pete and Robert,' she would remember later.

On Wednesday, 28 November 1945, shortly before midnight, Dwight Davis died from myocardial failure. He was 66.

Two days later, on Saturday, the funeral was held at 10 a.m. in the chapel at Fort Myer across the river in Virginia. Following the chapel service, the funeral procession, elaborately military as was due a former secretary of war, moved slowly through a gate into Arlington National Cemetery. A chaplain, a soldier bearing the guidon, several formations of marching soldiers, a military band, colour guards with flags of the Army and the United States, all this accompanied the flag-draped casket atop a horse-drawn caisson. Beside the casket walked the military and honorary pall bearers, including male family members and long-time tennis friends Bill Clothier and Julian Myrick.

Already in place at the grave and awaiting the procession was the firing party. The burial site (section 2, grave number 4962) was on a gentle rise which extended back to the bluff on which sat the yellow Custis-Lee Mansion. A half-mile to the south was the Tomb of the Unknown Soldier. Off to the north-east, across the Potomac, gleamed the graceful white buildings and monuments of official Washington.

At the completion of the brief graveside committal service, those attending were asked to stand for the rendering of military honours. Twenty-one guns fired a salute into the crisp November air, the waves of sound rustling the dry leaves on a nearby pin oak. A lone bugler, standing at the head of the grave, played Taps.

Some months later a tall, pale marker was erected at the grave. It was a soldier's tombstone. On the front was chiselled a representation of the Distinguished Service Cross, and underneath, the inscription, 'Dwight Filley Davis, Lieutenant Colonel, United States Army, 1879-1945'. On the back, 'Davis, Secretary of War 1925-1929, Governor General of The Philippines, 1929-1932'.

'It was ... as a public servant that Dwight Filley Davis contributed most to his country,' said an editorial in the *New York Sun*. 'Born with sufficient wealth to permit a life of leisure had he wished it, he threw himself wholeheartedly into the cause of good government and civic improvement in his native St. Louis, served with exceptional distinction in World War I, then went into broader fields of national affairs ... His was a fine example of how a wealthy and talented man can serve his city, his state and his nation.'

Yet in later years the world would primarily remember what Dwight Davis had done in 1900 as an earnest and idealistic young American tennis player. Wrote the British publication *Lawn Tennis and Badminton*, 'The gift of the cup was one of those happy inspirations – they come to men of vision – which in ways rarely understandable at the time, are afterwards found to have left their mark on the current of human life and relationships.'

ONLY A GAME?

T he war was over. At last the big silver bowl, its heavy tray and the heavier base of wood and silver could be taken from their wartime safe haven in the vault of the Bank of New South Wales. Now in December 1946, on the day after Christmas, the Davis Cup sat at the stadium court of the Kooyong Tennis Club in Melbourne, shimmering in the blistering Australian summer heat. A south breeze was blowing, but still it was hot.

Near the cup stood Sir Norman Brookes, waiting to address the crowd at this, the first challenge round since the end of the war and since the death of Dwight Davis. Shoulders now slightly stooped, hat in hand, the 69-year-old Brookes delivered an emotional tribute to his long-time friend, the cup's donor. Davis would always be remembered, said Brookes, through the great trophy which bore his name as long as tennis retained its place in the hearts of young men who met in international sports competition.

And then it was time for tennis.

In the first match the American Ted Schroeder, a net-rusher and volleyer (recently out of the American Navy), faced John Bromwich, the ambidextrous pre-war Australian star who had been wounded while serving in New Guinea. The home crowd had breathed a sigh of relief after American team captain Walter Pate announced that Schroeder would play the first singles match instead of the steady, baseliner Frank Parker who, earlier in the year, had won six zone and inter-zone singles matches. (In 1939, explained Pate later, he had seen that Bromwich, also a baseline player, with his long reach could 'out Parker Parker'.) Current US champion Jack Kramer, who had served during the war in the US Coast Guard, would play the other singles.

Schroeder lost the first set to Bromwich but decisively won the next two sets. After dropping the first three games of the fourth set, Schroeder appeared to 'rest' for the next three games, giving Bromwich the set 6-0, but running his opponent as much as possible. It was perhaps an extreme example of 'percentage tennis', a strategy Schroeder and team-mate Jack Kramer had picked up at the Los Angeles Tennis Club from a shrewd, tennis-playing engineer and inventor named Cliff

Roche. Roche taught, among other things, that a player should concentrate his energy on points and games he could win.

Schroeder came roaring back in the fifth set and was leading 5-3 when Bromwich hit a drop-shot in the ninth game. Schroeder rushed in and deftly slipped the ball just out of Bromwich's reach to take the match. The Australian crowd rose and gave the tall, hard-serving American a five-minute standing ovation. If fine tennis and crowd good-sportsmanship were indicators, the revived Davis Cup competition was off to an fine start.

Jack Kramer won his singles match against Dinny Pails and in the next day's doubles, Kramer and Schroeder upended their elders, the long-time team of Bromwich and Adrian Quist, to win the third match. The Davis Cup was going home. At the traditional banquet, Brookes said that Australia had got a look at a new kind of 'aggressive' tennis which 'should have a great influence on our future stars and may in the long run help us regain the coveted trophy'.

The American team had, for the first time, flown to a challenge round. Now for the return trip to the US, the big silver cup would also fly for the first time. The large hardwood case containing the cup, tray and base arrived at the airport. But there was a problem. No opening in the plane was large enough for the case to be eased through. The Australian National Airways' solution was to make two smaller boxes. ANA, along with several other airlines, also picked up the cost of transporting the trophy back to New York.

First, however, California wanted to celebrate. A reception on the steps of the Los Angeles City Hall was held to honour the cup and Kramer and Schroeder, the two local boys who had honed their games not far away at the Los Angeles Tennis Club. Two days later in New York a beaming Walter Pate got off a plane and posed for photographers holding the bowl. Pate, a contemporary of Dwight Davis's, had been on hand to see the first Davis Cup matches in 1900.

Buffed up and out of its wartime seclusion, the big silver trophy was back in business now as proud (if temporary) national icon, a silver symbol of supremacy at the confluence of sport and patriotism on the political stage. Former Australian prime minister Robert Menzies (an enthusiastic tennis player) had been on hand at the official Davis Cup banquet in January to bid the cup farewell. A month later in Washington, President Harry Truman presided at the draw for the 1947 order of play. Invited guests included Dwight Davis's son, Pete, and daughter, Cynthia. Though he was a horseshoe player himself, said the president, Mrs. Truman had been a tennis player back in Missouri and he had watched her play 'with a great deal of pleasure'.

For the next decade the challenge rounds would be monotonously the same: Australia defeating the US or US defeating Australia. Which was not to say that this new generation of power hitters was not providing riveting, crowd-pleasing tennis. And crowds there were – particularly in tennis-mad Australia. When Melbourne and Adelaide were the sites of challenge rounds, ever increasing numbers of temporary seats would be built – 15,000, then 17,000. But still people were turned away.

In 1954, eight years after the post-war resumption of competition, it was Sydney's turn to again host Australia's defence of the cup. The challenging American team – under captain (and former doubles star) Billy Talbert – arrived to find that new temporary stands would give the White City Stadium in Sydney an ear-shattering capacity of 27,500 – and still ticket money had to be returned to those who couldn't be accommodated. (In comparison, 40-odd years later, the new Arthur Ashe Stadium in Flushing, New York, would seat 23,500, the new number one court at Wimbledon, 11,000.)

The trophy itself had settled comfortably into Australia. It had been there four straight years now, honoured and displayed at important public events. Earlier in 1954, for instance, the young, 28-year-old queen, Elizabeth II, and H.R.H. Prince Philip had come to visit as part of the new monarch's six-month tour of the British Commonwealth. It was the first visit to Australia and New Zealand by a reigning British monarch. On the calendar of events was a tennis exhibition in Melbourne between the international teams of South Africa and Australia, not an official Davis Cup match, of course, since Australia, as the holding nation, did not play until the challenge round.

At the conclusion of the first exhibition match, the Davis Cup was trundled out onto the court, and the royal gaze fell upon the large silver bowl designed a half-century earlier (though no one present would have been aware of it) by a native of the English Midlands, a product of the admirable royal art training system and winner of a Queen's scholarship, Rowland Rhodes. Sir Norman Brookes presented Her Majesty with a golden miniature of the Davis Cup.

Before the Americans could take on Australia in the 1954 challenge round, they headed to Brisbane, Australia, to polish off the winner of the European Zone, Sweden, 5-0. Former Australian player Adrian Quist was covering the event for a Sydney newspaper. 'To me it seems a great pity that neither the Americans nor the Australians are ever pressed to reach the challenge round,' he wrote. Playing both singles and doubles for the US in the challenge round would be the urbane Philadelphian, Vic Seixas, and Tony Trabert, from Cincinnati. It had been three years earlier in 1951 that Trabert had played his first Davis Cup matches, had first heard those momentous words, 'United States serving ...' 'You take a deep swallow. It's hard to get the arm to move,' he would recall later.

In 1953, 19-year-old 'boy wonders' Lew Hoad and Ken Rosewall had played in the challenge round for the first time. In a spectacular, rain-soaked match Hoad had defeated the American, Trabert, in five sets. Now, on opening day of the 1954 challenge round in Sydney, the huge crowd was to see a rematch. This time Trabert came out on top, though losing two days later to Rosewall whom he had beaten the year before. With Vic Seixas winning his first singles match against Rosewall and the Seixas-Trabert doubles team defeating Hoad-Rosewall, the Americans retook the cup before the final day.

Australian captain Harry Hopman liked to include on each year's squad a couple of promising juniors, to 'squeeze the oranges', warm up the team stars, and generally get a taste of the unique team pressures of Davis Cup. In 1954 one of the juniors on hand was 18-year-old Roy Emerson, who had developed his game on a court he built with his dad out of clay ant hills on their dairy farm in Queensland. Emerson eventually would play in nine consecutive challenge rounds, more than any other Australian.

The US possession of the cup in 1954 was short-lived, for back it went to Australia the next year after a 5-0 rout at Forest Hills. The Harry Hopman junior development machine was producing a seemingly endless supply of talented young players – Frank Sedgman, Ken McGregor, Mervyn Rose, Neale Fraser, Mal Anderson, Ashley Cooper, Rod Laver, John Newcombe, Tony Roche, Fred Stolle, John Alexander – ready to keep the cup Down Under for the next 11 out of 13 years.

Challenge round matches in Australia were at Christmas time, and Norman and Mabel Brookes would entertain with a big holiday dinner for the team and other members of the Australian tennis establishment. The cup, out of the vault and ready for its official appearances, often would be on the sideboard in the Brookes dining room. There, on at least one occasion, it provided distraction for the Brookeses' young grandson, Norman, seated at the table between Adrian Quist and Harry Hopman. While more serious conversations were going on elsewhere at the table, the three competed to see who could flip the most plastic counters (poker chips) into the massive bowl.

Years later Neale Fraser, as Australian team captain, would occasionally have the cup at his home for victory cookouts – barbecues. It might sit in splendour in his sun room or on a table out on the lawn and, after the guests left, spend the night tucked snugly and safely under Fraser's bed.

Occasionally, when the cup was in the United States, it would make a pilgrimage to one of Dwight Davis's old haunts – the historic Casino in Newport where the US championships had been played in Davis's competition days. In 1954, the mellow old building with its picturesque shingles and lattice was turned into a tennis museum with a Hall of Fame honouring those who had been important to tennis through the years. The Hall of Fame had been the brain child of Jimmy Van Alen and his wife. Van Alen, an all around Casino aficionado, would also eventually be remembered for dreaming up a simplified scoring system with sudden-death tie-breaker.

Now, in 1956, in the second year of balloting, Davis and his doubles partner Holcombe Ward, had been voted into the new National Lawn Tennis Hall of Fame. Also enshrined this year were Davis's competition contemporaries Beals Wright, William Clothier and William Larned, as well as the first woman to be so honoured, May Sutton Bundy, an early US and Wimbledon champion. Malcolm Whitman had been voted in a year earlier, in the first group of honourees which also included Richard Sears, Dr. James Dwight, Oliver Campbell, Robert Wrenn and Joseph S. Clark, an 1880s US doubles champion. He and his doubles partner and brother had been the first two Americans to play at Wimbledon.

Holcombe Ward, a spry 77, was the only player from the first Davis Cup match still living. All the others – Whitman, Davis, Gore, Black and Barrett – were gone now. Arthur Gore went with his boots on, so to speak, having died in early 1927 (at the age of 59) after competing at Wimbledon just the summer before. Incredibly, he had competed at every Wimbledon since 1888. The dashing Scot, Ernest Black, had emigrated to Nova Scotia and had died in Halifax in 1931 at the age of 58. H. Roper Barrett, the non-playing captain of Britain's successful Davis Cup teams in the 1930s, had died in 1943 at the age of 69.

Eventually Dwight Davis's tennis-playing son-in-law, William McChesney Martin Jr., would serve as a Hall of Fame board member and later president after the Hall of Fame was combined with the National Tennis Foundation. Another son-in-law, artist Allen Hermes, would do a bust of Davis for the Hall of Fame museum, and a Davis grandson, John G. Davis, would later serve as vice-president of the Hall of Fame executive committee. Wrote Van Alen to Bill Martin, 'There is no doubt in my mind that your father-in-law's cup did more to increase the popularity of tennis throughout the world than any other one operation.'

Coincidentally, not far from Newport was Providence, Rhode Island, home of the Gorham Silver Co. which had acquired the Durgin Silver Co. in 1905 and eventually folded it into the Providence operations in 1931. On one of the cup's stays in the US, probably while the cup was at Gorham for repairs, plaster casts were made of the whole trophy – cup, foot, tray, base plaques.

Occasionally there were other reminders of those Durgin origins. In the summer of 1955, the USLTA had received a letter from the Amalgamated Silver Workers Union concerning one of its retired members, William Knoll. It seemed that the 83-year-old gentleman, living in a home for the aged on New York's upper West Side, dearly wanted to have a photograph of the Davis Cup to hang on the wall of his room. He had been, he said, the silver worker who had 'spun' the cup a half-century earlier. The USLTA sent him congratulations on his craftsmanship and a framed picture of the cup, which, he assured the association, he was hanging in a place of honour. At least two other Durgin employees – William H. Morton and a William Rowan – had, through the years, also been credited with being the cup's spinner. This crowd of spinners was, perhaps, testimony to the cup's fame.

The newest silver on the trophy, the fifteen 5- by 6½-inch silver plaques on the trophy's wood base, continued to fill with each year's winner and challenger (both country names and individual players), plus the names of other countries competing. In 1960 the name of a challenge-round newcomer – Italy – was engraved on the trophy. Led by Nicola Pietrangeli, Italy, which had played its first Davis Cup match in 1922, had at last made it through to the end.

The Italians lost to Australia, 4-1, but *fantastico!*, it was, nevertheless, a moment to be savoured like a smooth *gelato*. After all, Italy was only the third country (after Belgium, 1904, and Japan, 1921) to play in the challenge round other than the big four of Australia, France, Great Britain and United States. Pietrangeli, a resilient clay-court specialist who had won the French championships in both singles and doubles the previous year, would eventually compete in more Davis Cup ties, play more Davis Cup matches (120 wins, 44 losses) than any other player in the competition's history. (A 'tie', of course, is a team competition between countries, a term used primarily in Europe and Britain. A Davis Cup tie consists of five rubbers or matches.)

Four more nations made it into the challenge round for the first time in the 1960s – Mexico, Spain, India and Romania. The Dwight Davis who had said 'Don't keep the cup too long, Norman' would probably have approved of this geographical broadening of the challenge round. But would he have approved of some of the reasons why this had happened? Probably not, though who could say for sure. As a typhoon of change began to blow through tennis (and Davis Cup) during the next few decades, it would be a chancy game at best to guess what Dwight Davis would have thought of this or that development.

It could be argued, for instance, that Davis's great push to move tennis beyond the well-trimmed hedges of the country club and onto public parks courts would lead, inevitably, to this: a new crop of champions without private incomes who wanted to make money with their racquets, rather than use tennis as an entry into the business world, as Norman Brookes was still advising. And they wanted to make that money right out in front of everybody. There was dissatisfaction on all sides with the hypocrisy of under-the-table payments and 'jobs' with sponsoring companies.

There was money to be made playing tennis. Bill Tilden, Fred Perry, Ellsworth Vines, Don Budge had discovered this before the war, though their tours were small potatoes compared to what was to come once the shrewd tennis mind of Jack Kramer applied itself to the possibilities of play for pay. Kramer himself, it later developed, had first signed a pro contract with a tour promoter in September 1947, two days after teaming with Ted Schroeder at Forest Hills to fend off a challenge for the Davis Cup from Australia 4-1. The US national championships (which Kramer would win for a second year) were just getting underway. Kramer had become, as he would later put it, 'an illegal amateur formally, instead of the informal illegal amateur I had been'.

As quickly as a nation would develop Davis Cup and grand slam-tournament stars, they would be signed by professional tours, which later Kramer himself ran so successfully. Howls of anguish and anger arose from the offices of the world's tennis governing bodies and from the club rooms at Longwood and Germantown, at Forest Hills and Queen's, at Wimbledon and the Melbourne Cricket Club.

Howls well-modulated and well-bred, of course. For even more than the money, this was an affront to the code of the gentleman amateur. Davis Cup, to this camp, was the last bastion of amateurism. Ironically, with many of the world's stars siphoned off into professional tennis, now there was room for other players – and other countries – to succeed in Davis Cup.

By 1967 there were two men's professional tennis circuits. Late in the year a crack in the solid wall of tradition first appeared. Despite the threat of expulsion from the International Lawn Tennis Federation which still opposed 'open' tennis, the British ruling body, Lawn Tennis Association, announced that beginning in 1968, tournaments in Britain would be open to anyone, professional or amateur. This, of course, meant Wimbledon. Other national associations, and the ILTF, cautiously followed suit in 1968, though with complicated categories of who could or could not accept prize money. But much remained uncertain about the exact place of the Davis Cup in the new tennis firmament.

Other problems were easier to solve. The year-by-year engraved record of challenge round participants – which had filled the outside of the bowl and spilled over onto the tray – now had about filled the base as well. Challenge rounds in 1967 (Australia vs. Spain) and 1968 (United States vs. Australia) would fill the last empty silver plaque. This time it was a Melbourne manufacturing silversmith, T. Gaunt & Co., which supplied a new layer for the base. Might as well. The cup, after all, was spending most of its time Down Under.

Change piled upon change. At a meeting in London on 1 July 1971, the committee of Davis Cup nations voted in a rule change that would significantly alter – most said strengthen – the Davis Cup series. The challenge round would be replaced by a final round. No longer could one year's champion country take its ease while the rest of the world battled through round after round to win the right to challenge for the cup. The champion's 'standing out' until a challenger had been determined was a vestige of the early days of lawn tennis, dumped by the US championships and Wimbledon immediately before and after World War I.

First test of the new structure came in 1972. Good hosts take the rickety chair or the smallest lamb chop, so there was a certain amount of appropriateness in the fact that it was Dwight Davis's home country, the United States, which would be the first defending nation to have to play through the ranks. With wins over the Commonwealth Caribbean, then Mexico, then Chile, then Spain, the US was finally ready for the finals and the powerful (and often volcanic) Romanian team of Ilie Nastase and Ion Tiriac.

The Romanians, playing in Bucharest, had defeated Australia's Mal Anderson and Colin Dibley 4-1 in the other inter-zone final match. Australia was upset about the officiating – the bad line calls, the questionable second-serve foot faults, illegally long rests, a frightened umpire, partisanship from the officials so blatant that a linesman even massaged Tiriac's cramping leg during the long, third-day match with Dibley. Do not play the final in Bucharest, Australia cautioned the United States.

The US and Romania had first met in a challenge round in Cleveland in 1969 when Stan Smith, Arthur Ashe and Bob Lutz had defeated Nastase and Tiriac. In 1971 the two countries had met again, this time at a tennis stadium in the red-clay, pine-forest outskirts of Charlotte, North Carolina. Among the dramatic moments had been the US military band's accidental playing of the pre-Communist Romanian national anthem at the official ceremonies. Nastase and Tiriac were not amused. By the next day music for the current regime had been hustled down to Charlotte. Playing on hard clay, the US team of Stan Smith, Frank Froeling and Erik van Dillen had won 3-2.

Now, a year later, the Romanians were adamant that the finals be on their home ground, even though their semi-finals had been at home, whereas the US had played its semi-finals away, and in the past the champion had always defended the cup at home. The new rules were a bit hazy on this point. Hot wars had stopped the Davis Cup after its first 14 years, then after the next 21 years. Now, with the current stretch extending to 26 years, was the Cold War to halt the series again? The US (after what some claimed was arm-twisting from the US State Department) agreed to Bucharest. It would be the first Davis Cup final not played in either the US or Australia since Great Britain hosted the challenge round in 1937.

In the summer of 1972 Smith had won Wimbledon and Nastase had won

Forest Hills. In mid-October, at the flag-bedecked Progresul Sports Club in Bucharest, these two would meet again in a memorable battle for the *Cupa Davis*.

At the end of the first day of matches, Smith had defeated Nastase and Tiriac had beaten Tom Gorman to tie the score at 1-1. The next day's doubles matchup was a repeat of the previous year – Smith-van Dillen against Nastase-Tiriac. In 1971 the Romanians had won in three sets. The excited crowd looked for a repeat. This time, however, the American team prevailed 6-2, 6-0, 6-3, in what some tennis historians would rank as one of the most dramatic Davis Cup doubles matches ever (though probably not Romanian historians). On the third day, Smith's five-set victory over Tiriac nailed down the cup for the Americans, Gorman lost to Nastase and the final score was 3-2.

Throughout the three days the crowd had been loud and unruly, more like a soccer crowd unschooled in the tennis niceties of, for instance, not cheering when the other team's first serve goes into the net. Tiriac, who did know better, was vocally abusive to the tiny contingent of American spectators, and the line calls often were astonishing. As protection, the Americans, forewarned by the Australians, had attempted to keep their shots well inside the lines and sometimes, for instance on Smith's serves, even that did not result in accurate calls. Wrote Herbert Warren Wind in the *New Yorker*, 'The ethics of sport may not be the most important thing in the world, but the final at Progresul, for all its colour and thrills, was a travesty of a kind that no game can afford.'

And as topper to the whole improbable three days, Dwight Davis Jr. (Pete), a special guest at the event along with his wife and youngest son, John, was asked to say a few words on the final day. Pete, whose sports love had remained baseball (he had been a vice-president of the New York Mets) had never been particularly interested in Davis Cup. He also was not thrilled about having to make a speech. Nevertheless, he and John retired to a café area to put together some remarks. The day was bitterly cold, and the speech writers decided to fortify themselves with one or two 'thimbles full' of brandy. By the time they had returned to the arena, John had convinced his father that it would be wiser to forego his plan to lecture the crowd on its rudeness and incivility. Instead, Pete, with the aid of a translator, made a nice, proper little speech about his pleasure at being 'here in Budapest'. The translator corrected it to Bucharest but the damage was done. This word, among all the others, the crowd understood without translation. Puzzled by the boos, Pete finished and sat down – and only then learned about his gaff.

The painful convulsions of a tennis world trying to restructure itself continued through the 1970s. Pro tours demanded compensation for letting players participate at Forest Hills and Wimbledon. Contract pros were banned or were staging their own boycotts. In Davis Cup, nations refused to play other nations for political or human rights reasons, and players received threats from exiles because of policies of the government the team represented. And a continuing burr under the saddle for some tennis purists was the fact that Davis Cup players were now getting paid for representing their countries. Rather than encouraging, in Dwight Davis's words, a 'spirit of goodwill', 'a broad tolerance of others' viewpoints' and good sportsmanship that 'has no national boundaries', the Davis Cup was giving everybody just one more thing to argue about.

Some, like columnist Murray Janoff, wrote that it was time to put the beleaguered old trophy out of its misery. He quoted Dwight Davis Jr. as having told him a few years earlier that he was thinking about retiring the cup. (Nothing was said about whether the family had the right to do this in light of the original deed of gift.) But Pete Davis seemed to be having second thoughts now that someone else was saying the same thing. 'Now there's no need to do that [retire the trophy]. There's a lot of international prestige in the Davis Cup,' he told Janoff.

Yet the stretched-out Davis Cup schedule to accommodate as many as 55 countries (in 1974 and 1977), the new opportunities for players to make big money in tennis – it was all taking its toll on the historic old cup. 'In recent years it has diminished in significance because the best players have not always been available to represent their countries,' said the New York Times in early 1976.

Later in the year, when the USSR got suspended for refusing to play Chile in a 1976 semi-final match, American tennis writer Bud Collins discussed the long range effect upon Davis Cup, which he called 'a sort of United Nations in short pants'. Wrote Collins, 'The Soviet government objects to the Chilean government. Who doesn't, except maybe the hackers down at the Central Intelligence Agency. The Soviet protest is the kind of manoeuvre that is tearing the 76-year-old competition apart.'

And then there was always the problem of South Africa. Despite a strong team of Cliff Drysdale, Ray Moore, Bob Hewitt and Frew McMillan, South Africa's 1974 win of the cup was tarnished by the final-round default of India – a country, pointed out Collins, which itself had won no prizes for racial harmony.

'It's better to keep everybody together, playing even though bickering,' insisted Collins. 'The Davis Cup, overshadowed by the proliferation of big-money tournaments, is worth saving.'

Worth saving? Others agreed. For a stiff and rigid, ancient old piece of metal, the cup – this *tabula argenta* of tennis history – turned out to be surprisingly flexible. And what seemed to work, in the end, was a combination of changes involving players and procedures. Plus, of course, money.

At a press conference in October 1980 at the glittery Helmsley Palace Hotel in New York City, two significant changes were announced. The Davis Cup had acquired a commercial sponsor. Nippon Electric Co. (NEC), the Japanese telecommunications and electronics company, would be putting up $1 million in prize money beginning in 1981.

The other change had to do with structure. In 1973 the responsibility for running each year's competition (formerly handled by the previous year's champion) had been put into the hands of a committee of management elected by the competing countries – 'a logical sequel to the elimination of the challenge round,' said Australian sports writer Alan Trengove.

In 1978 the International Tennis Federation (which, like the United States Tennis Association, by now had stripped for speed by dropping the 'Lawn' from its title) had taken over the administration of the cup. The European and American Zones, dating back to 1923, had been joined by an Eastern Zone in 1955, and, in 1966, a division of the crowded European Zone into Sections A and B. But with more than 50 countries participating, the Davis Cup structure – and calendar – still creaked and groaned and popped at the seams.

Henceforth, it was announced in 1980, there would be a 16-country World Group atop the Davis Cup pinnacle. Countries would play through a manageable three rounds during the year, with the two third-round (semi-final) winners facing each other in a year-end final for possession of the cup.

Below the World Group would be the regional zones, and winners in those zones would move up the following year to replace the first-round losers in the next higher group. (Eight years later a new zone, Africa, would be added, and the zones would each be further divided into groups to accommodate the burgeoning number of countries wanting to play Davis Cup.)

And not only had the contract pros been allowed back in Davis Cup competition, but a flashy bunch of crowd-pleasing newcomers had begun showing up on team rosters – Björn Borg, John McEnroe, Yannick Noah, Pat Cash, Stefan Edberg, Boris Becker. Which was not to say that the fractious times were over. A new generation of high-income, (sometimes) tantrum-throwing players rebelled against everything from all-white tennis togs and historic concepts of sportsmanship to the authority of national tennis associations.

Yet eventually tempers cooled and tennis settled into its new era. Jack Kramer, whose tour payroll had once appeared likely to destroy Davis Cup, a decade later was himself serving on the USTA's Davis Cup committee. John McEnroe, that paradox of admirable, patriotic Davis Cup loyalty and inexcusable on-court behaviour, who had once been dropped from the American team for refusing to sign behaviour guidelines, rejoined the team two years later and ended up playing more Davis Cup for his country (years and ties) than any other American.

New tennis dynasties – Sweden and later Germany – began putting together new strings of wins of the cup. Other countries – Italy and Czechoslovakia – also savoured first time wins. The old-timers, though, still stuck their noses into the finals from time to time – even Great Britain, in 1978, in a final in the United States with the historical resonance of the first Davis Cup in 1900.

Australia gave another nod to the cup's history in 1983. All of Australia was euphoric over that country's first win, earlier in the year, of the America's Cup in yachting. It was the first time any country other than the US had won the venerable old silver mug. Captain Neale Fraser invited the victorious skipper of *Australia II* into the team dressing room during the finals against Sweden at Melbourne – not knowing that cross-pollination from the America's Cup had helped give Dwight Davis the inspiration for the Davis Cup in the first place. Australia won 3-2, and Brian Tobin, president of the Lawn Tennis Association of Australia, had the two famous pieces of sporting silver – the pitcher and the big bowl – photographed sitting together companionably, side-by-gleaming-side.

Other countries made it into the final round for the first time – Chile, Argentina, and in the 1990s, Switzerland and Russia. In Switzerland, a country which had been playing Davis Cup for 63 years, an astonishing *indoor* crowd of nearly 18,000 enthusiastic cowbell-ringing spectators would be on hand in Geneva in 1992 to see Jakob Hlasek and Marc Rosset defeat Brazil in the semi-finals, 5-0. The ecstatic Swiss then had to face the US in Ft. Worth, Texas.

'Maybe we're going to get crushed, 5-0, but don't tell me there's no chance,' said Rosset. (The score for the 1992 finals actually would be 3-1, US, with Andre Agassi and Jim Courier playing singles, Pete Sampras and John McEnroe, doubles.) 'The Davis Cup thing is friendship and togetherness. The spirit of the team is as important as the quality of the players,' said Hlasek.

To the rest of the world by now, Davis was just a name on a tennis trophy – sort of like *sterling* on the bottom. But back in St. Louis some still remembered a bit more about the man. In 1958 the city parks tennis tournament was officially named the Dwight Davis Public Parks Tennis Tournament in honour of the onetime park commissioner and booster of tennis for all. Winners from this tournament go on to compete nationally in the National Public Parks Tennis Association championships, the intercity competition that Davis began in 1916 and revived in 1923 while USLTA president.

The Dwight F. Davis Memorial Tennis Center in Forest Park opened in 1966 with 19 courts and seating for 2,200 (expandable to 3,500) around a small stadium court. Across town is the ten-acre Dwight Davis city park, dedicated in

1962. No tennis courts here – the action tends more toward basketball, soccer, softball and baseball. But there is a playground, Dwight Davis would be pleased to know.

In July 1900, a photograph of the big silver bowl in an American golf and tennis publication supplied to the curious the first visual image of the Davis Cup. Soon a wider audience was able to see photographic images of the trophy in books, newspapers and general-interest magazines. Now, in this hyper-visual age at the end of the trophy's first century, its electronic image is seen by millions around the world, as television cameras zoom in on the Davis Cup at courtside, sitting majestically on its high base.

Yet many still have only a vague – and imprecise – awareness of the name. One day Dwight Davis's grandson, John Davis, received a telephone call from a woman who said she had picked up at a garage sale a tennis trophy that Dwight Davis apparently had won in some tournament or other. She offered to sell it back to the family for a ludicrously large amount of money. 'After all,' she said with impatience, 'it *is* the Davis Cup.'

Of course, if your name is Davis – *that* Davis – you're allowed a certain amount of latitude. In the mid-1990s the clan Davis, descendants of the Samuel C. Davis who went to St. Louis to make the family fortune, began gathering in the summer for a volley-ball, sailing, get-to-know-your-cousins weekend called Tribal Rites. Recently the 'trophy' at the inevitable tennis tournament was an eight-ounce white Styrofoam cup.

It was called – what else – the Davis Cup.

CHAPTER 27

MALMÖ

A light snow has been falling in Malmö – the first snow of the season. It sifts into the cracks of the cobbled pavement and dusts the green copper roofs of the Swedish town's old brick churches.

This, Sweden's third largest city, sits on the water at the country's southern edge, a brief 45-minute hydrofoil ride across the *Öresund* from Copenhagen, Denmark. Malmö's normal population is 247,000. On this late November weekend, however, the town is swollen with visitors. Some have come on busses from outlying communities in southern Sweden to see the wildly popular new musical *Kristina Från Duvemåla*, a drama about the family-wrenching, massive Swedish emigration to the United States in the 19th and early 20th centuries.

Other visitors are here for a different drama, the 1996 Davis Cup World Group Final between Sweden and France. Interestingly enough, this drama too (in these late 20th century days of mega-sports earnings and high taxes) is awash in émigrés. On the French team, players Arnaud Boetsch and Guy Forget are currently legal residents of Switzerland, though Cedric Pioline, Guillaume Raoux and captain Yannick Noah still live in France. On the Swedish team, Stefan Edberg lives in London, while Thomas Enqvist, Nicklas Kulti and Jonas Bjorkman officially reside in Monaco. Only captain Carl-Axel Hageskog currently lives in Sweden.

The two countries are among the world's heavyweights in Davis Cup competition. Only the United States, Australia and Great Britain have won the cup more often than France and Sweden.

Sweden, which first entered Davis Cup competition in 1925 and first won the cup in 1975 during the halcyon days of Björn Borg, was the Davis Cup champion nation as recently as 1994. Half this year's team (Edberg and doubles specialist Bjorkman) were also on the 1994 team. Steady Sweden is one of only three nations that has stayed eligible for the World Group (i.e. not been eliminated in the previous year's first round and subsequent qualifying round) since the World Group was added to the competition's geographical zone structure in 1981. (The other two are Italy and the Czech Republic.)

France, which first played Davis Cup in 1904 but had its greatest run of successes with the Four Musketeers in the late 1920s and 1930s, won the cup in 1991 after a dry spell of 59 years. In 1991 also, France was led by captain Yannick Noah. Only Guy Forget had played in the earlier final although Boetsch was on the team. France and Sweden have never before met in a final. They most recently played in the quarter-finals in 1994, on the way to Sweden's successful win of the cup.

At the draw ceremony in Malmö at noon on Thursday the Davis Cup trophy makes its first official appearance. It had arrived by air from London two days earlier – a shipment of three stout metal cases on wheels and one cardboard box.

Now removed from the fitted cases and shrouds of protective flannel cloth, the five separate pieces of the trophy – the bowl, the foot into which the bowl fits, the tray, the two layers of the base – have been positioned on the stage. Sometimes, like today, the two empty shipping cases which hold the bases do double duty as platform for the trophy. For this they are swathed in specially made dark green velvet covers (the contents of the cardboard box).

An International Tennis Federation representative adjusts the plinths, centring one of the shell-and-flower *cartouches* between the plaques. She takes a pink silver polishing cloth from a paper sack and dabs at finger marks on the gleaming silver surface. 'Nobody's going to see the back,' she says. She treats the historic trophy with the easy familiarity of someone getting a cherished, but regularly used, piece of family silver ready for Christmas dinner.

On either side of the cup stand the security guards, Daniel and Annika, wearing dark green uniforms and light green berets. They will stick like glue to the trophy during its weekend in Malmö. Annika, as a French (of course) journalist remarks, does not look like your run-of-the-mill security guard. She is tall and pretty, with straight blonde hair – an archetype Swedish maiden. Fortunately for Daniel, she is also strong. Guarding the cup, as it turns out, involves frequently moving the trophy or wrestling it back into its cases. Total weight of the bowl, the tray and the two bases is 198 kilograms or 436 pounds.

Also on the stage are flags of the two competing nations made of dyed flowers – Sweden's yellow cross on a blue field, France's striped tricolour of red, white and blue. Tennis officials, the Lord Mayor of Malmö and a representative of NEC, the major corporate sponsor of the Davis Cup series, take their places at a table with microphones in the centre of the stage.

Another sponsor, the Opel division of General Motors, announces a new award for the Davis Cup series, the Opel/ITF Fair Play award. In future years during Davis Cup competition, significant acts or gestures of sportsmanship and fair play 'which constitute tennis's heart and heritage' will be acknowledged and rewarded. An Opel Citron 'all-purpose vehicle' will be presented to the tennis federation of the good sport's country. 'There may be many ties without a fair-play nomination,' cautions the company spokesman.

It is not clear whether off-court actions will also qualify. What about the host country that picks a relatively neutral court surface, one which does not necessarily give it a whopping advantage? (A few minutes later, during a press conference with the French team, Pioline, when asked about the court surface, says, with a somewhat surprised chuckle, that Sweden may have done just that.)

The two teams file in and sit in chairs on either side of the centre table. The French players wear jackets and ties, the Swedes wear jackets and dark sports shirts buttoned to the neck. All look a bit uncomfortable in civilian clothes. For some reason for a moment there is one player too many for the number of chairs on the French side, and bespectacled doubles player Guillaume Raoux clownishly wedges himself between two of his team-mates.

More introductions. Then ITF president Brian Tobin and Malmö Lord Mayor Kjell-Arne Landgren move over to the cup and prepare for the drawing. The two captains have already announced who will play doubles and the ranking of their singles players. Changes, however, may be made up until an hour before a match begins. It has already been decided that on the first day, Friday, the number one singles player for each country will play the number two player of the opposing team. On Sunday the competition will be reversed. This, of course, makes the showy, historical draw ceremony somewhat irrelevant, though it will decide which match is played first as well as provide good visuals for television.

Large pieces of paper with the names of the four singles players are placed in the cup and one name is drawn and read out – Pioline. France's tall, dark-haired number one will play Sweden's number two, Edberg, in Friday's first match. Pioline looks down at his toes. Edberg stares impassively ahead and shuffles his feet In 20 minutes the ceremony is over. Yes, the draw is good, comments Sweden's captain at the later press conference, since Edberg likes to have a fixed starting time.

Ah, Edberg. For the past year, like some medieval king making a grand procession about the realm, he has been making a farewell tour around the world's tennis realm, showered with gifts and accolades at tournament after tournament. Here, in his home country, the popular 30-year-old Swedish star is making his final appearance before retirement, 12 years after playing in his first Davis Cup match and after competing in 35 ties, including seven Davis Cup finals.

Some observers – though not talking particularly about tennis – have long cast about for ways to metamorphose sports from mere sweaty athletic contest to profound life experience. They write such things as 'the arc of a star athlete's career recapitulates the archetypal journey myth; he starts off naively in an Arcadian hick town, grows into wisdom and finally, through that wisdom, achieves Utopia'. Applied to Edberg, Arcadia would be his home village of Västervik, 430 kilometres north-east of Malmö, and Utopia would be the convention centre (formerly a Saab factory), the venue for this year's Davis Cup finals.

This, then, according to the script, is to be Edberg's weekend, his party. And how do you feel about being the bad guys and ruining Edberg's final hour of glory? French captain Yannick Noah is asked at the press conference. 'We all respect Stefan very much,' says Noah. 'He has been a role model for a lot of people. If he had a party at his place [he smiles and pauses – much laughter] but since he decided to have the party here, we're going to try and spoil that party.'

There are questions from reporters to Forget and Noah about 1991 when France previously won the cup. Those finals were in France (Lyon) and 'the pleasure of winning is even greater when you can share it,' says Noah. Even this time, though only about 700 French fans are on hand, 'a lot of people at home will be following us,' says Noah. (He's right. Later figures from French television will show that 64 percent of those watching television Sunday night in France were watching the final France-Sweden match.)

And that interest reaches beyond Europe to the whole extended French-speaking world – 'in Africa, in the islands', adds Noah who was himself born in the Cameroons (where he was discovered as a potential tennis talent by American Davis Cup star and future team captain, Arthur Ashe).

Photographers move forward and the bowl reflects a blizzard of camera flashbulbs. Players pose behind the cup, to the side of the cup, leaning on the tray. Edberg is asked to pose with the cup alone. 'Two giants,' someone murmurs, 'the trophy and Edberg.'

This, of course, is one of the things the cup does particularly well – hold still for endless photographs. This time there is a new 1990s twist. After the hall is nearly empty, one man holds a nearly invisible piece of thin cord out about six feet from the trophy while another takes photographs from three different angles. The cord is to make sure the camera is at exactly the same distance for each photo. The three photos will be merged together to make a dimensional, hologram-like image for the new Davis Cup web page on the Internet.

Computers. Web pages. Not surprisingly, much has changed since Holcombe Ward reached inside floppy tennis hats for that first Davis Cup draw in 1900 on the rustic front porch of the Longwood Cricket Club. What is surprising is how much has stayed the same.

Though players are now paid handsomely by their country federations for playing Davis Cup; though players, like most athletes in world class competitions, are routinely tested for drugs (samples were flown from Malmö to the US and a lab at the Indiana University Medical School reported all clean) ; though 124 nations played Davis Cup in 1996 (65 percent of Earth's nearly 200 countries); though an intricate structure of multi-level zonal and group competitions has been constructed to enable that many teams to compete; and though all of these changes would astound the competition's pioneers, the basics have stayed the same.

Davis Cup is still an annual competition. Several times over the weekend ITF president Brian Tobin will announce emphatically that it will continue to be an annual competition, though there are regular suggestions that it be held less often, like golf's Ryder Cup. (Nothing new here, either. Every once in awhile, at least since the 1930s, the suggestion has been made – and batted down – that Davis Cup competition be held every two, three or four years.)

Just as in 1900, five matches are played over three days – two singles matches on day one, one doubles match on day two, two singles matches on day three. Underneath expensive logos on expensive tennis shirts, hearts of players in this normally individualistic sport still beat faster when the score is called out Advantage France or Advantage Sweden and not Advantage Edberg or Pioline or Enqvist.

Doubles is still amazingly important – not surprising in this competition begun by a man who was a doubles tactician and had great success in this part of the game. 'This is when doubles becomes a big deal,' Noah will say after the weekend is all over. 'You don't get that elsewhere anymore.' Selection of playing surface still matters just as much as it did in 1900 when Arthur Gore and Roper Barrett grumbled about Longwood's long grass and soggy turf.

And that country still has an edge that can consistently toggle on the button of patriotism or otherwise convince its best players to compete. Great Britain, after losing the first two Davis Cup competitions, demonstrated this in 1903 when the Doherty brothers finally could – or would – sail across the Atlantic and compete. They captured the trophy. The United States, after winning the cup for the 31st time in Moscow in 1995, demonstrated this the following April when not one of its four top players (Sampras, Agassi, Courier or Chang) could – or would – compete in the second round. The defending nation lost to the Czech Republic.

'Recruiting, that's the hardest part,' American Davis Cup captain Tom Gullikson had said ruefully in Boston a few months before Malmö. 'So many people are pulling them [tennis's superstars] so many different ways. You've just got to make it [playing Davis Cup] a priority.'

As he spoke the trophy itself sat sparkling nearby. The winning nation gets possession of the trophy for the following year, and the cup was making one of its final appearances in the US. Since April the cup's presence in the US had been a bittersweet one, as is often the case when the nation holding the cup is defeated in early rounds. Who wants to have on constant display a spectacular silver reminder that the winner's crown of laurel leaves embarrassingly has slipped down over one eye.

The cup, therefore, had spent much time during the year quietly packed away in the vault of the United States Tennis Association office outside New York City. Though it had been on hand, of course, for the US's first-round matches (and win) against Mexico in California, it had not made the trip to Prague for the quarter-finals. It had been on display briefly at the Atlanta (Georgia) sports SuperShow preceding the 1996 Olympics and at several ceremonies at the International Tennis Hall of Fame in Newport, Rhode Island. However, at the 14 days of the US Open it had been pulled out and displayed only once – and that at a private party, not where ordinary ticket-buying tennis fans could see it.

Gullikson's comments in Boston were at an occasion of particular historic resonance. Shreve, Crump & Low, the venerable Boston jewellers from whom the cup had been ordered back in 1900, was throwing a party to celebrate not only the reopening of a suburban branch store but to celebrate the firm's 200th anniversary. In fact, in honour of this special birthday, Shreve's was staging two special events: this Chestnut Hill store reopening and the exhibit *Trophies & Treasures* at the Bostonian Society, an elegant small museum in the brick building in south Boston that was once the Massachusetts State House.

For the Bostonian Society exhibit, Shreve's president Kevin Jenness and curator Catherine Zusy had pulled together some of the most famous pieces of silver which the store had sold through the years. The dozen or so pieces were a varied lot and included the commemorative vase presented to Massachusetts Senator Daniel Webster in 1835 by his grateful constituents; a trophy for the 1892 race of fishing boats from Gloucester to Boston; and a small engraved box presented to a Boston dentist who pioneered in the use of ether in surgery.

But at the reception preceding the exhibit's opening, two large sports trophies had been the stars. One was the Cy Young trophy, a large silver baseball balanced on crossed ebony baseball bats on loan from the Baseball Hall of Fame in Cooperstown, New York. It had originally been presented in 1908 to American (and Boston) baseball hero Denton T. (Cy) Young, the first pitcher to win more than 500 games. Since his death in 1955, the trophy had been the symbol of the Cy Young award, presented annually to the major leagues' best pitchers.

The other, of course, was the Davis Cup, which had added a tray (1920) and two tiers of plaques (1935 and 1969) since Shreve's sold the original bowl to young Dwight Davis. Alone in a large glass case at the end of the room, the cup looked magnificent in the soft low light from the room's chandeliers. Just steps away were double doors leading to a balcony overlooking the site of the 1770 Boston Massacre, which preceded the American Revolution. From this balcony the Declaration of Independence had been read to the citizens of Massachusetts. This building, said the society's president, 'exudes history from every brick and pore'.

This night, however, the ghosts of Revolutionary War heroes mingled with ghosts of more recent vintage, commented the society's director as she stood by the Davis Cup – ghosts with names like Norman Brookes, Bill Tilden, Henri Cochet, Fred Perry, René Lacoste and Arthur Ashe. Many who leaned forward with their wine glasses and hors d'oeuvres to peer through the protective glass at the engravings had never seen the trophy before.

'It's enormous,' said one.

'It's palatial – it has "presence",' said another.

One who had seen it many times before but who had come to study it again was John Sears, a tall Bostonian with his own connection to Davis Cups past. He was the grandson of the first US tennis champion, Richard Sears, and the great-great grandson of David Sears, on whose estate Richard Sears and his friends started the Longwood Cricket Club, site of the first Davis Cup competition.

Twenty-three members of the extended Sears family had been tennis champions, said John Sears (Bostonians know such things) but alas, there is no Sears name engraved on the cup. Richard Sears and second cousin Dr. James Dwight were champions a generation too early. Dr. Dwight, of course, had been as important as anyone in organising and hand-feeding the international competition during its tender early years. He had finally received his own silver Davis Cup miniature in 1909.

A week later the cup had been moved out to Shreve's remodelled store in Chestnut Hill, the Boston suburb in which the Longwood Cricket Club is now located. The original site at Longwood and Brookline Avenues had been sold, over a period of years beginning in 1908, to the Winsor School, a private girls school. The school uses the approximate site of those first Davis Cup matches as a sports field.

The cup sat at the front of the store, high on a console behind counters filled with pricey gold baubles and holding its own nicely, thank you, in a room filled with such things as Christofle silver and Bacarat crystal. Because the rectangle of counters kept its admirers at a distance, on this night there would be no peering at the engravings, no reading of this portable feast of tennis history carved in silver. Yet because it was up above eye level anyone who had a mind to, could see clearly, for once, the details around the bowl's bottom – the ridges and whorls bathed in light reflected upward from the tray.

Among the special guests on this occasion was Dwight F. Davis III, in town also to visit his son, Dwight F. Davis IV, a fourth generation Davis at Harvard. DFD III, one of the cup donor's 14 grandchildren, said that when he was eight or nine years old, he had asked his grandpa why he had given the Davis Cup anyway. 'Dwight,' he said his grandfather replied, 'I thought if men of different nations could get together and compete on the tennis court they would get along and the world would become a better place for it.'

Other speakers during the brief formal program were equally lofty. 'For us at Shreve's,' said the store's current president Kevin Jenness, 'the Davis Cup is really the Holy Grail.'

'Davis Cup is by far my favourite form of tennis,' said the evening's master of ceremonies, tennis writer and broadcaster Bud Collins. It was always 'a thrill', he said, to see the trophy, 'and I've never seen it look better'. From the speakers there were stories about Davis Cup dramas during the Cold War, about drinking beer rather than champagne from the cup when the Australians won, about the 1995 US victory in Moscow, about the qualities of patriotism and team consciousness that gave Davis Cup competition its unique atmosphere. Davis Cup competition was the place to look 'if you want to see genuine smiles on the faces of multi-millionaires', said Gullikson. 'Next year, we're going to win the Davis Cup back!' (Much applause.)

Also on hand was Stanyan Lupien, grandson of cup designer Rowland Rhodes. The two middle-aged men, Davis and Lupien, shook hands in front of the cup, the one on the left, Davis's grandson, of slight build, with sandy hair and glasses, and on the right, Rowland Rhodes' grandson, a ruddy, robust man with close-cropped white hair. Though his grandfather's role in the trophy's creation had long been part of family legend, Stan Lupien had never before seen this famous example of his grandfather's art. As for Rowland Rhodes and his employers, the Durgins, none lived to see the large sporting cup they produced reach international prominence. Rhodes died in 1903 at the age of 38. Both William B. Durgin and his son George died two years later.

Grail. Symbol of international goodwill. Elegant example of design and craftsmanship. Portable feast of tennis history. In Malmö the Davis Cup is playing all of these roles. Because the stadium is small (under 6000 seats) the cup is not down at courtside as it often is during Davis Cup competitions.

Instead, a special sturdy platform, covered with pleated black cloth, has been built for the cup at the top of a wide stair ramp, on the west side of the court, beneath the decorated Honorary Stand. Here sit the tennis federations' presidents, sponsors and special guests, including Sweden's Prime Minister Göran Persson and his family. (Sweden's King Carl Gustav, the great-grandson of famous tennis-playing King Gustav V, is not expected to attend.)

This is no fragile hot-house flower, this trophy. All during the three days of competition it has been remarkably accessible to tennis fans. They pull out spectacles and kneel down by the plaques and try to find a country, a year. They balance precariously on seats to get photos. Parents squeeze children forward for a better view and point out to them famous names from the sport's past.

They look down inside the bowl and see faint tracings of the words *International Lawn Tennis Challenge Trophy* around the rim. (The inside of the bowl is currently without its original gold wash, not re-applied during the most recent refurbishment.) If they know where to look on the outside of the bowl (behind the first 'e' in *Challenge*) they can find the engraved record of the first Davis Cup match in 1900. And if they look very, very hard, they may see, on the bowl's surface, a few tiny dings and dents – proof of a good life lived, like laugh lines on the face of a famous, ageing beauty.

Faithful guards Daniel and Annika patiently answer questions: yes, it is made of solid silver; yes, it is very heavy; yes, it will run out of room for names in three years. (After the 1996 final is engraved only one blank plaque – to be engraved top and bottom – will remain. This means a new, third tier for the base by 1999.)

The tennis, during the first two days of the final at Malmö, has been tough and balanced. It has set up the classic, the always desired, at least by impartial lovers of tennis if not by clapping, clomping patriotic partisans, Davis Cup *dénouement*: critical matches on the third day. Yet who could have predicted that this third day would turn out to be a Davis Cup record setter and one of the most remarkable days of tennis ever.

Back on day one, Friday, there had been the drama of Edberg down on the ground in pain with a twisted ankle. During the first set of the first match, Edberg was at the net, moving to his right when he appeared to just roll over on his ankle. The crowd groaned. The ankle was taped and Edberg was able to resume play but was no match for Pioline. France won 6-3, 6-4, 6-3.

In the second match of the first day the home crowd had erupted in cheers as Thomas Enqvist at last won Sweden's first set of the competition. And this, as it turned out, was prophetic for the rest of the match. Despite a tie-break in the third set, Enqvist overpowered France's Arnaud Boetsch, 6-4, 6-3, 7-6. The score was France 1, Sweden 1 going into the second day's doubles.

Skilled doubles veteran Guy Forget and Guillaume Raoux, the combination which had won Davis Cup matches against Denmark, Germany and Italy earlier in the year, took down Sweden's Jonas Bjorkman and Nicklas Kulti in four sets, 6-3, 1-6, 6-3, 6-3. The score stood at France 2, Sweden 1. The cheering, chanting French fans, with their bright red and blue wigs and tricolour painted faces, were ecstatic. They had flown in on chartered planes with tricolour mufflers around their necks to bang their drums and wave their flags.

Their battle cry – sung at the top of their lungs over and over and over again like some advertising jingle gone mad – was a song often heard at French sporting events, 'Ce soir, on vous met de feu ...' – 'Tonight, we put you in the fire ...' sung to a tune which sounded to American ears like 'The Beer Barrel Polka'.

Now, on this the final day, Sweden is in that feu (fire). It must win the first match between the two countries' number one players, Enqvist and Pioline. As for the second match, rumours float about town: Edberg will play. Edberg won't play.

In Lilla Torg, the small square of restored medieval buildings in Malmö's old section, Christmas shoppers mill about on this the first Sunday in December. They warm their hands over high braziers of coals and receive packets of sweets from the white-robed young women who are this year's candidates to be the town's mythical Christmas St. Lucia.

Earlier in the day a winter sun had been shining, its pale golden light flickering along the canals and down the streets of the city. And the sky was, for a time, not a muffled winter grey but crisp, clear blue – the blue of the Swedish flag. Perhaps an omen for the home team.

At 1.05 p.m. the Enqvist-Pioline match begins. Enqvist, ranked ninth in the world and Pioline, ranked 21st, have never before played each other. The big, 22-year-old Enqvist, built like the young Dwight Davis, splays shots out much like Davis used to do when his game was not on. Enqvist loses the first set 3-6 and drives an easy forehand into the net to lose a second set tie-break. In the third set, after a dramatic third game in which the score is deuce more than ten times, Enqvist begins to pull even with now accurate, sizzling down-the-line backhands.

The Swedish crowd, sedate the first two days compared to the exuberant French, has come alive. 'Too-muss, too-muss,' the fans chant over and over to encourage the struggling Enqvist. Some, with painted blue and yellow faces, wear Viking helmets with long, wicked horns.

Enqvist wins the third set 6-4 and breaks Pioline's serve to win the following set as well. His ecstatic fellow Swedes jump to their feet. The score is now two sets all. The late afternoon sky is dark beyond the thin ribbon of windows high across the north end of the building as the fifth set begins.

Pioline is far from out. In Davis Cup, unlike in normal tournament play, captains may coach during matches. Yannick Noah, dreadlocks swinging in intensity, leans forward in his chair next to the umpire stand and shouts encouragement to his tall, gangly player. Pioline takes the lead 5-3 and is ready to serve for the match and the cup. Possibly the condition of Edberg's ankle is moot.

But Enqvist holds on. Capitalising on Pioline errors he breaks Pioline's serve, to pull up to 5-4. The grandstands rock as shouts and stamping from the excited Swedish crowd rattle off the arena's yellow metal walls. Annika, the guard, frequently reaches forward to steady the cup until the rumble of stamping subsides.

The two powerful top-spin specialists continue to trade shots from the back of the court, working their way to 6 games all. In Davis Cup competition there is no tie-break in the fifth set of a match. The winner must win the old fashioned way – by two games. The two play on. With the score 7-7, Pioline loses his serve with a double fault. French fans groan. Enqvist goes ahead to win the match 9-7. The final score is 3-6, 6-7 (10-8), 6-4, 6-4, 9-7. Sweden has tied the competition at 2-2. For the 14th time in Davis Cup history, the champion nation will be decided in the fifth match.

It is then announced officially – Edberg will not play. Nicklas Kulti, who had played doubles for Sweden the previous day, will substitute in the match against France's Arnaud Boetsch. Outside it is dinner time in snug Swedish homes, but here in the Malmö Mässan there is still more remarkable tennis to be played.

Four times before Kulti, 25, and Boetsch, 27, have played and Boetsch has won three of these encounters. However, this Plexipave surface is better suited to Kulti's power game. Kulti, who earlier in his career won three ATP Tour events, has won only one singles match since June and is ranked 65th in the world. On this night, however, he is clearly rising to the occasion, taking the lead 2-1 at the end of three sets.

On and on they battle. And then it happens. With Boetsch leading 5-3 in the fourth set tie-break, Kulti pulls up lame with a cramp. A cramp! The crowd watches in shared agony as he hobbles to the sidelines, trying to walk it off.

There can be no time-out. In Davis Cup, play may be stopped only for injuries, and a cramp is not technically considered an injury but rather a function of conditioning. After the crowd buys him a little extra time with extended cheering, Kulti stoically continues. In fact, he somehow wins two more points before Boetsch at last takes the tie-break making it two sets all. Again, on this amazing day, a match is going into five sets.

Swedish coach Carl-Axel Hageskog, who happens to have been the team trainer during Sweden's 1994 cup victory, goes to work on Kulti's leg when the players rest briefly as they change ends. Meanwhile, in the French camp on the other side of the umpire's stand, Noah is reminding Boetsch that cramps come and go and that Kulti will get better.

And he does. Buoyed by cheers from the Swedish fans – Edberg along with the rest of the Swedish bench joins in the deafening chants of 'Kul-ti, Kul-ti' – the Swede powers his way to a miraculous 7-6 lead in the fifth set. Now, with the score at 0-40, all Kulti needs is one more point to claim the set, the match – and the cup.

But it is not to be. Boetsch manages to save his serve and pull even at 7-all. Chefs and waitresses from the hospitality areas elsewhere in the building have come up onto the stairways to watch. Kulti's leg is stiff as he walks back to the baseline.

Then the cramp strikes again. Kulti's face contorts in pain and Noah, ever the sportsman, jumps up to quiet the cheering French crowd in the stands behind him. Kulti, almost totally incapacitated now, soldiers on. It's 9-8 France and on his last serve Kulti can hardly toss the ball in the air.

Boetsch puts him out of his misery and takes the final point to win 10-8. The clock reads 22.58 (10.58 p.m.) – nearly ten hours from when the day's matches began. France has won the Davis Cup for the eighth time. And incredible as it seems, for the first time in Davis Cup history, the winner of the cup has been determined in the fifth set of the fifth and final match.

The French players and the French fans are delirious. Both teams come out onto the court and Yannick Noah, understanding the poignancy of Sweden's loss on this day that was to be Edberg's 'party', hoists the Swedish star onto his shoulders and jogs about on the court in tribute. The audience cheers even more wildly.

The net comes down and the heavy trophy is carried out to the centre of the court. One of the guards removes his beret and uses it to quickly wipe away fingerprints on the bowl's rim. Presentations, pictures, and then the *Marseillaises*.

Allons enfants de la patrie,
Le jour de gloire est arrivé

sings the French team, heads back, mouths ecstatically wide open, as they stand in a line behind the large trophy clutching their 12-inch high individual replicas. A day of glory, indeed.

A traditional part of Davis Cup since the first competition in Boston in 1900 has been the final banquet for the two teams. Tonight the event is in the 16th-century town hall of Malmö. Because of the marathon day of tennis, those attending do not sit down at the long festive tables in the large Knut Banqueting Chamber until after midnight.

Candles in tall silver candelabra flicker in the mirrors at one end of the high-ceilinged room. Heavy gold damask drapes hang from the high arched windows which look out over *Stortorget*, the central square of Malmö's old town. There are introductions of officials at the head table and many *Skoals!* as glasses are raised high. There is a saying, says one speaker, that 'Davis Cup turns boys into men. I think that is very true today'.

Speakers praise the event as being the most dramatic final in Davis Cup history. Newspaper reports in coming days will agree. 'One of the most tensely emotional sporting events in my experience,' David Miller will write in *The Times* (London). Simon O'Hagan, in the *Independent*, will call it 'unarguably the greatest final in the competition's long and illustrious history' and will write about 'the unique quality of Davis Cup tennis – the sort of tension, and scope for heroism that as any Ryder Cup golfer will tell you only comes when individuals are doing it for a team'.

In the Malmö banquet hall, two long tables in the centre of the room, reserved for the two teams, have remained empty. Suddenly, at 1.24 a.m., side-doors burst open and in comes the Swedish team to great applause. Thirty minutes later the French team arrives. In jackets and ties now, and accompanied by wives and girlfriends, they all look amazingly fresh and rested.

Yannick Noah, who has been through all of this before not only as victorious captain in 1991 but as a member of the runner-up French team in 1982, goes to the microphone. 'What I love about Davis Cup is it is not about contracts, schedules and business,' he says. 'This tradition is much bigger than dollars.'

An hour or so earlier at the post-match press conference, he had expanded on the team aspect of the competition. Though it takes character, he said, to win grand slam tournaments, 'what you do in Davis Cup is sacrifice for others ... that's why the Davis Cup is great'. And if that sacrifice means giving up four money-winning weeks on the circuit, and if some of the world's top players don't want to do that, 'too bad'. 'This team makes my life special,' he added. 'They are the ones sweating and bleeding.'

At the banquet more gifts are presented, including a rocking chair for Edberg, who tries it out, twiddling his thumbs. Much laughter. The players exchange gifts. Boetsch and Kulti – the winner and his tenacious opponent who hours earlier had been doing that sweating and bleeding – stand and shake hands and talk together briefly.

Meanwhile, the silver trophy which Dwight Davis donated nearly 100 years earlier to foster just such moments as this, sits alone in an alcove at the far end of the room. Flanking it on either side are massive *faux* marble pillars. Not needed in this room tonight are its faithful guards Annika and Daniel.

Nobody here is going to steal the trophy. After all, the people in this room, like the thousands of players, captains, coaches, trainers and off-court dreamers who have fought to win the Davis Cup ever since 1900, know that there would be no fun in getting it that way.

EPILOGUE

I n October 1996, two months before the final at Malmö, a 92-year-old Frenchman died in St. Jean de Luz, France. René Lacoste was the oldest surviving player to have played in a Davis Cup final. He had been one of the famed Four Musketeers who had first won the cup for France in 1927, though later generations would know him primarily for the crocodile-emblazoned sportswear which his company marketed (his tennis nickname was 'the crocodile'). He and Dwight Davis were acquaintances.

In December 1996, after winning the cup in Sweden, the French team brought the trophy back to Paris for a reception at the Elysée Palace hosted by French President Jacques Chirac. Later there was a parade in two open cars down the Champs Elysées packed with thousands of fans, many of whom had watched nearly ten hours of television coverage of the spectacular Sunday final two days earlier.

And after that, in a supremely Gallic gesture, the team drove to the Roland Garros Tennis Stadium and placed, at the foot of a statue of René Lacoste, Dwight Davis's silver cup.

Notes

CHAPTER 1 Beginnings

Page 9   *Muddy River*: maps, box 1900, Boston Public Library.

Twenty-six trains: *Brookline Chronicle*, 11 August 1900.

Page 10   *sixth largest*: Ranking ahead of St. Louis in the 1880 census were New York, Philadelphia, Brooklyn, Chicago and Boston. The US census of 1870 ranked St. Louis as fourth largest, but newspapers, later historians – and an incensed Chicago – found 1870 population figures suspect (James Neal Primm, *Lion of the Valley, St. Louis, Missouri*, 287-288).

British Consul: Davison Obear, *Sixty Years of Tennis In St. Louis, 1881-1941*, 4.

from Brookline: *Souvenir of the Semi-Centennial Anniversary of the Founding of the House of Saml C. Davis & Co.*, 1.

'spare harnesses and parts': Ware, *Emigrant's Guide To California*, as quote by Dan Murphy and Mary L. Van Camp, ed., in *Oregon Trail, Voyage of Discovery*, 7.

Samuel C. Davis & Co.: *Souvenir ...*, 1-4.

Page 11   *sloshed over the side guards*: Francis Parkman, *Oregon Trail*, 1; also *Official State Manual for Missouri 1947-1948*, 20-21; Federal Writers Project, *Missouri*, 245.

three sons: 1850 Census for St. Louis County, Missouri, 3rd Ward, sheet 297. No Charles is listed in the household in the 1860 census and no mention of a Charles has been found in family records.

fashionable new street: Richard Allen Rosen, 'Rethinking the Row House: The Development of Lucas Place, 1850-1865', *Gateway Heritage*, Summer 1992, 20-23.

Washington University: Donn Walter Hayes, 'History of Smith Academy of Washington University' (Ph.D. dissertation, Washington University, 1950), 2, 19; 'Washington University'; Walter B. Stevens, *History of St. Louis*, 50-52; Ralph E. Morrow, *Washington University in St. Louis: A History*, 3.

'collection of fossils': John T. Davis, 'Journal May-July 1862', Journey by Riverboat to Fort Benton', 14 May, Accession No. 82-0017, Missouri Historical Society, St. Louis.

buffalo: ibid., 22 July.

'the states': ibid., 27 July.

moved back East: *Souvenir ...*, 4.

Page 12   *admitted to the bar, early death*: Harvard Law School Library Archives, Cambridge, Massachusetts; Boston City Directory, 1868, 1869, 1870.

Filley boys: Henry R. Stiles, *The History and Genealogies of Ancient Windsor, Connecticut*, Connecticut Historical Society, Hartford, Connecticut.

'Great West': Hayes, 'History of Smith Academy', 144, quoting resolution adopted upon the death of James Smith in 1877.

stove and tinware: Primm, *Lion of the Valley*, 243; Charles H. Cornwell, *St. Louis Mayors, Brief Biographies*, as quoted by Winter, *Civil War in St. Louis*, 119; *substantial wealth*: Primm, *Lion of the Valley*, 236.

Benton circle: Primm, *Lion of the Valley*, 242; *one of the founders*, 279; Ernest Kirschten, *Catfish and Crystal*, 460.

mayor reluctantly: Charles Van Ravenswaay, *St. Louis: An Informal History of the City and Its People*, 423; *aversion to ... gloves*, 447.

Missouri went into convulsions: Primm, *Lion of the Valley*, 239-286.

Page 13   *no slaves were sold*: Primm, *Lion of the Valley*, 245; Van Ravenswaay, *Informal History*, 475.

part of ... Post-Dispatch: Kirschten, *Catfish and Crystal*, 270, 281-82.

exposed and captured: Harry Langenberg (who got the story from his mother and grandmother, one of the Filley daughters), interview with author.

Committee of Safety, shooting melee: Primm, *Lion of the Valley*, 248-250; Charles M. Harvey,

'Missouri from 1849 to 1861', *Missouri Historical Review,* October 1907, 31-34; Captain George S. Grover, 'Civil War in Missouri', *Missouri Historical Review,* October 1913, 12; Walter B. Stevens, 'Lincoln and Missouri', *Missouri Historical Review,* January 1916, 74-75.

Page 14 *Southern sympathizers:* Primm, *Lion of the Valley,* 259-262.

no business telling churches: Abraham Lincoln to General S. R. Curtis, 2 January 1863, *Complete Works of Abraham Lincoln* VIII, 168-170.

'I will not have control': Lincoln to O. D. Filley, 22 December 1863, *Complete Works of Abraham Lincoln* IX, 269-271; Lincoln to Secretary of War E. M. Stanton, 11 February 1864, *Complete Works of Abraham Lincoln* X, 4-5; Howard K. Beale, ed. *The Diary of Edward Bates 1859-1866,* 323.

abolished slavery: Primm, *Lion of the Valley,* 274-276.

five border slave states: The other four were Kentucky, Maryland, Delaware and the new state of West Virginia.

'most imposing': Souvenir ..., 7-13; *Pictorial Saint Louis,* 54; Missouri Historical Society, *Glimpses* IX, 4, 126; *SL Globe Democrat,* 28 December 1949; Primm, *Lion of the Valley,* 352-353. The building was demolished in the early 1950s.

Page 15 *'beer would never do':* Primm, *Lion of the Valley,* 365, indirectly quoting Harry Turner.

more than $1 million: unidentified clipping [14 April 1894], Necrology Scrapbook, vol. II-C, Missouri Historical Society.

CHAPTER 2 'O Queen of Schools'

Page 17 *clock:* Donn Walter Hayes, 'History of Smith Academy of Washington University' (Ph.D. dissertation, Washington University, 1950), 56, photo following 237; *350 boys:* 86.

'sufficient knowledge', 'competent ladies': Smith Academy Catalog 1889-1890, 21-22, Washington University Archives, St. Louis.

seven years here: Smith Academy Catalogs 1888-1889 to 1894-1895; Smith Academy Record Book 1885-1890, 128.

Smith, donor of funds: Hayes, 'History of Smith Academy', 2, 5, 144.

William Greenleaf Eliot: ibid., 192; James Neal Primm, *Lion of the Valley,* 522.

Page 18 *'upon the morning grass':* Hayes, 'History of Smith Academy,' 16, 226-228. A typewritten copy of the poem was found pasted into the cover of an old Smith Academy catalogue by Ph.D. candidate Hayes. 'At Graduation – 1905' has been published in *The Complete Poems and Plays of T. S. Eliot* (London: Faber & Faber, 1969), 592.

poet revisited: Alzina Stone Dale, *T. S. Eliot, The Philosopher Poet,*26.

family motto: Hayes, 'History of Smith Academy,' 146; Peter Ackroyd, *T. S. Eliot, A Life,* 15.

Eliot's laws: Lyndall Gordon, *Eliot's Early Years,* 8.

shakier in arithmetic: Smith Academy Grade Book 1878-1890, Washington University Archives.

Macaulay, Cicero: Smith Academy Catalog 1894-1895, 22-31.

when reciting: Hayes, 'History of Smith Academy', 72.

'servant may be waiting': ibid., 33.

'any university examinations': Charles Paine Curd, *The History and Work of Smith Academy,* 1897, 7, Washington University Archives.

Page 19 *tuition:* Smith Academy Catalog 1894-1895, 14.

dates on streetcars: Helen Davis Hermes, interview with author.

silver spoon: Dr. Terry (?) to Charles Van Ravenswaay, 1951, CVR File, Missouri Historical Society, St. Louis.

move the nation's capital: Primm, *Lion of the Valley,* 289.

rival Chicago: Encyclopaedia Britannica, 11th ed., s.v. 'St. Louis'.

population: ibid.; Primm, *Lion of the Valley,* 280, 345.

'subterranean activity': Harper's New Monthly Magazine, March 1884, 497.

'blighting, noxious': Charles Savage, *Architecture of the Private Streets of St. Louis,* quoted in Julius K. Hunter, *Westmoreland and Portland Places,* 20.

Page 20 *1,400-acre*: Caroline Loughlin and Catherine Anderson, *Forest Park*, 11.

royal road: Primm, *Lion of the Valley*, 402.

largest chunk: Map of Westmoreland and Portland Place Residents, n.d., Isaac H. Lionberger Papers, box 3, folder 2, Missouri Historical Society; Hunter, *Westmoreland and Portland Places*, (16), 33.

'not left to chance': Hunter, *Westmoreland and Portland Places*, 34.

area's first house: ibid., 187.

palazzo-style residence: ibid., 102-103, 187-188; *most expensive house, Olmsted... design*: 187; Leon Strauss (current owner), interview with author.

Page 21 *over to his sons*: Lee Hall, *Olmsted's America*, 237, 240-241.

into a coma, Bright's disease: unidentified clippings [13 April, 14 April 1894], Necrology Scrapbook vol. II-C, Missouri Historical Society, St. Louis.

funeral: unidentified clipping, [16 April 1894], Necrology Scrapbook.

'uncommon degree': Minutes of special meeting, St. Louis Club, 13 April 1894, Missouri Historical Society.

Page 22 *'spiritual purity'*: unidentified clipping, Necrology Scrapbook.

richest man in the state: unidentified clippings [13 April, 14 April 1894], Necrology Scrapbook.

will was filed: unidentified clipping, Necrology Scrapbook.

other widows: Hunter, *Westmoreland and Portland Places*, 82.

son Dwight's age: Smith Academy Catalog 1894-1895, 16.

kept busy: Hunter, *Westmoreland and Portland Places*, 82.

Page 23 *'window' in Sarah's tent*: Helen McKay Steele et al., *Indianapolis Woman's Club 1875-1940*, 41.

freshman class: Washington University Catalog 1895-1896, 26.

meeting Boston sister-in-law: North Shore Blue Books 1896, 1898; *Magnolia Leaves*, vol. IV, no. 2, July 1884, Essex Institute, Salem, Massachusetts.

for a cruise: Harry Langenberg, interview with author.

the Oceanside: Joseph E. Garland, *Boston's Gold Coast, The North Shore 1890-1929*, 41-43, 47.

Appletons in London: Joseph Dwight (nephew of Dr. James Dwight) to Fred A. Wilson, Nahant, n.d., Library, International Tennis Hall of Fame, Newport, RI; George E. Alexander, *Lawn Tennis: Its Founders & Its Early Days*, 53-60; Richard D. Sears, 'Lawn Tennis In America', in *Tennis, Lawn Tennis, Rackets, Fives* (The Badminton Library of Sports and Pastimes), 315-316; Lance Tingay and George Alexander, 'Roots: 1874-1918', in *Bud Collins' Modern Encyclopedia of Tennis*, Bud Collins and Zander Hollander, ed., 1-9.

Others claimed: And there are even more contenders for the title of first game in the US. Tennis historian George Alexander cites a documented incident of an Army officer's wife playing tennis at Camp Apache in Arizona Territory in October 1874 with a set purchased in May 1874 in Canada (Alexander, *Lawn Tennis*, 56-57; Tingay and Alexander, *Bud Collins' Modern Encyclopedia of Tennis*, 9).

Page 24 *'fog has gone'*: Joseph E. Garland, *Boston's Gold Coast*.

first took up the game: 'U.S.L.T.A Officers Nominated,' *American Lawn Tennis*, 15 January 1923, 600; S. Wallis Merrihew, 'Dwight Filley Davis', *American Lawn Tennis*, February 1946. In the 1946 obituary of Davis, longtime *ALT* editor Merrihew says he corresponded with DFD at the time of the founding (resuscitation actually) of *American Lawn Tennis* in 1907, asking about origins of the Davis Cup and, presumably, about DFD's tennis beginnings.

courts were laid out: Membership Book 1893-1894, Essex County Club, Manchester, Massachusetts; George C. Caner Jr., *History of the Essex County Club 1893-1993*, 32-33, 162, 164 quoting 1894 *Wright & Ditson Official Lawn Tennis Guide*; Garland, *Boston's Gold Coast*, 121.

1895 he entered: New York Evening Sun, 23 August 1898; Frank V. Phelps, 'Dwight Davis Tennis Tournament Record', October 1996, mms.

Hotel Wentworth: J. Parmly Paret, 'A Summer With the Tennis Experts', *Outing*, August 1898, 487-489.

50 of the 82 entries: NY Times, 21 August 1895; '*swarm*': NY Times, 20 August 1895.

win one set: Phelps, 'Davis – Tournament Record'; 'Fifteenth USLTA Men's Singles Championships ... 1895' (drawsheet), reprinted in William Talbert and Pete Axthelm, *Tennis Observed: The USLTA Men's Singles Championships 1881-1966*, 70.

Joe Wear: 1895 drawsheet, Talbert and Axthelm, *Tennis Observed*, 70; Smith Academy catalogs 1889-1890, 17-18; 1894-1895, 53, Washington University Archives.

Page 25 *'got over his 'grouch''*: Lark, 15 July 1896, clippings from Paret Scrapbook vol. IV, William M. Fischer Lawn Tennis Collection, St. John's University, Jamaica, New York.

US Nationals in 1896: Phelps, Davis Tournament Record; 1896 drawsheet, Talbert and Axthelm, *Tennis Observed*, 71; NY Times. 20 August 1896.

'look at his hair': *The Harvard (Class) Album -1899*, 9, Harvard University Archives, Cambridge, Massachusetts.

St. Mark's: Questionnaire for Harvard class report, n.d. HUD 300.505 box 595, Harvard University Archives.

'dying century': 'Class History', *The Harvard (Class) Album – 1900*, 5.

CHAPTER 3 A Serve is Born

Page 26 *back at his feet*: Holcombe Ward, 'The American Twist Service', *Fifty Years of Lawn Tennis in the United States*, 83-86.

Davis observed: ibid.; Arthur S. Pier in 'Some Tennis Champions – Deciding Moments in their Great Matches', *American Magazine*, August 1910, 470, also gives Davis as well as Ward credit for developing the new serve.

'reverse twist': J. Parmly Paret, 'A New Era in Lawn Tennis', *Saturday Evening Post*, 4 November 1899, 367; Ward, 'The American Twist Service,' 83. In later years this 'reverse twist' would be called a slice. The serve Ward was developing, with Davis's help, would be known, of course, as the American twist.

Paret analyzed: Paret, 'A New Era in Lawn Tennis', 366-368; 'Era of the Harvard Group', *American Lawn Tennis*, January 1951, 12.

'constant hesitation': Paret, 'Era of the Harvard Group', 12.

Page 27 *'brutal sport'*: Lyndall Gordon, *Eliot's Early Years*, 21.

'languish and die', 'fight battles': ibid.

clubs: Dwight F. Davis, Class of 1900 Sec. Files HUD 300.505 box 617, Harvard University Archives, Cambridge, Massachusetts.

'Institute-Pudding ... crowd: Kim Townsend, *Manhood at Harvard*, 94, and also for discussion of the intricacies of waiting and final clubs.

grades horrible: Dwight F. Davis student record, UAIII 15.75.12, Harvard University Archives.

recommendations: C. P Curd and W. W. Gale to Harvard, [June] 1895, Dwight F. Davis student folder, UAIII 15.88.10, Harvard University Archives.

Page 28 *'rich in tennis courts'*: *Official Lawn Tennis Bulletin*, 22 August 1894, 77.

790 men: P. E. Presbrey, 'Secretary's Report For 1901', *Lawn Tennis*, February-March 1902, 111.

'tennis honors': Harper's Weekly, 27 August 1898, 854.

'two golden ages': Paret, 'Era of the Harvard Group', 12.

cold oatmeal: John M. Barnaby II, *The 'H' Book of Harvard Athletics*, vol. II, Geoffrey H. Movius, ed., 733.

'game was played': NY Times, 5 August 1895.

perched in trees: J. Parmly Paret, 'A Summer With The Tennis Experts', *Outing*, August 1898, 485.

Page 29 *shoulder ... wrist*: for instance, J. Parmly Paret, 'Recent American Development of Lawn-Tennis', Harper's Weekly, 24 April 1897, 425. Ward's scrapbooks are in the archives of the Seabright Lawn Tennis and Cricket Club, Rumson, New Jersey.

'fine points': NY Times, 5 August 1895, 3.

'not ... permitted to enter': 'The National Tennis Championship', Harper's Weekly, 27 August 1898, 854.

'*hitch well*': *NY Evening Sun,* 23 August 1898.

Page 30   '*lawn tennis experts*': as quoted in James West Davidson and Mark Hamilton Lytle, *After The Fact*, 2nd ed. (NY: Knopf, 1986), 249.

'*brilliant*' ... *match*: *NY Sun,* 23 August 1898.

Page 31   *muttering; 'six of the most perfect*': Malcolm D. Whitman, 'Net Play: A Determining Factor', *Fifty Years of Lawn Tennis in the United States,* 74.

younger player pressed: *NY Journal,* 24 August 1898.

'*inexcusable errors*': Holcombe Ward, 'American Methods,' *Lawn Tennis At Home and Abroad,* A. W. Myers, ed., 208.

'*very young player*': unidentified clipping, [24 August 1898?], J. Parmly Paret Scrapbook (?) (1894-1901), William M. Fischer Lawn Tennis Collection, St. John's University, Jamaica, New York.

'*a new star*': *NY Journal,* 24 August 1898.

'*disastrous end*': *NY Sun,* 6 October 1898.

Page 32   *injured his foot*: *American Lawn Tennis,* 13 October 1898, 277.

CHAPTER 4   The 'Ould Mug' Spawns a Cup

Page 33   '*famous colt team*': undated clipping from *Brooklyn Eagle* [summer 1899], Paret Scrapbook, William M. Fischer Lawn Tennis Collection, St. John's University, Jamaica, New York.

hours drilling: J. Parmly Paret, *Lawn Tennis & Croquet,* 7 November 1900, 430.

Page 34   '*necessarily weak return*': Holcombe Ward, 'The Theory of the Modern Game of Doubles', *The Book of Sport,* vol. II, William Patten, ed., 301-308.

'*conquer these moods*': *Golf and Lawn Tennis,* 1 March 1900, 37.

getting his Dwights mixed up: *Golf and Lawn Tennis,* 15 June 1900, 250.

'*Harvard Cyclone*': *Brooklyn Eagle,* 22 October 1899.

'*vicious pleasure*': John M. Barnaby II, *The 'H' Book of Harvard Athletics,* vol. II Geoffrey H. Movius, ed., 740.

Page 35   *just 56*: Robert Minton, *One Hundred Years of Longwood,* 14; *Wright & Ditson Official Lawn Tennis Guide, 1899.*

headed for California: Dwight F. Davis, 'The Establishment of an International Trophy', *Fifty Years of Lawn Tennis in the United States,* 69.

first all-professional baseball: Geoffrey C. Ward and Ken Burns, *Baseball: An Illustrated History* (NY: Knopf, 1994), 21-23.

more matches: *American Lawn Tennis,* reprinted in *Lawn Tennis,* 6 December 1899, 435.

avidly following: Davis, 'The Establishment ...', 70.

'*fluke, foul and fizzle*': Jerome Brooks, *The $30,000,000 Cup,* 134.

Columbia ... *launched*: *NY Times,* 11 June 1899.

Page 36   '*Sir Tea*'; '*ould mug*': Brooks, *$30,000,000 Cup,* 153.

festivities for Admiral Dewey: ibid. 153.

'*demoralize sport*': ibid. 145.

Page 37   '*two and two together*'; *far-reaching consequences*: Davis, 'The Establishment ...', 70; *Official Bulletin USLTA,* April 1927, 10. S. Wallis Merrihew corresponded with Davis to get information about the origins of the cup for volume 1, number 1 of his *American Lawn Tennis,* 15 April 1907.

among the travelling party: Elizabeth Wright Strelinger (Beals Wright's daughter, George Wright's granddaughter), interview with author.

'*even to the bowlers*': *NY Times,* 30 July 1899, 15.

confidentially: Davis, 'The Establishment ...', 70.

Championship of America: A self-proclaimed championship. The first recognised USA championship was held at Newport in 1881.

new overhand serve: 'The Game Is Brought To America', *Fifty Years of Lawn Tennis in the United States,* 20.

'*propriety of paying*': A. Wallis Myers, *The Complete Lawn Tennis Player,* 316-317.

Page 38 *three had come*: 'Former Visits of Foreign Players', *Official Souvenir Programme, International Lawn Tennis Championships* 1902, Holcombe Ward Papers, Seabright Lawn Tennis and Cricket Club, Rumson, New Jersey; official draw sheet, 'Seventeenth USLTA Men's Single Championships, The Casino, Newport, R.I., 1897'.

mystery donor: NY Times, 10 February 1900.

Dr. Dwight ... sent a letter: A. Wallis Myers, *The Complete Lawn Tennis Player*, 318.

Page 39 *'blue ribbon trophy'*: *Boston Herald*, 10 February 1900.

formal acceptance: *NY Times*, 22 February 1900; *Golf and Lawn Tennis*, 1 March 1900.

friend Richard Olney: *NY Times*, 5 February 1923; USLTA *Bulletin*, April 1927.

suggested rules: *Boston Herald*, 10 February 1900; *Golf and Lawn Tennis*, 25 April 1900, 200; *Lawn Tennis and Croquet*, 23 May 1900, 74-75.

Page 40 *shortened ... to 'Davis Cup'*: 'On the Tennis Courts', *NY Tribune Illustrated Supplement*, Spring 1900.

CHAPTER 5 Shaping the Cup

Page 41 *eagle, building, awnings*: *Selling Quality Jewels Since 1800: A History of Shreve, Crump & Low Co.*, 25-26; site visit.

trace its history: *Selling Quality Jewels*, 3-21; miscellaneous documents, Shreve Archives, Boston.

Longwood Bowl: Robert Minton, *One Hundred Years of Longwood*, 11.

winter or spring of 1900: Catherine Zusy, an independent researcher and exhibit curator, has been most helpful in confirming details about the trophy. She also has been able to find no order books for this period for Shreve, Crump & Low or Durgin giving the price of the bowl and exactly when it was ordered.

Page 42 *'moonbeam-coloured'*: *World Book Encyclopedia* (surprisingly enough pushed to unusual lyricism by the metal), s.v. 'silver'.

Durgin, the man: 'William B. Durgin Co.: Half Century of Business Success', *Concord Evening Monitor*, 1 October 1904; genealogy department, Vital Records, New Hampshire Health and Human Services, Concord. Many clippings about the Durgin Co. were generously shared by Ann Rolfe who has been researching the company for many years.

Newell Harding: Charles H. Carpenter Jr., *Gorham Silver 1831-1981*, 29; letter from R. T. Supple, 20 November 1921, Durgin Scrapbook 1921-1931, catalogue number 671, D959sc, New Hampshire Historical Society, Concord. Scrapbook includes clippings of interviews with early Durgin employees.

$200: William J. Green to John B. Abbott (both later Durgin presidents), n.d., Concord Public Library Historical Materials Collection, box 15:1-7, at New Hampshire Historical Society, manuscript department, Concord; R. T. Supple letter, 20 November 1921, Durgin Scrapbook, New Hampshire Historical Society.

bustling town, not ...thumping: James O. Lyford, ed. *History of Concord New Hampshire*, 626-631, 637.

first ... small shop: *Concord Daily Monitor*, 29 June 1875.

bought their tools: *Hands That Built New Hampshire: The Story of Granite State Craftsmen, Past and Present*, 144.

Gorham ...drop press: Carpenter, *Gorham Silver*, 48.

Page 43 *bar of silver over his shoulder*: Charles Tidd to John F. Reilly, 28 October 1943, Concord Public Library Historical Materials Collection, box 15:1-7, at New Hampshire Historical Society.

'good husky man': *Concord Monitor-Patriot*, 23 June 1925, interview with John B. Abbott.

'stickler': Typescript in Concord Public Library Historical Materials Collection, box 15:1-7, at New Hampshire Historical Society, n.d. [1926?] possibly copy of newspaper article.

new ... brick building: photographs, New Hampshire Historical Society (originally Perry Collection 6, 20, 32); *Concord Daily Monitor*, 29 June 1875.

company's 18 ... workmen: *Concord Daily Monitor*, 29 June 1875.

Page 44 *paid the minister*: *Concord Patriot*, 20 September 1923, Durgin Scrapbook, New Hampshire Historical Society.

shrewd, best of reputations: R. G. Dun & Co., New Hampshire, vol. 14, p. 110, 218, 352. Collection, Baker Library Harvard University Graduate School of Business Administration, Boston.

turned down ... order: *Concord Evening Patriot*, 18 October 1921; *New Hampshire Labor Review*, July 1927 ('William B. Durgin Co.', vertical file, Concord Room, Concord Public Library), though apparently plated silver from other manufacturers was carried in the ground floor sales room in the Durgin building in the 1870s (*Concord Daily Monitor*, 29 June 1875).

Durgin line: Unidentified newspaper clippings and interview with William Green in 'Granite Chips' column in *Concord Evening Monitor & New Hampshire Patriot* [1926?], 'Durgin Co.', vertical file, Concord Public Library; *William B. Durgin, Artisan in Sterling Silver*, collection 739 D959, New Hampshire Historical Society.

gold rings: *Concord Daily Monitor*, 29 June 1875.

souvenir spoons: *Concord Evening Patriot*, 3 August 1921.

iron pot: Green interview in 'Granite Chips'.

curious residents: ibid.; M. Craigue to John F. Reilly, 19 July 1943, Concord Public Library Historical Materials Collection, box 15:1-7, at New Hampshire Historical Society.

parade: Lyford, ed., *History of Concord*, 1135-1140.

60 men: *Concord Monitor*, 19 September 1885, Judge Elwin L. Page notes, Concord Public Library Historical Materials Collection, box 15:1-7, at New Hampshire Historical Society.

racing down the stairs, pick his teeth: Ed Sanders to John F. Reilly, 30 May 1943, 14 April 1951, Concord Public Library Historical Materials Collection, box 15:1-7, at New Hampshire Historical Society.

Page 45 *health, son George*: Dun Reports, vol. 14, 218, 352; George Durgin obituary, *Concord Evening Monitor*, 29 May 1905.

rest of the country: Dun Reports, vol. 14, 352; Watson Tinker to John F. Reilly. 12 May 1944, Concord Public Library Historical Materials Collection, box 15:1-7, at New Hampshire Historical Society.

English influence, stub files: Mildred Craigue (daughter of Henry Craigue) to John F. Reilly, 19 July 1943, Concord Public Library Historical Materials Collection, box 15:1-7, at New Hampshire Historical Society.

preferred to 'factory': 'Granite Chips' newspaper column, 21 July 1927, Durgin Scrapbook, New Hampshire Historical Society.

cricket team: unidentified clipping, 22 August 1921, Durgin Scrapbook, New Hampshire Historical Society.

sailed for England: *Concord Monitor*, 3 June 1887 (Judge Page notes).

Rowland Rhodes: geneology department, Vital Records, New Hampshire Health and Human Services, Concord.

Madonna and Child: Most details about Rhodes' life are from 'Extracts from the Life of Rowland Rhodes', a manuscript prepared by his widow Helen (or Ellen) W. Stanyan Rhodes, dated 3 June 1917, accession number 1977-17 (M), 1-2.55 misc 19B-38, New Hampshire Historical Society.

Victoria medal: medal and documentation, Stanyan Lupien (grandson of Rowland Rhodes), interview with author.

Page 46 *printed announcement*: accession number 1977-17 [M], 1-2.55 misc 19B-38, New Hampshire Historical Society.

'get in out of the wet': Helen Rhodes, 'Extracts from the Life ...'

Page 47 *married*: marriage certificate, Vital Records, New Hampshire Health and Human Services.

Cy Prime: The piece, now in the family's collection, was included in the 1939 exhibit 'New England Genre,' covering the period 1776-1900, at the Fogg Art Museum, Harvard University. 'Genre art depicts the ordinary art of ordinary people', explained the exhibit catalog, and for this artists were selected who 'embodied the spirit of New England'.

design for the new sporting trophy: The drawing is in the collection of the International Tennis Hall of Fame, Newport, Rhode Island. The finished weight of the bowl is 217 ounces, without the base (S. Wallis Merrihew, *The Quest of the Davis Cup*, 308; 'Valuation of Goods – Davis Cup Trophy' for International Tennis Federation, 28 February 1984).

'violating first principles': *Official Lawn Tennis Bulletin*, 26 September 1894, 135.

Page 48 *war feathers*: Katharine Morrison McClinton, *Collecting American Nineteenth Century Silver* (New York: Charles Scribner's & Sons, 1968), 152.

Old English D: 'Marks Used By Durgin', compiled by D. B. Garvin, 1975, mms., New Hampshire Historical Society.

'rockribbed hills': *Republican Statesman*, 19 January 1924.

new century begin: Arthur Ford to John F. Reilly, 24 May 1945, Concord Public Library Historical Materials Collection, box 15:1-7, at New Hampshire Historical Society.

terrapin forks: Revised Price List Fancy Flatware, 15 August 1898, William B. Durgin Co., Durgin Scrapbook, New Hampshire Historical Society.

four-storey brick: 1891 photograph, New Hampshire Historical Society; *Concord Monitor*, 7 and 9 August 1890 (Judge Page notes).

William Morton: Morton letter to the editor, *Concord Monitor-Patriot*, January 1935; John Abbott quoted in unidentified clipping, January 1935, 'Durgin Co.', vertical file, Concord Public Library; Gardner Corbin, v.p. Concord Silversmiths, letter to the editor, *Sunday Boston Herald*, 2 August 1936. In later years, as the Davis Cup series increased in prominence, others would also be given (or take) credit for spinning the bowl, see Chapter 26.

Page 49 *frequent annealing*, and other production details: David Rogers, Gorham Co., interview with author.

no one would think to mention: *Concord Evening Monitor*, 1 October 1904.

CHAPTER 6 Racquets at the Ready

Page 50 *graduate*: Dwight F. Davis student record, UAIII 15.75.12, Harvard University Archives, Cambridge, Massachusetts.

'drives to the net': *The Harvard (Class) Album -1900*,17-18, Harvard University Archives.

Page 51 *French emperor, $40 annually:* Robert Minton, *One Hundred Years of Longwood*, 2.

'childish things': Malcolm D. Whitman, 'Net Play: A Determining Factor,' *Fifty Years of Lawn Tennis In The United States*, 77.

imposing ... moustache, and other British player descriptions: miscellaneous photographs, for instance in S. Wallis Merrihew, *The Quest of the Davis Cup*, 3.

Page 52 *sands of Dinard*: *Lawn Tennis and Croquet*, 30 May 1900, 91; A. W. Myers, *Lawn Tennis at Home and Abroad*, 148-151.

'tennis longevity': Myers, *Lawn Tennis at Home and Abroad*, 41.

embroidered with the Royal Standard: *Lawn Tennis*, 1 August 1900, 255.

Page 53 *'in Doubles with E. D.'*: *Lawn Tennis*, 25 July 1900, 242.

'with brilliant effect': *Lawn Tennis*, 1 August 1900, 255, 258; 6 February 1901, 476. Years later at least one tennis history would miss *Lawn Tennis's* irony and report the send-off send-up as literally true.

English ... ranked: *NY Times*, August 7, 1900; *Boston Evening Transcript*, 7 August 1900.

not as important: Holcombe Ward, 'American Methods', *Lawn Tennis at Home and Abroad*, A. W. Myers, ed., 192.

stopped playing singles: *NY Times*, 24 March 1900.

not like ocean travel: *Golf and Lawn Tennis*, 10 May 1901, 137. Both Dohertys played at Dinard in September, and in August Laurie won the German championship at Homburg though R. F. did retire from his singles match and scratch at Puteaux in July (miscellaneous clippings, Doherty Scrapbook (beginning 1892), Wimbledon Library, Wimbledon Lawn Tennis Museum, London;

Lawn Tennis and Croquet, 12 September 1900, 363).

Page 54 *only ... Eaves: NY Times,* 24 March 1900.

'teach our young players': Brooklyn Eagle, n.d. 1899, Paret Scrapbook, William M. Fischer Lawn Tennis Collection, St. John's University, Jamaica, New York.

on hand to greet: Boston Herald, 6 August 1900.

'beggar description': Merrihew, *The Quest of the Davis Cup,* 12.

CHAPTER 7 The First Match

Page 55 *clubhouse:* Robert Minton, *One Hundred Years of Longwood,* 5, 17.

draw ceremony: line drawing, *Boston Globe,* 7 August 1900.

'good fellows': Boston Herald, 7 August 1900.

Page 56 *'make a good showing': Boston Post,* 7 August 1900.

'hard hitters': Boston Herald, 7 August 1900.

'ill-advised': Boston Globe, 7 August 1900.

'not the slightest doubt': Brookline Chronicle, 4 August 1900.

'very close tennis': NY Times, 7 August 1900.

'screw' service: Sportsman, 20 August 1900, as quoted in *Lawn Tennis & Croquet,* 22 August 1900, 309.

conditions very even: Boston Herald, 7 August 1900.

Chambers: Minton, *One Hundred Years,* 7-8; *Longwood Cricket Club Directory,* 1969, 3.

iron roller: Minton, *One Hundred Years,* 5.

Page 57 *'arts and wiles': Boston Herald,* Thursday, 9 August 1900.

cricket ... replaced hay: Minton, *One Hundred Years,* 2.

grandstand seating, rows of ... chairs: line drawing, *Boston Globe,* 10 August 1900.

expatriates: Boston Globe, 8 August 1900.

'rash steps themselves': Boston Globe, 10 August 1900.

'to gaze upon': A. Wallis Myers, *The Complete Lawn Tennis Player,* 244.

25 women: Longwood Cricket Club Bylaws and Membership, 1900, 16, 17-27, Archives, Longwood Cricket Club, Chestnut Hill, Massachusetts.

Page 58 *'marvelled considerably': Boston Evening Transcript,* 8 August 1900.

hit it out: Boston Globe, 9 August 1900.

CHAPTER 8 'With Weeping and with Laughter'

Page 59 *'blank amazement': Boston Morning Journal,* 9 August 1900.

something new ... to the ball: Boston Globe, 9 August 1900.

applause for visitor's: Brookline Chronicle, 11 August 1900.

rarity: Paul Metzler, *Tennis Styles and Stylists,* 2.

players scrambled: Boston Morning Journal, 9 August 1900.

'grand tennis': Boston Herald, 9 August 1900.

Page 60 *linking ... player with country: Boston Post,* 9 August 1900.

'egg-shaped lump', 'escape him all together': Boston Morning Journal, 9 August 1900.

'any elaborate care': Boston Globe, 9 August 1900.

'rub down and brush up': Boston Evening Transcript, 10 August 1900. Nearly three decades later, E. D. Black told S. Wallis Merrihew that the rests had been very much in the American team's favour 'as they play themselves right out in each set and the rest fixes them up for the next. The effect was quite the opposite with us' (*The Quest of the Davis Cup,* 16).

any succeeding sets: Dr. Dwight would later propose that only one rest be allowed, and that after the third set. 'As to its duration I am indifferent – five, seven or ten minutes.' He emphasised, however, that he was not for a game 'in which a poorer player can win simply by greater endurance ...' (*Lawn Tennis and Croquet,* 24 April 1901).

relied on ground strokes: Boston Morning Journal, 9 August 1900.

100 standees: Boston Herald, 10 August 1900.

Page 61 *pointed out Mansfield*: Boston Globe, 10 August 1900.

same side of the court: Lawn Tennis and Croquet, 29 August 1900, 326, 328.

'thrilling contest': Boston Globe, 10 August 1900.

'Stay at Home': Boston Post, 10 August 1900.

Page 62 *headed for the … barn*: line drawing, Boston Herald, 11 August 1900.

consultations: Golf and Lawn Tennis, 11 March 1901, 107.

drawing: Boston Herald, 10 August 1900.

banquet: S. Apphira, 'England v. America', Lawn Tennis and Croquet, 29 August 1900, 329.

poor showing understandable: Lawn Tennis and Croquet, 3 October 1900, 410.

Page 63 *'sensation'*: Golf and Lawn Tennis, 19 September 1900, 379.

no basis to this complaint: Lawn Tennis and Croquet, 3 April 1901, 506-507; Golf and Lawn Tennis, 25 April 1901, 201-203.

diagram: Lawn Tennis and Croquet, 5 September 1900, 356.

garden party: Lawn Tennis and Croquet, 7 November 1900, 431.

'cruel surprise': S. Apphira, 'England v. America', Lawn Tennis and Croquet, 29 August 1900, 328-329.

probably Gore: J. Parmly Paret, 'International Supremacy at Lawn Tennis,' Lawn Tennis and Croquet, 7 November 1900, 429. Barrett's complaints would get full airing eight years later in A. W. Myers, The Complete Lawn Tennis Player, 242-245.

'outplayed the Americans': 'Ins and Outs', Lawn Tennis and Croquet, 7 November 1900, 327.

American viewpoint: Paret, 'International Supremacy', Lawn Tennis and Croquet, 7 November 1900, 429-430

Page 64 *'Qui s'excuse'*: Lawn Tennis and Croquet, 22 August 1900, 309.

Even the Messrs. Doherty': Morning Post, n.d., Doherty Scrapbook (beginning 1892), Wimbledon Library, Wimbledon Lawn Tennis Museum, London.

'does not seem possible': Brookline Chronicle, 11 August 1900.

better organized: Golf and Lawn Tennis, 29 September 1900, 540; Lawn Tennis and Croquet, 7 November 1900, 431.

Page 65 *'With weeping and with laughter'*: Lawn Tennis and Croquet, 22 August 1900, 308. Actually, it was left up to the reader to fill in the word 'pants'. Said a tongue-in-cheek note from the editor, 'We cannot allow this line to be completed. This is not a fashion magazine.'

'noblest Roman': Golf and Lawn Tennis, 28 September 1900, 538.

CHAPTER 9 Off to England

Page 66 *'new century'*: Lawn Tennis and Croquet, 5 September 1900, 343.

much interest: Lawn Tennis and Croquet, 29 August 1900, 326-327.

'brilliant player': Lawn Tennis and Croquet, 5 September 1900, 342.

Page 67 *missed his spikes*: Golf and Lawn Tennis, 28 September 1900, 539.

'making capital of it': Parmly Paret to Holcombe Ward, 1 October 1900, Holcombe Ward Papers, Seabright Lawn Tennis and Cricket Club, Rumson, New Jersey.

'race for progress': Lawn Tennis and Croquet, 7 November 1900, 428.

deed of gift: Minutes, USNLTA, 7 February 1901, copy in 'Davis Cup' file, William M. Fischer Lawn Tennis Collection, St. John's University, Jamaica, New York.

'published blank … forms': Lawn Tennis, 10 June 1901, 14.

Astor … historic trophies: unidentified clipping, spring 1901 (?), Ward Papers; Golf and Lawn Tennis, 24 August 1901, 457.

miniature 'pots': Dr. James Dwight to Holcombe Ward, 23 March, n.y., Ward Papers; item 414A DUR. [Durgin], 'Miniature Davis Cup' (1924) with photograph, Archives, Gorham Company.

Page 68 *fox hunting*: Lawn Tennis and Croquet, 6 February 1901, 477.

'quite enough': Lawn Tennis and Croquet, 3 April 1901, 507.

'takes a month': *Lawn Tennis and Croquet*, 6 March 1901, 492.

rising in several European countries: *Outing*, 10 May 1901, as quoted in *Lawn Tennis*, 10 May 1901, 1.

'any country has the right': *Golf and Lawn Tennis*, 11 March 1901, 101.

'dread the ocean trip': *Lawn Tennis* (NY), 10 May 1901, 2; *Golf and Lawn Tennis*, 11 March 1901, 136-137.

'close economy': Parmly Paret to Holcombe Ward, 1 October 1900, Ward Papers.

$8: *Wright & Ditson Official Lawn Tennis Guide, 1904*.

Page 69 'Lookout my boy': George Wright to Holcombe Ward, 3 May 1901, Ward Papers.

explained ... Presbrey: *Lawn Tennis and Croquet*, 10 July 1901, 205.

'mouth water': *Lawn Tennis and Croquet*, 3 July 1901, 186.

black shoes: *Golf and Lawn Tennis*, 13 July 1901, 354, 361.

Page 70 'not nearly so brilliant': Eustace Miles, *Lawn Tennis and Croquet*, 3 July 1901, 185.

'Davis everywhere': *Lawn Tennis and Croquet*, 3 July 1901, 191.

'impossible to describe': ibid.

Doherty statistics: Alan Little, *Wimbledon Compendium, 1995*, 172.

'very pretty': 'The Lawn Tennis Champions', unidentified clipping, Doherty Scrapbook (beginning 1892), Wimbledon Library, Wimbledon Lawn Tennis Museum, London.

Page 71 'steadiness': *Lawn Tennis and Croquet*, 3 July 1901, 185.

not using ... stratagems: *Lawn Tennis and Croquet*, 3 July 1901, 190.

'Dohertys Wednesday': cable, Holcombe Ward to French & Ward, n.d., Ward Papers.

11-course dinner: signed menu, *Lawn Tennis and Croquet*, 10 July 1901, 207.

'mysteries of the famous service': *Lawn Tennis and Croquet*, 3 July 1901, 181-182.

drill hat: 'England Beats America at Lawn Tennis', unidentified clipping, Doherty Scrapbook (1892).

Page 72 'so clean': ibid.

Tuesday and Wednesday match details: *Lawn Tennis and Croquet*, 3 July 1901, 190; 10 July 1901, 210.

'schoolboy smile': 'England Beats America ...,' Doherty Scrapbook.

'hardware kings': unidentified clipping, Doherty Scrapbook.

'beaten': cable, Holcombe Ward to French & Ward, 3 July 1901, Ward Papers.

not ... challenge after all: G. R. Mewburn to James Dwight, 13 July 1901, reprinted in *Lawn Tennis and Croquet*, 17 July 1901, 228.

Page 73 'foolish to send': *Golf and Lawn Tennis*, 29 July 1901, 381.

'team next year': *Lawn Tennis and Croquet*, 17 July 1901, 228.

'unhappy chapters': ibid., 229.

CHAPTER 10 Round Two

Page 74 cannon: unidentified clipping, Doherty Scrapbook (beginning 1892), Wimbledon Library, Wimbledon Lawn Tennis Museum, London.

current US doubles champions: As three time winners Ward and Davis did take permanent possession of the historic Astor cups, made by Tiffany. Davis's trophy is in the collection of the International Tennis Hall of Fame, Newport, Rhode Island.

knee injury: Arthur S. Pier, 'Some Tennis Champions', *American Magazine*, August, 1910, 470.

before the singles match: *NY Times*, 15 August 1901.

practicing hard: *Boston Herald*, 29 July 1902.

gashed foot, schedule change: *NY Times*, 6 August, 8 August 1902.

Page 75 regain title: Alan Little, *Wimbledon Compendium, 1995*, 172.

without strain: *Boston Herald*, 29 July 1902.

'muscular': Grace Glueck, Paul Gardner, *Brooklyn People and Places, Past and Present* (New York: H. N. Abrams, 1991), 213.

'velvet,' hands and knees: *NY Times*, 6 August 1902.

tickets ... free: S. W. Merrihew, *The Quest of the Davis Cup*, 23.

weight: G.W. Hillyard, as quoted in John Barrett, ed., *ITF World of Tennis, 1995*, 366.

Page 76 *Laurie's strength*: Bud Collins and Zander Hollander, ed., *Bud Collins' Modern Encyclopedia of Tennis*, 16.

Reggie not Laurie: *NY Times*, 6 August 1902.

reverse singles: As *Lawn Tennis and Croquet* later explained to its readers, regulation 7 stated, 'A player shall not be called upon to play more than one match a day except with the unanimous consent of the captains of the opposing sides, and the committee of management' (3 September 1902, 410).

Staten Island hills: *NY Times*, 8 August 1902.

General Slocum: *NY Times*, 6 August 1902; 'Doherty Brothers Coolly Defeat Ward and Davis,' unidentified clipping, Doherty Scrapbook (1892), Wimbledon Library. Two summers later, on 15 June 1904, the *General Slocum*, carrying 1,400 passengers on a church outing, was destroyed in a horrendous fire (Edward Robb Ellis, *Epic of New York City*, New York: Coward-McCann, 1966, 468-470).

7,000: *NY Times*, 9 August 1902. Other newspapers and Team Captain Collins' report to LTA (*Lawn Tennis and Croquet*, 24 September 1902, 481) estimated the crowd as nearly 10,000. Merrihew, *Quest of the Davis Cup*, 23, thought the number was closer to 6,000.

'in this country': *NY Times*, 9 August 1902.

Ted Jr. attending: *NY Times*, 7 August 1902.

recent injury: *NY Times*, 9 August 1902.

white hats: 'Doherty Brothers Coolly Defeat ...', Doherty Scrapbook.

Page 77 *disconcerting*: *NY Times*, 9 August 1902.

over-anxious: 'Doherty Brothers Coolly Defeat ...', Doherty Scrapbook.

passing shots: *NY Times*, 9 August 1902.

tortoise: *NY Times*, 9 August 1902.

ill effects 'Doherty Brother Coolly Defeat ...', Doherty Scrapbook.

Page 78 *scalps*: *NY Times*, 22 August 1902.

Duchess: 'Englishmen Coming Again Next Year', unidentified clipping, Doherty Scrapbook.

exasperatingly: *NY Times*, 22 August 1902.

'lacks ... steadiness': 'Englishmen Coming Again Next Year', Doherty Scrapbook.

Page 79 *'boodler'*: DFD to Holcombe Ward, 10 December 1902, Holcombe Ward Papers, Seabright Lawn Tennis and Cricket Club, Rumson, New Jersey.

'Ware & Ward': Ward was considering teaming up with player Leo Ware, though it was Beals Wright who became Davis's replacement.

'only for exercise': *SL Post-Dispatch*, 17 June 1903.

Davis career statistics: Frank V. Phelps, 'Dwight Davis Tennis Tournament Record', October 1996, mms.

Page 80 *terminated*: Pier, *American Magazine*, August 1910, 470. It is not known whether Pier got this information from an interview with Davis.

'twinkling of an eye': unpublished mms., Whitman family collection.

Page 81 *'muckraking'*: The term comes from a speech given by President Theodore Roosevelt in April 1906, says author Richard Hofstadter. By that time Roosevelt, though a progressive and a reformer, was concerned about the excesses of 'the literature of exposure, which ... was beginning to flood the nation.' Roosevelt took the term from the Man with the Muck-rake in Bunyan's *Pilgrim's Progress* 'who could look no way but downward with the muck-rake in his hand.' The muck of political and business corruption needed to be 'scraped up,' said the president, but 'an epidemic of indiscriminate assault upon character does not good, but very great harm.' (Richard Hofstadter, ed., *The Progressive Movement 1900-1915*, 18-19.)

'many successes': Paret, 'Styles of Play and Skill of the Experts', *Spalding's Lawn Tennis Annual, 1902*, 27-28.

CHAPTER 11 Meet Me in St. Lou-ie

Page 82 *met on class day*: *Boston Evening Globe*, 6 July 1904.

wealthy: *NY Herald*, 6 July 1904.

fourth in his class: Records, Registrar's Office, Washington University. Davis's class had 37 graduates. His cumulative grade point average at graduation was 87. At the end of his junior year he had ranked second in the class of 42 students.

sisters: 1880 Census for Newton, Middlesex County, Massachusetts, vol. 21, E.D. 474, sheet 23, line 25.

'pretty little romance': *Boston Journal*, 6 July 1904; family interviews with author.

Page 83 *Edwards Whitaker*: Julius K. Hunter, *Westmoreland and Portland Places*, 31, 122-23.

civic leaders hoped: Yvonne M. Condon, 'St. Louis 1904', in *Historical Dictionary of World's Fairs and Expositions, 1851-1988*, John E. Findling, ed., 179.

Theodore Roosevelt, Fair details and statistics: ibid. 178-185.

' ... *Lou-ie, Lou-ie*': though the song was sung this way, the actual spelling in the song title was the more proper 'Meet Me In St. Louis, Louis' (David Ewen, *American Popular Songs*, New York: Random House, 1966).

myths: Condon, 'St. Louis 1904', 185; James Trager, 'Food and Drink, 1904', *The People's Chronology CD* (New York: Henry Holt, 1994).

Paris Exposition: David Wallechinsky, *The Complete Book of the Summer Olympics*, 691.

Page 84 *Sullivan*: *World's Fair Bulletin*, October 1904, 16.

City Beautiful: Donald Bright Oster, 'Nights of Fantasy,' *Bulletin of the Missouri Historical Society*, April 1975, 181; Richard Hofstadter, *The Age of Reform*.

Municipal League: '100 Years of Civic Activism, A Brief History of the National Civic League' in *1993 National Civic League Annual Report*, 10-13.

Sand Gardens: Linda Oliva, 'A Boston Sand Garden Kicks Off the Playground Movement', 36-39, Charles E. Hartsoe, 'From Playgrounds to Public Policy', 47, *Parks & Recreation*, August 1985.

into Americans: R. B. Duff, 'The Playground Movement In The United States and Its Influence' (master's thesis, Indiana University, 1910), 12.

Charlotte Rumbold: Oster, 'Nights of Fantasy', 185-193, 204.

women's clubs elsewhere: Duff, 'The Playground Movement ...', 33.

Wednesday Club and playgrounds: Charlotte Rumbold, *Report of the Park Commissioner*, April 1908, 26-27.

1903 benefit tournament: Mary McKittrick Markham Diaries and Scrapbooks, journal 13 June 1903, box 1, Missouri Historical Society, St. Louis.

Page 85 *Joe Wear*: *NY Times*, 5 June1941; *Davis Cup Media Guide*, 1996, 46-47

considered them all Olympic: Bill Mallon, *A Statistical Summary of the 1904 Olympic Games*, 1; *History of the Louisiana Purchase Exposition*, 565.

Olympic records: Wallechinsky, *The Complete Book of the Summer Olympics*, 690-691.

all 'Olympic Games' winners: *World's Fair Bulletin*, October 1904, 17; *History of the Louisiana Purchase Exposition*, 565, 570, 573; Mallon, *A Statistical Summary*, 1-3, 40-42.

later IOC records: Wallechinsky, *The Complete Book of the Summer Olympics*, 690-691.

nationally ranked: *USTA 1997 Tennis Yearbook*, 75.

only one non-American: Mallon, *A Statistical Summary*, 40.

tried to recruit European: *NY Times*, 7 February 1904.

would not be sending: *NY Times*, 13 March 1904. Belgium and France did challenge in 1904 (Alan Trengove, *The Story of the Davis Cup*, year-by-year appendix, 334).

Page 86 *weight*: *NY Herald*, 21 June 1903.

Olympic winners: Mallon, *A Statistical Summary*, 40-42; *History of the Louisiana Purchase Exposition*, 570, 573; *World's Fair Bulletin*, October 1904, 17; Wallechinsky, *The Complete Book of the Summer Olympics*, 393, 690-693.

Missouri Bar: Archives, Missouri Bar Association, Jefferson City, MO.

married: wedding certificate and announcement, William McChesney Martin Jr. Papers, box 60, folder 1, Missouri Historical Society; *NY Herald,* 16 November 1904, 9; marriage register, Emmanuel Protestant Episcopal Church, Geneva; *lengthy trip:* Harvard College, *Class of 1900, Secretary's Second Report,* 1906, 60, Harvard University Archives, Cambridge, Massachusetts. Davis, not the first man to have trouble remembering the exact date of his marriage, often gave the year erroneously as 1905. Particularly reliable on family dates is Davis's entry in Harvard College, *Class of 1900 Twenty-Fifth Anniversary Report* (1925), probably thanks to efficient secretaries in the War Department.

'jolly well licked': W. Cameron Forbes, *Journal,* vol. I, 173, W. Cameron Forbes Collection, Houghton Library, Harvard University, Cambridge, Massachusetts.

'at home': at home card, Martin Papers, box 60, folder 1, Missouri Historical Society.

Page 87   *from his honeymoon: SL Post-Dispatch,* October 1925.

Rolla Wells: James Neal Primm, *Lion of the Valley,* 381-384. Primm considers Wells only a moderate reformer, on the trail of only obvious theft, bribery, and other illegalities, never believing that 'his own large fortune and those of his friends were based in part upon unfair exploitation of the community' (384). Possibly the same argument could have been made about Davis, with regards to the banking, railroads and real estate aspects of the family fortune.

'riffraff,' 'illiterate': Lincoln Steffens, *The Shame of the Cities,* 21, originally published in *McClure's,* October 1902, as 'Tweed Days in St. Louis', co-authored by Claude Wetmore, former city editor of the *Post-Dispatch.* Primm claims that Wetmore actually wrote the article which Steffens edited (*Lion of the Valley,* 389).

'rascals': Steffens, *Shame of the Cities,* 70 (originally published in *McClure's,* March 1903, as 'The Shamelessness of St. Louis').

politics a sport: Steffens, *Shame of the Cities,* 4, 'Tweed Days'.

Page 88   *Campbell:* Hunter, *Westmoreland and Portland Places,* 54; Primm, *Lion of the Valley,* 376.

St. Louis Transit Co.: Steffens, *Shame of the Cities,* 27-36 ('Tweed Days'); Primm, *Lion of the Valley,* 380-381.

House of Delegates: SL Post-Dispatch, 17 May 1911.

governed the city: Primm, *Lion of the Valley,* 321.

saloon keepers: SL Post-Dispatch, 16 October 1925.

five small parks: SL Post-Dispatch, 21 May 1911; *Annual Report of the Park Commissioner,* April 1908, 4.

'combine,' not get anyone to second: SL Post-Dispatch, 16 October 1925.

'would-be reformer': Harvard College, *Class of 1900, Secretary's Fourth Report,* June 1915, 112.

living here: birth announcement, Martin Papers, box 60, folder 1, Missouri Historical Society.

died tragically: family interviews with author.

16 Portland Place: Hunter, *Westmoreland And Portland Places,* 129, 144, 145, 192, 193, 208; John and Virginia Byrne (current owners), interview with author. In the late 1920s the house's second owner added a tennis court; it was not there while the Davises lived there.

Page 89   *National Municipal League:* In 1987 the organisation became the National Civic League.

Page 90   *'too friendly': SL Post-Dispatch,* 17 May 1911.

'free-bridge' issue: Caroline Loughlin and Catherine Anderson, *Forest Park, 106*; Primm, *Lion of the Valley,* 422-424.

'had to beg him': SL Post-Dispatch, 17 May 1911.

'disaster of ... rich and ... Harvard': SL Republic, 4 June 1911.

Keep Off The Grass signs: Annual Report of the Park Department, April 1912, 9; April 1915, 3.

Page 91   *'sacrifice the grass': SL Post-Dispatch,* 21 May 1911.

park sleepover: Loughlin and Anderson, *Forest Park,* 135.

'pitiless' : Annual Report of the Park Department, April 1912, 16.

seedlings: ibid., 5; Loughlin and Anderson, *Forest Park,* 88, 91.

Lucas Garden: Annual Report of the Park Department , April 1912, 4.

'*majestic beauty*': ibid., 3.

Page 92 *historians would call:* Loughlin and Anderson, *Forest Park,* 152.

16th in playground expenditures: Yearbook of the Playground Association of America for 1909, quoted by Duff, 'The Playground Movement', 20, 21.

German ... insisted; 'streets ... still crowded': Annual Report of the Park Department, April 1912, 15.

'*little lads*': SL Republic, 4 June 1911.

'*crowd forty tennis courts*': ibid.

Fairground courts: ibid.; *Annual Report of the Park Department,* April 1912, 5.

first free public parks courts: Annual Report of the Park Commissioner, April 1908, 7. Even earlier, in 1891, a St. Louis sports entrepreneur who had seen lawn tennis in New York and Philadelphia, laid out courts in Forest Park where, for a fee of 25 cents, members of the public received shoes, balls, racquets and an hour of court time. (Unidentified St. Louis newspaper clipping, c.1927, quoting the booklet 'Forest Park Lawn Tennis Campus'.)

24 tennis courts: Annual Report of the Park Department, April 1912, 5.

insist on crediting: for instance Davis's former doubles partner Holcombe Ward, later USLTA president, in a tribute to Davis in a 1941 booklet *Sixty Years of Tennis In St. Louis,* Obear, ed., 5; also newspaper articles published later at the time of Davis's national and international political prominence.

32 new courts: Loughlin and Anderson, *Forest Park,* 110; *4.30 a.m., Annual Report of the Park Department,* April 1913, 8.

Page 93 *not rich man's game: Annual Report of the Park Department,* April 1913, 8.

not taken his $3000 salary: SL Globe-Democrat, 14 October 1925, quoting Rodowe Abeken, former parks recreation superintendent, and attorney Edward Foristel.

CHAPTER 12 Tournaments for All

Page 94 *retired:* Harvard College, *Class of 1900, Secretary's Fourth Report,* June 1915, 111, Harvard University Archives, Cambridge, Massachusetts.

Page 95 '*worthy of Christy Mathewson': Reedy's Mirror,* 18 December 1914, 51.

William Marion Reedy: John Flanagan, 'Reedy of the *Mirror*', *Missouri Historical Review,* January 1949, 128-144.

'*suave, diplomatic': Reedy's Mirror,* 18 December 1914, 51.

racquets championship: Lord Aberdale, *The Wills Faber Book of Tennis & Rackets* (London: Stanley Paul, 1980), 350-351.

'*father of organised park athletics': SL Globe-Democrat,* 14 October 1925.

'*battles of peace': Annual Report of the Park Department,* 1912-1913, 4.

Page 96 '*saloons and dance halls*': ibid.

national municipal leagues: Annual Report of the Park Department, April 1914, 6.

'*super-odoriferous building': Annual Report of the Park Department,* April 1912, 11.

desperately wanted elephants: SL Post-Dispatch, 2 December 1913,1.

zoo's board of control: Loughlin and Anderson, *Forest Park,* 129.

Miss Jim: Primm, *Lion of the Valley,* 433; Loughlin and Anderson, *Forest Park,* 126, 128, 130.

Davis's ... arguments: Primm, *Lion of the Valley,* 434; Loughlin and Anderson, *Forest Park,* 130.

Page 97 *including Davis:* Donald Bright Oster, 'Nights of Fantasy: The St. Louis Pageant and Masque of 1914', *Bulletin of the Missouri Historical Society,* April 1975, 178.

values could be served: ibid., 191-193.

four nights: Caroline Loughlin and Catherine Anderson, *Forest Park,* 116 (one night was rained out).

eye-popping production: James Neal Primm, *Lion of the Valley,* 427-430; Loughlin and Anderson, *Forest Park,* 115-117; Oster, 'Nights of Fantasy', 175, 200.

'*since the World's Fair': Annual Report of the Division of Parks and Recreation,* April 1915, 5.

'*in every new high school*': Minutes of Annual Meeting, USNLTA, 11 February 1916, 66.

Page 98   *growing surplus:* ibid., 65, 67.

    'resting on our shoulders': ibid., 67.

    Longwood Cricket Club: Minutes of Annual Meeting, 13 March 1916, Minute Book 1911-1916, Archives of Longwood Cricket Club, Chestnut Hill, Massachusetts.

    Maurice McLoughlin: Collins and Hollander, *Bud Collins' Modern Encyclopedia of Tennis*, 87, 523.

    'spectators': NY Times, 2 April 1916, 4.

    'balloted for their membership': SL Globe-Democrat, 26 March 1916.

    'scraping for pennies': SL Republic, 27 February 1915.

    bond issue: Annual Report of the Park Department, April 1914, 10-11; April 1913, 5.

CHAPTER 13 Meanwhile, with the Cup (1)

Page 99   *default:* NY Times, 5 August 1903; A. Wallis Myers, *The Complete Lawn Tennis Player*, 259; S. Wallis Merrihew, *The Quest of the Davis Cup*, 35; Alan Trengove, *The Story of the Davis Cup*, 31.

    only time brothers: Bud Collins and Zander Hollander, *Bud Collins' Modern Encyclopedia of Tennis*, 453.

    'Boston crowd': NY Times, 13 March 1904.

    'that darned bath': Alan Trengove, 'Supreme Strategist', *Fireside Book of Tennis*, 72.

    'reflected in the ... silver': Mabel Brookes, *Crowded Galleries*, 61.

Page 100 *taken into custody:* Brookes, *Crowded Galleries*, 125.

Page 101 *vault of ... Black, Starr & Frost:* Merrihew, *The Quest of the Davis Cup*, 310.

CHAPTER 14 War

Page 2   *voted ... to enter the war:* Washington Post, 6 April 1917; Samuel Eliot Morison, *The Oxford History of the American People*, 860.

    tears: US Rep. Jeannette Rankin, in Part I of the four-part radio series *Women In Congress*, Robert A. Franklin, producer (Princess Anne, Maryland: WESM-FM, University of Maryland, Eastern Shore, 1996). Rankin was the only legislator to vote against US participation in both World Wars.

    'It is painful': 31 March 1854, as quoted by Martin Gilbert as an epigraph to Section One, *Atlas of World War I*.

    'safe for democracy': Henry Steele Commager, ed., *Documents of American History*, 308-312.

    56 sunk: Gilbert, *Atlas of World War I*, 86.

    was in London: NY Telegram, 16 October 1925; unidentified clippings, 29 December 1916, 'Dwight F. Davis', vertical file, Missouri Historical Society, St. Louis.

Page 103 *back into shape:* SL Globe-Democrat, 14 October 1925.

    Famous & Barr farm: SL Globe-Democrat, 8-9 February 1986.

    Plattsburg: Morison, *Oxford History*, 853.

    nearly 28,000: Robert L. Carter, *Pictorial History of the 35th Division* (unpaged).

    feet under Paris tables: Charles B. Hoyt, *Heroes of the Argonne*, 26.

    tea for breakfast: ibid., 25.

    almost one million: David McCullough, *Truman*, 111.

    Springfield and Eddystone: Hoyt, *Heroes of the Argonne*, 35.

    see Paris: ibid., 32.

Page 104 *pocket ... south of Verdun:* Mark C. Carnes and John A. Garraty, *Mapping America's Past*, 165 (map).

    memorised eye charts: McCullough, *Truman*, 105.

    Meuse-Argonne offensive: Narrative of the 35th's five days in this campaign is based primarily on text, pictures and maps in *Order of Battle of the United States Land Forces in the World War* (212-221); the regimental histories *Pictorial History of the 35th Division* (Carter), *Heroes of the Argonne* (Hoyt) and *From Vauquois Hill to Exermont* (Clair Kenamore); and *My Experiences in the World War*, vol. II (John J. Pershing).

ideal ... to defend: Pershing, *My Experiences,* II 282.

battle lines unchanged: ibid., 280.

Page 105 *trunks splintered:* David S. Thomson, *Pictorial Biography: HST,* 42-43 (photograph).

24-mile front: Pershing, *My Experiences,* II 294.

about noon: Carter, *Pictorial History of the 35th Division,* map 26 September.

no one following: Kenamore, *From Vauquois Hill,* 131-133; Helen Davis Hermes, interview with author.

Page 106 *'adjutanting a brigade':* Kenamore, *From Vauquois Hill,* 133.

captured beer: ibid., 122-123.

Pershing message: ibid., 154.

'amidst its dead': ibid., 155.

'stiff crust': ibid., 156.

heavy losses: Carter, *Pictorial History of the 35th Division.*

blunt objections: Kenamore, *From Vauquois Hill,* 139.

Page 107 *'dead man's last contribution':* ibid., 188.

Montrebeau Wood: ibid., 203.

'lost its punch', 'however incompetent': ibid., 204. Kenamore also points out, with some disgust, that a brigadier general who joined one of the division's brigades in October, ten days after it came out of battle, was awarded the Distinguished Service Medal for his handling of the brigade during the Argonne-Meuse offensive (246). See also Kenamore Appendix A, 251-253 and Hoyt, *Heroes of the Argonne,* Chapter XIV.

brigade headquarters: Hoyt, *Heroes of the Argonne,* 110.

engineers ... picked up rifles: Carter, *Pictorial History of the 35th Division;* Hoyt, *Heroes of the Argonne,* 110-111.

Page 108 *'devoid of fear':* General Orders 81, Headquarters 35th Division, A.E.F., 14 October 1918, as quoted in Harvard College, *Class of 1900 Twenty-Fifth Anniversary Report* (1925), 190, Harvard University Archives, Cambridge, Massachusetts.

'vastly superior numbers': citation for distinguished-service cross, 3 March 1923, as quoted in Harvard College, *Class of 1900 Twenty-Fifth Anniversary Report* (1925), 190.

before dawn: Hoyt, *Heroes of the Argonne,* 120.

'better to have come out': DFD to Nelson Cunliff, as quoted in unidentified clipping, vertical file, Missouri Historical Society.

1,000 dead: Kenamore, *From Vauquois Hill,* 240. In 1921 the state of Missouri erected near Cheppy a monument to those who died in the battle of the Argonne.

Page 109 *Americans ... killed or wounded:* Carnes and Garraty, *Mapping America's Past,* 165; Gilbert, *Atlas of World War I,* 112.

'bodies withered': 'The Swimmers', *Saturday Evening Post,* 19 October 1929; the phrase, probably Wilson's 'making the world safe for democracy'.

85 machine-guns: Hoyt, *Heroes of the Argonne,* 120-121.

1,200 horses : ibid., 122.

miserable months: Kenamore, *From Vauquois Hill,* 247.

tennis tournament at Cannes: Al Laney, *Covering the Courts,* 28-31; George Carens, 'Williams and Washburn', 192-194, Allison Danzig, 'Richard Norris Williams 2d', 194-195, both in *Fireside Book of Tennis.*

'fiercely and victoriously': George A. White, 'Cradle Days in the Legion', typescript of four-part series which appeared in *American Legion Weekly,* 19, 26 November, 10, 17 December 1920, 5.

Page 110 *'without enthusiasm':* ibid., 7.

would be considered founders: notarised roster from Paris Caucus, American Legion Archives, National Headquarters, Indianapolis, Indiana; Miles Z. Epstein, 'Seventy-Five Years for God and Country', *American Legion Magazine,* September 1994, 42-46.

'credit to the doughboys': as quoted in *SL Globe-Democrat,* 14 October 1925.

'I can't find the parade': Hermes, interview.

staff ... photograph: Carter, *Pictorial History of the 35th Division*.

Traub ... relieved of command: Hoyt, *Heroes of the Argonne*, appendix (12).

CHAPTER 15 Washington Calls

Page 111 *county commissioner*: David McCollough, *Truman*, 159; Harry S. Truman, *Memoirs I*, 136.

Henry J. Allen: Clair Kenamore, *From Vauquois Hill to Exermont*, 189; miscellaneous records, Kansas State Historical Society, Topeka.

Cape Girardeau: SL *Times*, 25 March 1920.

platform: SL *Times*, 27, 29 March 1920.

Page 112 *'with proper reservations'*: DFD to John H. Holliday, chairman of Davis-For-Senate Committee, 2 February 1920 (as reprinted in SL *Globe-Democrat*, 4 February 1920).

he was against: SL *Globe-Democrat*, 28 March 1920.

'straddler': SL *Post*, 30 April 1920.

80,000 votes: unidentified clipping, 5 April 1920, DFD Senate Campaign Scrapbook (unpaged), family collection; *'moist'* : different clipping, same page.

'not in favour of the 18th amendment': DFD to Holliday, 2 February 1920.

fancy dress ball: Harry Langenberg Jr., interview with author; SL *Post-Dispatch*, 13 October 1925.

candidate-at-home: SL *Post*, 9 May1920.

glamorous shot: brochure, campaign scrapbook.

even Shon: Helen Davis Hermes, interview with author.

Page 113 *'not brilliant'*: Zoë [Akins] to 'Ninon' n.d., Thekla Bernays Papers, Missouri Historical Society, St. Louis.

'personal word', *'fight for clean politics'*: SL *Globe-Democrat*, 3 August 1920.

'too scarce': SL *Globe-Democrat*, 1 August 1920.

St. Louis by 20,000 votes: ibid.

'reeked with fraud': SL *Globe-Democrat*, 4 August 1920.

'house-cleaners movement': DFD to W. K. Bixby, 15 November 1920, William Keeney Bixby Papers, Missouri Historical Society.

Page 114 *largest representation*: Julius K. Hunter, *Westmoreland and Portland Places*, 42.

ballet performances: Mary Taussig Hall, interview with author.

grandmother: Cynthia Davis Martin and Helen Davis Hermes, interviews with author.

stuffed turtle: Hermes, interview.

awe at the sight: William Julius Polk Jr., interview with author.

Shon, 'nursery children': Martin and Hermes, interviews.

sit up straight: Hall, interview.

Page 115 *arthritis, grey mists*: family interviews.

'my own wife': *Much Ado*, November 1925.

Page 116 *'earnest personality'*: Robert S. Brookings to Herbert Hoover, n.d., Commerce Files, box 178, Herbert Hoover Papers, Herbert Hoover Library, West Branch, Iowa.

'pure office detail': Herbert Hoover to DFD, 21 March 1921, box 178, Hoover Library.

'rehabilitation of foreign commerce': NY *Times*, 18 March 1921, 2.

Not that the Times: editorials 5 and 7 January 1921.

vigorous future activity: NY *Times*, 18 March 1921.

snag the WFC job: The Reminiscences of Eugene Meyer Jr., vol. 1, part 2, 412-413, Oral History Collection, Columbia University, New York.

'director of a bank': NY *Times*, 23 March 1921.

Page 117 *'to inspire confidence'*: NY *Times*, 23 December 1921 (loan totals through November).

as they had expected: Meyer, Oral History.

'in stimulating Veterans' play': Julian Myrick, Minutes of Annual Meeting of the United States Lawn Tennis Association, 3 February 1923, 120, USTA Archives, White Plains, New York.

'*heartiest demonstration of the meeting*': *NY Times*, 4 February 1923.

Page 118 '*more than that*': Minutes of USLTA Annual Meeting, 3 February 1923, 45.

lost no time: Minutes of USLTA Executive Committee, 3 February 1923, 15.

in the future: *NY Times*, 5 February 1923.

being refurbished: Minutes of USLTA Executive Committee, 17 March 1923.

'*similar to ... Public Links*': Minutes of USLTA Executive Committee, 3 February 1923, 15.

Walker Cup: John Gleason, 'A Great Amateur', *Golf Journal*, July 1997, 50-53; Rose Ann Collins, 'Two Great Sports Trophies, From St. Louis With Love', *St. Louis Commerce*, September 1980, 102-108. A Walker grandson and namesake, George Herbert Walker Bush, would not only take up golf and tennis, but also politics – and become president of the United States.

play until midnight: 'Municipal Lawn Tennis Increasingly Popular,' *American City Magazine*, May 1923, 506.

Page 119 *American Olympic Association*: Minutes of USLTA Annual Meeting, 3 February 1923, 104. Tennis would be an Olympic sport for one more Olympics (1924) before taking a 64-year hiatus until 1988 (Bud Collins and Zander Hollander, *Bud Collins' Modern Encyclopedia of Tennis*, 644).

'*friendly negotiation*': Minutes of Annual Meeting, 3 February 1923, 105.

full agenda: ibid.; Minutes of USLTA Executive Committee, 3 February, 17 March 1923.

'*regard them as amateurs*': *NY Times*, 4 February 1923.

draw Davis into ... controversy: E. H. Outerbridge to DFD, 2 August 1923, Outerbridge to Malcolm Whitman, 13 February 1931, Malcolm Whitman Papers, collection of Frederick Crocker Whitman (Whitman's son); Dwight F. Davis, 'Tennis – Everybody's Game', *American Legion Monthly*, July 1926.

assistant secretary of war: *NY Times*, 1 March 1923.

CHAPTER 16 Thunderbolts and Tennis Balls

Page 120 *nearly two miles*: 'The Old Executive Office Building,' pamphlet published by the Executive Office of the President, Office of Administration. See also *The Old Executive Office Building: A Victorian Masterpiece*.

Distinguished Service Cross: John E. Strandberg and Roger J. Bender, *The Call of Duty: Military Awards and Decorations of the United States of America*, 60-66.

quick to point out: *NY Times*, 8 March 1923.

receiving criticism: Bob Cox, assistant librarian, American Legion National Headquarters, communication with author.

Pershing proud: John J. Pershing, *My Experiences in the World War*, vol. I, 342.

one of 259: 1923 Annual Report of the Secretary of War to the President, 166, 167; 1925 Report, 165;

Page 121 '*is a cinch*': Minutes of USLTA Executive Committee, 17 March 1923, 15.

'*with deep regret*': ibid., 21; *NY Herald*, 16 March 1923.

keep his hand in: Minutes of USLTA Executive Committee, 15 September and 15 December 1923.

Wightman Cup: Hazel Wightman, 'The Women's International Trophy', *Fifty Years of Lawn Tennis in the United States*, 179. The Wightman Cup competition, between the US and Britain, opened the new Forest Hills stadium in 1923. Though Mrs Wightman originally anticipated involving other countries, it remained a competition between just the US and Great Britain until it was disbanded in 1989.

'*raise his stock*': Theodore Roosevelt Jr. diary, vol. 3, 19 and 23 February 1923, Manuscripts Division, Library of Congress, Washington, DC.

opportunity to reciprocate: DFD to Ted Roosevelt Jr., 1 March 1923, T. Roosevelt Jr. Papers, Special Correspondence, Manuscript Division, Library of Congress.

'*plate of string beans*': Roosevelt diary, vol. 2, 4 September 1922.

Page 122 '*Ogden Reed*': Roosevelt diary, vol. 1, 3 November 1921.

'*Grace Vanderbilt*': ibid., 14 January 1922.

'clap from the blue': Roosevelt diary, vol. 3, 2 August 1923.

column of naval officers: ibid., 8 August 1923.

not yet ... begun to unravel: Robert K. Murray, The Politics of Normalcy: Governmental Theory and Practice in the Harding-Coolidge Era, 100-113.

had been a disaster: for an overview see Terrence J. Gough, 'Soldiers, Businessmen and US Industrial Mobilisation Planning Between the World Wars', War & Society, May 1991, 63-98.

Page 123 'in the national defense': NY Times, 19 April 1923, 21.

'harmonious and effective': NY Times, 22 May 1923.

'instinct for power': Jordan A. Schwarz, The Speculator: Bernard M. Baruch in Washington, 1917-1965, 4.

'rather than to business leaders': Schwarz, The Speculator, 335-336.

he wrote privately: ibid.

'will be eliminated': NY Times, 29 September 1923.

'can lose a war': NY Times, 16 December 1923.

Page 124 'Industrial War College': Terrence J. Gough, 'Origins of the Army Industrial College: Military-Business Tensions After World War I', Armed Forces & Society, Winter 1991, 266.

'properly conservative': memo from Lieutenant Colonel J. H. Burns to Colonel H. B. Jordan, 25 January 1936, file AIC 352, Subject Files, Records of ICAF, RG 334, National Archives, Washington, DC (memo was not sent to Commandant, AIC until 1941); Gough, 'Origins of the Army Industrial College', 265.

after listening to arguments: Burns to Jordan, 25 January 1936; J. M. Scammell, History of the Industrial College of the Armed Forces 1924-1946, 22-24; Francis W. A'Hearn, 'The Industrial College of the Armed Forces: Contextual Analysis of an Evolving Mission, 1924-1994' (Ph.D. dissertation, Virginia Tech, 1997). A helpful guide through this material has been John A. Dodds, an Air Force attorney at the Pentagon and a 1992 graduate of the Army Industrial College after it became the Industrial College of the Armed Forces (ICAF). Dodds has done much research on the history of the institution, particularly the Baruch connection.

already convinced Secretary Weeks: Gough, 'Origins of the Army Industrial College', 264-265; remarks by General Harley B. Ferguson, Founder, Army Industrial College, 19 March 1937, Army Industrial College Lectures, vol. 15, 836.

valuable ally: though James E. Hewes Jr. in his book about US secretaries of war/defence (From Root to McNamara) has nothing to say about Davis's later administration as secretary of war – singling out, among the inter-war secretaries, the respected John Weeks and the flashy Patrick Hurley – he does give Davis credit for starting the Army Industrial College while assistant secretary (54).

'little school': Bernard Baruch, 'The War Industries Board', lecture delivered 12 February 1924, at Army War College (typescript, National Defence University Library), 15.

attempted putsch: Gough, who is Chief, Historical Support Branch of The Centre of Military History, unearthed this showdown on 20th Street for 'Origins of the Army Industrial College', 267-268.

Munitions Building: James Good, Capital Losses.

ten officers: Dwight F. Davis, 'Procurement,' lecture delivered 11 February 1924, at Army War College (typescript, National Defence University Library), 3. There are, however, only nine men in the photograph of the first graduating class of the AIC (Theodore Bauer, History of the Industrial College of the Armed Forces, [C-6]).

sent Weeks a memo: memo dated 19 February 1924, cited in Harold W. Thatcher, Planning for Industrial Mobilisation, 1920-1940, Q.M.C. Historical Studies no. 4 (Washington: Historical Section, Office of the Quartermaster General, 1943), 24-25; Major General James H. Burns (USA, Ret.) to Major General A. C. Smith, 22 August 1953, file HIS 350.03, Special Studies Mobilisation, History of Military Mobilisation in the United States Army, 1775-1945, Records of the Office of the Chief of Military History, Records of the Army Staff, RG 319, National Archives.

Page 125 *'stay off his turf'*: Gough, 'Origins of the Army Industrial College', 268.

'should be kept so': Address of Assistant Secretary of War Dwight F. Davis at Opening of The Army Industrial College, 21 February 1924 (typescript, National Defence University Library), 5.

ranked as high in importance: Colonel Harry B. Jordan, 'A School of Supply Strategy', *Army Ordnance*, XIX, September-October 1938, 75-78.

on the White House lawn: photograph, 1924 Davis Cup Photo Album, William M. Fischer Lawn Tennis Collection, St. John's University, Jamaica, N.Y.

'athletic competition': Coolidge letter to DFD, 1 March 1924, as quoted in *NY Herald*, 6 March 1924; memos 28 February, 3 March 1924, Calvin Coolidge Papers, microfilm roll 33, 25 (War Department).

Page 126 *'retain the cup'*: Minutes of USLTA Executive Committee, 15 December 1923, 9.

Page 127 Iliad *at his elbow*: Lance Morrow, *Time*, 9 March 1998, 88.

'ideal tennis temperament': Parmly Paret, *Outing*, November 1898.

'for the coming diplomat': *NY American*, 17 March 1923.

'standing on our heads': DFD to Colonel Robert Burkham, 21 November 1923, Julius J. Goldberg Collection, Missouri Historical Society.

'various new jobs,': DFD to Burkham, 6 December 1923, 24 November 1924.

Page 128 *War Department as well*: Alfred F. Hurley, *Billy Mitchell: Crusader for Air Power*, 94. This book is a particularly useful overview of the whole Mitchell affair.

'excellent war record': John Weeks to Calvin Coolidge, 4 March 1925, Coolidge Papers, microfilm roll 34, 25 (War Department).

if one were needed: Calvin Coolidge to Dwight Morrow, 11 March 1925, as quoted in Hurley, *Billy Mitchell*, 99.

Page 129 *6,000-word statement*: Burke Davis, *The Billy Mitchell Affair*, 119.

'almost treasonable administration': as quoted in Hurley, *Billy Mitchell*, 101.

'full and impartial investigation': *NY Sun*, 11 September 1925.

'That's bully': Associated Press, 10 September 1925.

'by Acting Secretary Davis': *NY Times*, 13 September 1925.

'sprung a surprise': ibid.

ice water, stocking feet: *NY Times*, 13 September 1925 (Section 10, Sports).

CHAPTER 17 Air Power, Fire Power, Political Power

Page 130 *'background of his times'*: Jerry Israel, *Dictionary of American Biography*, s.v. 'Davis, Dwight Filley,' sup. 3, 218.

Air Board began hearings: *NY Times*, 22 September 1925.

4,500-word statement, got a laugh, 'step-child': ibid.

Page 131 *met at Union Station*: Burke Davis, *The Billy Mitchell Affair*, 227.

generally supportive of Mitchell: Burke Davis, *Mitchell Affair*, 229-232.

applauded by many spectators: *NY Times*, 1 October 1925.

Page 132 *court-martial 'contemplated'*: *NY Times*, 6 October 1925.

made it official: *NY Times*, 13 October 1925.

oath of office, banner headline: *SL Globe-Democrat*, 14 October 1925.

Middle Western 'type': *Providence Journal*, 16 October 1925.

'tennis cabinet': *NY Telegram*, 16 October 1925.

Page 133 *someone else would be appointed*: 'The Daily Mirror of Washington,' *Evening Post*, 30 October 1925.

debonair: Isaac Don Levine, *Mitchell: Pioneer of Air Power*, 347.

'isn't a vaudeville show': Burke Davis, *Mitchell Affair*, 235-236.

limit the number of spectators: ibid.

'discredit upon the military service': *NY Times*, 21 October 1925.

'educate the American people about aviation': Assistant Defense Counsel Clayton Bissell, as quoted in Burke Davis, *Mitchell Affair*, 236-237.

threatened to call: NY Times, 31 October, 5, 6 November 1925.

hissed the name, also named Davis: NY Times, NY World, United Press, 12 November 1925.

'Dwight F. Davis Day: SL Post Dispatch, 19 November 1925.

Page 134 *evening's programs*: 'Program for Civic Reception,' 'Dwight F. Davis,' vertical file, Missouri Historical Society.

'prepare against war': Associated Press, 20 November 1925.

'first broad aeronautical policy': Alfred F. Hurley, *Billy Mitchell: Crusader for Air Power*, 105.

'another decade and more': Levine, *Mitchell*, 364.

'children dependent upon him': DFD to Coolidge, [23 January 1926] as quoted in NY Times, 26 January 1925.

Page 135 *'drive home his point'*: Associated Press, 20 December 1925.

Davis approved: Maurer Maurer, *Aviation In the U.S. Army, 1919-1939*, 191-196.

'a man you could absolutely trust': The Reminiscences of F. Trubee Davison, 110, Oral History Collection, Columbia University, New York.

'next to the same lady': ibid., 190.

didn't help a bit: Helen Davis Hermes, interview with author.

consulting doctors: Boston Sunday Post, 18 October 1925.

took ill: Associated Press, 22 December 1925.

'delicate health': Boston Sunday Post, 18 October 1925.

friendship ... prized: Helen Davis Hermes and Cynthia Davis Martin, interview with author.

Page 136 *stop to her new activity*: Good Housekeeping, March 1935, 224-225; Ishbel Ross, *Grace Coolidge and Her Era*, 93-94.

shooting craps: Hermes, interview.

led by Herbert Hoover: Hermes and Martin, interview.

'game – St. Mark's': for instance entry Wednesday, 26 May 1926, Appointment Books of Secretary of War, vol. 15, RG 107 entry 98, National Archives, Washington, DC.

no favours of any kind: NY Times, 20 May 1926.

'got his goat,' 'soldier athlete': NY Times, 4 August 1926.

Page 137 *secretary of war's office*: The Old Executive Office Building: A Victorian Masterpiece, fig. 44; Washington Post, 2 February 1888; NY Tribune, 11 March 1928; site visit.

visitors streamed in: random entries 1925-1929, Appointment Books of Secretary of War, RG 107, NA; NY Times, 8 July 1927.

'antithesis of militarism': NY Times, 9 January 1927.

Page 138 *'chummy talk'*: Associated Press, 13, 15 February 1928; NY Times, 15, 16 February 1928.

preparing for bed: NY Times, 9 July 1927.

school outside Paris: NY Times, 19 September 1926.

Page 139 *'do not intend to make any'*: DFD to Calvin Coolidge, 30 June, 6 July 1927, Coolidge Papers, microfilm roll 34, series 25 (War Department).

'stronger than ever next winter': DFD to Everett Sanders, 9 August 1927, Coolidge Papers, microfilm roll 34, series 25.

'Tanks': Arch Whitehouse, *Tank: The Story of Their Battles and the Men Who Drove Them from Their First Use in World War I to Korea*, 33-34.

'crude and makeshift': Mildred Hanson Gillie, *Forging the Thunderbolt: A History of the Development of the Armored Force*, 20-21.

formations of soldiers on foot: Kenneth Macksey, *The Tank Pioneers*, 76.

'did not attend': NY Times, 21 August 1927; Associated Press, London, 20 August 1927. Gillie, in *Forging the Thunderbolt* (20), claims Davis did attend the maneuvers. However, no contemporary reports in England or the US have been found to support this. The National Archives' Timothy Nenninger ('Organizational Milestones in the Development of American Armor, 1920-1940', mms., 25) points out that, though Military Intelligence Division records (RG 165, National Archives) include many reports on the British mechanized force, they contain no mention of

Davis. In the 9 August 1927 letter to Coolidge's secretary Everett Sanders sent from France, Davis says that 'after one day in England to visit the [war] cemetery there,' he will sail for home (Coolidge Papers, microfilm roll 34, series 25). No mention of any Salisbury Plain maneuvers.

Page 140 *he decided*: Also helpful on Davis's role are Israel, *Dictionary of American Biography*, s.v. 'Davis,' sup. 3, 218, and Paul M. Robinett, *DAB*, s.v. 'Chaffee, Adna Romanza,' sup. 3, 151.

ordered his chief of staff: General Charles P. Summerall to G-3, memo 7 November 1927; Adjutant General Central File, 1926-39, RG 407, AG 354.2, National Archives, as cited in Nenninger, 'Organizational Milestones,' 25.

permanent mechanized force: NY Times, 14 December 1928.

CHAPTER 18 Meanwhile, with the Cup (2)

Page 141 *not be sporting*: NY Times, 7 March 1919.

not ... Lenglen: NY Times, 14 May 1921.

sailed seat cushions: NY Times, 3 September 1921.

ordered a ... tray: S. Wallis Merrihew, *The Quest of the Davis Cup*, 309-310.

Page 142 *made by ... Durgin*: Concord Evening Patriot, 3 August 1921.

1923 ... Australia: Davis Cup, tray engravings.

American continents: 'The Argentine' challenged (but defaulted) in 1921, and, as Argentina, competed in 1923; Mexico and Cuba competed for the first time in 1924.

two ... zones: NY Times, 21 December 1922.

26 countries: International Tennis Federation, *Davis Cup Media Guide, 1997*, 69.

'Tilden's court': Joan Bower, Germantown Cricket Club, interview with author; Frank Deford, 'Bill Tilden,' 14, Frank V. Phelps, 'The Cricket Clubs of Philadelphia,' 17, both in *History of Philadelphia Tennis, 1875-1995*.

'Made at Durgin's': Concord Daily Monitor and New Hampshire Patriot, 13 September 1927.

Page 143 *down Fifth Avenue, Davis bid farewell*: NY Times, 17 September 1927.

waived the duty: NY Times, 25, 26, 27 September 1927.

CHAPTER 19 Hoover Takes Charge

Page 144 *Tilden ... off the team*: NY Times, 21, 24 July 1928.

contacted President Coolidge: Richard Evans, 'Stages For the Ages,' 1987 USTA tournament programs, quoting Ted Tinling.

Collom ... reinstating: NY Times, 26 July 1928.

Page 145 *'ungracious act'* : NY Times, 26 July 1928.

'is guilty of professionalism': Denver Post, 29 July 1928, as quoted by Associated Press.

surprise ... announcement: Herbert Hoover, *Memoirs*, 190; Ishbel Ross, *Grace Coolidge and Her Era*, 223; NY Times, 3 August 1927.

'absurd if he did': William R. Castle Jr. Diaries, 29 August 1927, microfilm holdings, Herbert Hoover Library, West Branch, Iowa.

pass on the news: ibid., 31 August 1927.

Page 146 *'chances ... none at all'*: Castle diaries, 26 November 1927.

'hanging from ... every limb'; boom ... brought to a halt: NY Times, 19 February 1928.

putting their money: Alice Roosevelt Longworth, *Crowded Hours*, 327.

offered his congratulations: NY Times, 16 June 1928; Associated Press, Chicago, 26 July 1928.

here at Kill Devil Hills: Memorial ceremony details, Fred Howard, *Wilbur and Orville*, 429-430; NY Times, 18 December 1928; Eric Hodgins, 'Heavier Than Air,' *The New Yorker*, 13 December 1930, 30-31.

Page 147 *12 horsepower*: Leonard S. Hobbs, *The Wright Brothers' Engines and Their Design*, 28; Howard, *Wilbur and Orville*, 105-107.

'prosperity throughout the world': NY Times, 18 December 1928.

Page 148 *dead before he could be lifted*: ibid.

> *retreat from Moscow*: Hodgins, *New Yorker*, 31.

> *'receptive frame of mind'*: *NY Times*, 10 January 1929, also 9 January, 12 February 1929; Appointment Books of Secretary of War, 9 January 1929, vol. 21, RG 107 entry 98, National Archives, Washington, DC.

> *private memo*: Franklin Fort to Hoover, n.d., Campaign & Transition, General Correspondence-Fort, box 20, Hoover Papers, Hoover Library.

> *by telephone*: *NY Times*, 23 February 1929; Joseph Nathan Kane, *Facts About the Presidents*, 192, though earlier there had been a phone in a booth near the president's office.

> *letter of resignation*: DFD to Calvin Coolidge, 26 February 1929, Campaign & Transition, General Correspondence-Davis, box 20, Hoover Papers; Coolidge to DFD, 27 February 1929, DFD to Coolidge 2 March 1929, Coolidge Papers, microfilm roll 34, series 25 (War Department).

> *'some little time yet'*: Herbert Hoover to DFD, 13 February 1929, Campaign & Transition, General Correspondence-Davis, box 20, Hoover Papers.

> *new secretary of war*: Hoover, *Memoirs*, 191, 218; *NY Times*, 1 March 1929.

> *diplomatic post in Europe*: *NY Times*, 16 May 1929.

> *supporters wrote*: miscellaneous memos, Campaign & Transition, Cabinet Appointments, box 84, and Presidential Secretary's File, box 521, Hoover Papers.

> *going to London*: Castle diaries, 22 October 1927.

Page 149 *never on the short list*: Hoover to Henry L. Stimson, cable 21 February 1929, Stimson to Hoover, cable 23 February 1929, Campaign & Transition, General Correspondence-Stimson, Hoover Papers; *NY Times*, 11 April 1929.

> *'confidence this end'*: Hoover to Stimson, cable 21 February 1929; Lawrence Richey to Christian Herter (for relay to Stimson), telegram 4 February 1929; Stimson response (relayed by Herter), 14 February 1929, General Correspondence- Herter and Stimson, Hoover Papers.

> *'virtually had to select'*: Henry L. Stimson, 'Memorandum of Events Since Becoming Secretary of State,' dictated 28 August 1930, reel 2, vol. 10, (transcription p.7), Henry Lewis Stimson Papers, Yale University Library (microfilm, Herbert Hoover Library). Others thought James Good, Davis's successor as secretary of war, had been behind Davis's selection (Castle diary, 18 May 1929). Castle said he did not understand why Davis had accepted.

> *'springboard to higher office'*: *SL Post Dispatch*, 15 May 1929.

> *highest paid*: *NY Herald Tribune*, 16 May 1928; *World Almanac*, 1930, 39. Though justices of the Supreme Court received $20,000 (chief justice $20,500), they were not 'under the president' even though appointed by the president.

> *actually a telegram*: George Akerson to DFD, 10 May 1929, Presidential Secretary's File, box 521, Hoover Papers. 10,

> *lunch at the White House*: *SL Post-Dispatch*, 15 May 1929; *NY Times*, 16 May 1929.

> *had accepted*: *NY Times*, 16, 18 May 1929. Also among those vying for the post of governor-general was Douglas MacArthur (Carol Petillo, *Douglas MacArthur*, 148; Stanley Karnow, *In Our Image*, 265-266). Cabled MacArthur to Davis 21 May 1929: 'Behalf the Army in the Philippines I extend heartiest felicitations on your appointment as Governor General and anticipate with sincere pleasure the resumption of a personal association which proved so delightful in the past.' (Dwight F. Davis Personal Name File, Part 4, entry 21, box 149, RG 350, National Archives, Washington, DC).

CHAPTER 20 Sharing the Sidewalk

Page 150 *Manila's Pier 7*: *Manila Commerce & Bulletin*, 9 July 1929; *NY Times*, 9 July 1929; *Washington Post*, 8 July 1929.

> *typhoon*: Associated Press, 8 July 1929.

> *Washington for comment*: 'Suggestions for basis of Inaugural Message,' delivered to DFD by

General Francis L. Parker, 6 June 1929; DFD to Parker, telegram, 22 June; Parker to Secretary of War, memo, 24 June and response, 29 June; Secretary of State Henry L. Stimson to Parker 1 July; Parker to DFD, cablegram, 2 July 1929, all from Dwight F. Davis Personal Name File, Part 2, entry 21, box 149, RG 350, National Archives, Washington, DC.

Page 151 *overflowing*: Frederic S. Marquardt, *Before Bataan and After*, 113-114; Lewis E. Gleeck Jr., *The American Governors-General and High Commissioners in the Philippines*, 242.

statements in writing: *Manila Bulletin*, 9 July 1929.

'did not engage in any sports': ibid.

'is usually missing': *SL Globe-Democrat*, 29 July 1929.

back in the United States: World Wide photo, 3 September 1929.

'far beyond its importance': DFD to Patrick J. Hurley, 28 March 1930, DFD Personal Name File, Part 2.

Page 152 *'not to break the trust'*: ibid.; see also Godfrey Hodgson, *The Colonel: The Life and Wars of Henry Stimson*, 139.

younger leaders: 28 March 1930, DFD Personal Name File, Part 2.

'how little we know in Washington', *'off the sidewalks'*: DFD to Hurley, 7 August 1930, DFD Personal Name File, Part 2.

'whirlwind of racial hatred': ibid.

Alice ... coached: Henry L. Stimson, 'Memorandum of Events Since Becoming Secretary of State,' dictated 28 August 1930, reel 2, vol. 10, (transcription p. 7), Henry Lewis Stimson Papers, Yale University Library, New Haven, Connecticut (microfilm, Herbert Hoover Library).

Page 153 *boycotting American cigarettes*: International News Service, 8 April 1930.

'Has Islands' Heart': *American Chamber of Commerce Journal*, October 1930.

Shon traveled to Seattle: radiogram, 25 September 1930, DFD Personal Name File, Part 2.

'will know someone booked': General F. L. Parker to Howard Lewis, 2 January [1930], DFD Personal Name File, Part 2.

Page 154 *Brookes ... visit*: Mabel Brookes, *Crowded Galleries*, 246.

remodelled: DFD to W. Cameron Forbes, 3 October 1930, January 1931, bmsAM1364, W. Cameron Forbes Collection; Forbes to DFD, 26 January 1931, Forbes to Stimpson, 23 March 1931, Forbes Letterbook (book 5) p. 440, W. Cameron Forbes Collection, Houghton Library, Harvard University, Cambridge, Massachusetts.

unfailingly politely: for instance DFD to Forbes, 1 July 1929, 22 April 1931, Forbes Collection.

'era of good feeling': Forbes to Stimson, 23 March 1931, Forbes Letterbook, p. 436, Forbes Collection.

passengers on tour boats: unidentified clipping, December 1931, St. Louis Mercantile Library; Marquardt, *Before Bataan and After*, 119-120.

'fearlessly suppressed': *NY Times*, 9 July 1929.

Page 155 *'Manila's top-heavy bureaucracy'*: Marquardt, *Before Bataan and After*, 116-117.

'errant officials': H. Ford Wilkens, 'Dwight F. Davis: Governor-General of the Philippines,' *Current History*, June 1931, 348.

'loss of free trade privileges': DFD to Parker, 23 November 1929, DFD Personal Name File, Part 2.

'all the Far East': DFD to Hurley, 13 September 1930, DFD Personal Name File, Part 2.

in just his first year: Marquardt, *Before Bataan and After*, 118.

motor boat to facilitate landings: Parker to Quartermaster General, memo, 3 May 1933; Sargent Thomas Hankins to Captain Hans Ottzenn, 28 June 1933; K. F. Baldwin memo, 26 October 1933, DFD Personal Name File, Part 4.

Page 156 *'nightly pow-wows with the tribes'*: *Journal of American Chamber of Commerce*, July 1930, quoted in Gleeck, *The American Governors-General*, 247.

'any ship we ever had': *Cruisin' Around with The Governor General on the U.S.S. Pittsburgh, Spring 1931*, commemorative publication, 112-113, series XII, William McChesney Martin Jr. Papers, Missouri Historical Society, St. Louis.

'corking fast match': *Cruisin' Around*, 22, and for other details on the tour.

fencing-like movements: souvenir program, Jogyakarta, 30 March 1931, family collection.

Page 157 *'ordinary official letter'*: *Malay Mail*, 17 March 1931, reprinted in *Cruisin' Around*, 63.

'brief but lavish festivities': *Time*, 6 April 1931, 22-23.

'on transportation alone': *Milwaukee Journal*, 23 July 1931.

two and a half times better: Gleeck, *The American Governors-General*, 252.

Page 158 *'ill equipped'*: ibid., 247.

'oppressed peasantry': ibid., 252-253.

'unsound foundation for roads': ibid., 252; *NY Times*, mail dispatch 10 June 1931, 17 July 1931.

'since he assumed office': *NY Herald Tribune*, 23 July 1931.

'treasury deficit behind me': *El Debate*, n.d., quoted by Walter Robb in the *Washington Star*, 2 August 1931.

'remain in office indefinitely': *Philippine Herald*, n.d., quoted in *NY Times*, 6 September 1931.

long leave of absence: *NY Times*, 6 September 1931; *Filipino Nation*, October 1931.

Page 159 *'petulant', 'churn-dog'*: Ted Roosevelt to Eleanor Butler Roosevelt, 19 November 1931, container 5, Family Correspondence, Theodore Roosevelt Jr. Papers, Manuscript Division, Library of Congress, Washington, DC. The Roosevelt family letters for fall 1931 provide a fascinating view backstage at a presidential appointment. Douglas MacArthur was among those whose help was enlisted. 'If you write him, remember his name is MacArthur,' Eleanor cautioned her husband, in a note that all uncertain spellers could appreciate (handwritten note signed E at bottom of MacArthur to Mrs. Theodore Roosevelt, 5 November 1931, container 29, Special Correspondence, T. Roosevelt Jr. Papers).

'up with Harding': Ted Roosevelt to Eleanor Roosevelt, 21 November 1931, T. Roosevelt Jr. Papers.

objections to the sometimes mercurial': Gleeck, *American Governors-General*, 279, quoting Stimson's diary.

'let it be Alice': as quoted in *NY Times*, 16 December 1931.

'had his leg pulled': Gleeck, *American Governors-General*, 279, quoting Stimson's diary.

'did his part': EBR pencil note at the bottom of DFD to Ted Roosevelt, 1 March 1923, container 27, Special Correspondence, T. Roosevelt Jr. Papers.

'proud to be a tyrant': *NY Times*, 21 November 1931.

Page 160 *economically developed Philippines*: *Philippines Herald*, 8 July 1931; *American Chamber of Commerce Journal*, December 1931; Marquardt, *From Bataan*, 130-132; Gleeck, *American Governors-General*, 255.

'almost inconceivable': *NY Times*, 21 November 1931.

'most successful governor-general': Gleeck, *The American Governors-General*, 371.

'they want Dwight Davis': *Philippine Herald*, 20 November 1931, quoted in *NY Times*, 21 November 1931.

CHAPTER 21 Family Matters

Page 161 *get out of the market*: family interviews.

ship reached North America: F. L. Parker to D. J. Hanscom, American Mail Line, 4 December 1931, Dwight F. Davis, Personal Name File, Part 4, entry 21, box 149, RG 350, National Archives, Washington, DC.

'end after all': DFD to Ted Roosevelt Jr., 19 June 1932, container 27, Special Correspondence, Theodore Roosevelt Jr. Papers, Library Of Congress, Washington, DC.

move ... Mellon: Dwight F. Miller, Herbert Hoover Library, communication to author.

my chief, President Hoover: Associated Press, 8 July 1931; *Philippine Herald*, 11 July 1931; *NY Times*, 9 July, 5 November 1931; *Washington Star*, 9 January 1932.

Page 162 *not been considered a foolish man*: 9 July 1931.

ready for a rest: *Washington Star*, 19 January 1932.

distant cousin: Roosevelt genealogy, *Theodore Roosevelt Association Journal*, Winter 1990, 45. They were fifth cousins.

tendered his resignation: DFD to Herbert Hoover, Hoover to DFD, 9 January 1932, DFD Personal Name File, Part 4.

stopping in Boston: Bureau of Insular Affairs memo, 12 January 1932 (misdated 1931), DFD Personal Name File, Part 4.

'and return then': DFD to Ted Roosevelt, 11 March 1932, Special Correspondence, T. Roosevelt Jr. Papers.

Legion of Honour: NY Times, 3 February 1932.

Page 163 *'In these songs'*: unpublished mms., Whitman family papers.

'ordinary, friendly game': Bunny Austin, interview with author; A.W. Myers, *Memory's Parade*, 159.

only two ways public men: Myers (who was present at the luncheon), *Memory's Parade*, 157-158; *NY Times*, 2 March 1932. DFD sometimes ruefully joked about being remembered only as the Davis Cup donor, say family members.

Page 164 *an excellent seat was found*: Herbert Reed, *Scribner's*, July-December 1933, 27. Details from this earliest version have changed as the story has passed down through the years through the family, but the point has stayed the same.

'what's important in life': William McChesney Martin Jr. to author, 25 October 1985.

greeted with great applause: NY Times, 31 July 1932, 30 November 1945.

Page 165 *victory was snatched*: Al Laney, *Covering the Court*, 171-172; *NY Times*, 1, 2, 7, 10 August 1932; Trengove, *Story of the Davis Cup*, 107-110

wished he'd never donated: John Van Ryn, interview with author; Bud Collins, *Boston Globe*, 24 November 1996.

question whether international sports: NY Times, 7 August 1932.

tightened the rules: Trengove, *Davis Cup*, 110.

cure: DFD to Ted Roosevelt, 19 June 1932, Special Correspondence, T. Roosevelt Jr. Papers; Helen Davis Hermes, interview with author.

right into the stomach: Hermes interview.

Berlin clinic, died: Associated Press, 11 October ; *SL Globe-Democrat*, 12 October; *NY Times*, 12 October 1932; family interviews.

hurried back to St. Louis: SL Post-Dispatch, 13 October 1932.

'my dear friend': SL Post- Dispatch, 14 October 1932.

Page 166 *Meridian Plantation*: SL Globe-Democrat, 5 February 1934.

came down for the hunting: Mary Taussig Hall, interview with author.

'hope I miss': Hermes interview.

ice cream cone: Hermes and Cynthia Davis Martin, interviews with author.

easy to talk to: Lord Sherfield (Roger Makins), interview with author.

Page 167 *copious tears*: John G. Davis, interview with author.

the banks closed: W. P. Cooney to William McChesney Martin Jr., 6 March 1945, William McChesney Martin Jr. Papers, Missouri Historical Society, St. Louis; *Time*, 19 December 1932, 12.

Broadway shows: Cynthia Davis to William M. Martin, telegram 18 March 1937, Martin Papers.

enthusiastic about the theater: miscellaneous letters, Martin Papers,

Page 168 *would always be proud*: Hermes interview.

Grace Coolidge: St. Louis Globe-Democrat, 8 April 1936.

'never hurt me': Dwight F. Davis, 'Things I Did Not Say,' *Good Housekeeping*, March 1935, 224-225.

'charming as ever': Theodore Roosevelt Jr. diary, vol. 3, 24 September 1923, container 1, Theodore Roosevelt Jr. Papers, Manuscript Division, Library of Congress, Washington, D. C.

Page 169 *nearly $3 million*: Associated Press, 4 December 1936.

English manor house: George Miller, International Brotherhood of Electrical Workers, interview with author; 'Bayberry Land,' typescript based on information from Bob Keenan, Bayberry Land archives; *Kansas City Star*, 5 August 1932; *Hampton Express*, 21 November 1980; site visit. In 1949 Pauline Sabin Davis, to the astonishment of fellow Southampton residents, sold Bayberry Land to the Joint Industry Board of Electrical Industry for use as a vacation and education center for IBEW members.

'more hypocrisy': *NY Herald,* 11 December 1932.

'Joan of Arc': N.A.N.A., *Boston Globe,* 30 June 1932.

married: Associated Press, 8 May 1936.

CHAPTER 22 Meanwhile, with the Cup (3)

Page 170 *'plinth'*: The first layer of the base was bought from Tiffany & Co. and made in London in 1935 (as indicated by silver hallmarks on the base). This two-year delay (the engravings on the base plaques begin with the 1933 British victory over France) possibly indicates a period of uncertainty among Davis Cup Nations about how to continue the engraved silver record.

record 31: International Tennis Federation, *1997 Media Guide,* 69.

handsome New Yorker: Shields passed along his good looks to his granddaughter, actress Brooke Shields, wife of 1980s-1990s American Davis Cup player Andre Agassi. Sam Hardy was one of the California Hardy brothers who had competed against Dwight Davis and other East Coast players in 1899 during the West Coast tennis tour which helped give Davis the idea for an international competition and trophy.

save himself for ... Davis Cup: *NY Times,* 4 July 1931; Sidney B. Wood Jr., 'How I Won Wimbledon by Default,' excerpt from 'Aged In The Wood,' mms. Wood once told tennis historian Frank Phelps he considered himself a 'half-Wimbledon champion.'

U.S ... lost: Sidney B. Wood Jr., interview with author.

Page 171 *bare ... knees*: Bunny Austin, interview with author.

'bade it godspeed': Associated Press, 30 July 1933; *NY Times,* 29 July, 31 July 1933.

champagne toasts: Fred Perry, *Autobiography,* 62-66.

CHAPTER 23 Brookings

Page 172 *repeater watch and chronograph*: *American Lawn Tennis,* 20 April 1936, 16; *Lawn Tennis and Badminton,* 1 August 1936; United Press, 27 July 1936. The watch has been donated by the Davis family to the International Tennis Hall of Fame.

'who happened to be the donor': *Lawn Tennis and Badminton,* 1 August 1936.

still had some bite to it: William J. Clothier II, interview with author.

Page 173 *chagrin of ... younger opponents*: Clothier interview; *American Lawn Tennis,* 5 September 1936, 10.

'turn more quickly': *SL Globe-Democrat,* 29 September 1935.

'autocratic methods': *American Lawn Tennis,* 20 November 1938.

Page 174 *Delano resigned*: Donald T. Critchlow, *The Brookings Institution, 1916-1952,* 135. Frederic A. Delano was Franklin Delano Roosevelt's uncle, a brother of FDR's mother (index, Frederic A. Delano Papers, online index of FDR Library, Hyde Park, New York, maintained by Marist College).

four days later: Minutes, Annual Meeting of the Board of Trustees, 21 May 1937, Minutes and Agendas, 1927-1984, box 2, Archives, Brookings Institution, Washington, DC.

internationalist outlook: Critchlow, *Brookings,* 136-137.

'Rah! Rah! Davis Cup': Moulton to DFD, 11 August 1937, 'Davis, Dwight F.,' Board of Trustees Files, accession no. 83-003, Brookings Archives.

four areas: Harold G. Moulton to J. S. Myrick, 17 December 1945; resolution adopted by Board of Trustees following the death of Dwight F. Davis; other miscellaneous letters, Davis file, Brookings Archives.

'too speculative': DFD to Moulton, telegram 24 August 1943, Davis file, Brookings Archives.

Page 175 *'in this country'*: Harvard College, *Class of 1900, Secretary's Ninth Report,* 1940, 71, Harvard University Archives, Cambridge, Massachusetts.

work of Brookings: DFD to Moulton, 23 October 1937, Davis file, Brookings Archives; DFD to Herbert Hoover, 23 October 1937, Herbert Hoover Papers, box 45, Herbert Hoover Library, West

Branch, Iowa.

21 possibilities: DFD to Hoover, 23 October 1937, Hoover Papers.

brick house on Decatur Place: 'History of the Codman-Davis House,' brochure, Royal Thai Embassy, Washington, DC. The house is now the official residence of the Ambassador of Thailand.

'Uncle Dwight': Sheila Smith Cochrun, interview with author.

Page 176 *'That was an order':* Lord Sherfield (Sir Roger Makins), interview with author.

estate in trust: SL Globe-Democrat, 11 August 1937.

Sam died: SL Globe-Democrat, 16 June 1940.

CHAPTER 24 Meanwhile, with the Cup (4)

Page 177 *greatest ever:* Allison Danzig, for one, in 'The Story of J. Donald Budge' in *Budge on Tennis,* 28, 30.

Budge and ... von Cramm: Don Budge, interview with author; Al Laney, *Covering the Court,* 229-241; Danzig, 'The Story of J. Donald Budge' in *Budge on Tennis,* 28-31; Don Budge and Frank DeFord, *Don Budge: A Tennis Memoir,* 3-19; Egon Steinkamp, *Gottfried von Cramm: Der Tennisbaron,* 9-12; Ted Tinling, *Love and Faults;* 148-151; NY Times, 6 August 1937.

Page 178 *crowd's amusement:* Bunny Austin, interview with author.

'too long for it to stay away': NY Sun, 27 July 1937.

double-decker bus; champagne: NY Times. 6 August 1937.

by careful strategy; picked these ... four: Budge interview; Budge and DeFord, *A Tennis Memoir,* 101-103.

Page 179 *'a grand slam':* Allison Danzig, NY Times, 18 September 1938.

bridge: Alan Trengove, *The Story of the Davis Cup,* 130. (Danzig doesn't ruin his metaphor by explaining it, of course.)

1939: NY Times, 5 September 1939; Associated Press, 1 September 1939; Ed Fabricius, 'Davis Cup Ties in Philadelphia,' *History of Philadelphia Tennis 1875-1995,* 22-23; Vic Seixas, interview with author. Seixas, who lived down the road from the Merion Cricket Club, was head ballboy for these matches and would himself play seven years of Davis Cup during the 1950s.

'in excellent hands': NY Times, 6 September 1939.

CHAPTER 25 Taps

Page 180 *'would have starved to death':* Richard Austin Smith, 'Bill Martin: A Talent for Timing,' *Fortune,* October 1955, 154.

called Grandpa: Harvard College, *Class of 1930, Twenty-Fifth Anniversary Report,* 264, HUD 330.25, Harvard University Archives, Cambridge, Massacusetts.

returned to public life: Associated Press, 7 May 1940.

Page 181 *'brains not physiques':* SL Globe-Democrat, 8 March, 26 May 1942.

pamphlet of regulations: War Department, *Army Specialist Corps Regulations (Tentative)* (Washington, DC.: Government Printing Office, 1942), 'Davis, Dwight F.,' Board of Trustees Files, Archives, Brookings Institution, Washington, DC.

'chocolate soldier,' 'infra dig': The Reminiscences of Harvey Bundy, 256-257, Oral History Collection, Columbia University, New York.

'dignity of their own uniform': Henry L. Stimson and McGeorge Bundy, *On Active Service In Peace And War,* 455-457, with quotations from Stimson's diaries.

Corps ... abolished: Associated Press, 31 October 1942.

'noble in purpose': Stimson and Bundy, *Active Service,* 457.

one of 16 bombs: John Barrett, *One Hundred Wimbledon Championships,* 102.

Page 182 *'Roll on the day':* NY Herald Tribune, 19 January 1941.

name their son for ... president: Lord Sherfield (Roger Makins) and Dwight Makins, interviews with author.

Pauline ... resigned position: Associated Press, 19 December 1943.

Davis's health: Moulton to DFD, 6 January 1942, 'Davis, Dwight F.,' Board of Trustees Files,

Brookings Archives; Certificate of Death, District of Columbia Bureau of Vital Statistics, 28 November 1945.

'in the way of the gardener': DFD to Harold Moulton, 30 June 1943, Brookings Archives.

'good fettle': Moulton to DFD, 18 July 1945, Brookings Archives.

Page 183 *'sports they had loved'*: Mabel Brookes, *Crowded Galleries*, 246-247.

condition worsened: Moulton to DFD, 21 November 1945, Brookings Archives.

children gathered: Helen Davis Hermes, interview with author.

myocardial failure: Certificate of Death, 28 November 1945.

funeral: Department of Defense, Internment Records, Arlington National Cemetery; *Washington Star,* 29 November 1945; *SL Globe-Democrat,* 30 November 1945; *American Lawn Tennis,* February 1946; Master Sargent Michael Buckley, Protocol for Secretary of Defense, communication with author; site visit.

Page 184 *'Lieutenant Colonel'*: Pauline Davis to William McChesney Martin Jr., 26 January 1946, Martin Papers, Missouri Historical Society, St. Louis. Pauline asked Martin to find out for her what rank should be used on Davis's tombstone.

'his state and his nation': NY Sun, 1 December 1945.

'human life and relationships': Lawn Tennis and Badminton, 15 December 1945, 349.

CHAPTER 26 Only a Game?

Page 185 *Bank of New South Wales*: Neale Fraser to author, 24 October 1997.

emotional tribute: American Lawn Tennis, February 1947, 7-8.

always be remembered: 'The Much Traveled Cup,' official program, *Davis Cup Challenge Round, Forest Hills, N.Y., 1947,* 29.

'out Parker Parker': Walter Pate, 'The Recovery of the Davis Cup,' *Atlantic Monthly*, August 1947, 38.

appeared to 'rest': Associated Press, 26 December 1946; *Time,* 6 January 1947.

'percentage tennis': Jack Kramer with Frank DeFord, *The Game,* 27-42; Julius Heldman, 'The Style of Jack Kramer,' *Fireside Book of Tennis,* 279-282.

Page 186 *'regain the coveted trophy'*: United Press, 29 December 1946.

case to be eased through: Pate, *Atlantic Monthly,* 40.

Los Angeles Tennis Club: Kramer with DeFord, *The Game,* 27-31.

holding the bowl: NY Times, 12 January 1947.

'great deal of pleasure': NY Times, 4 February 1947.

Page 187 *stadium seating:* This would be a record for tennis crowds until 30,500 saw the Billie Jean King-Bobby Riggs rhinestone-spangled 'Battle of the Sexes' indoors in Houston in 1973. Actually, says King, her Ted Tinling-designed dress, now at the Smithsonian, had tiny mirrors not rhinestones sewn on it (*Tennis,* August 1998, 28).

golden miniature: Mabel Brookes, *Crowded Galleries,* 89.

'are ever pressed': Alan Trengove, *The Story of the Davis Cup,* 186.

'take a deep swallow': Tony Trabert, video interview with John Barrett and Barry Williams.

Page 188 *'squeeze the oranges', clay ant hills*: Roy Emerson, interview with author.

flip the ... counters: Norman Gengaults-Smith (grandson of Norman Brookes), interview with author.

under Fraser's bed: Neale Fraser, interview with author.

Page 189 *second year of balloting: NY Times,* 29 May 1956.

first ... Americans to play at Wimbledon: Frank V. Phelps, 'Joseph Sill Clark, 1861-1956,' *History of Philadelphia Tennis,1875 -1995,* 8.

'than any other one operation': James Van Alen to William McChesney Martin Jr., 4 May 1974, box 49, folder 2, series VII, William McChesney Martin Jr. Papers, Missouri Historical Society, St. Louis.

plaster casts were made: Sara Kirtlink, Gorham Co., interview with author. The casts were included in the Gorham archive material given to the John Hay Library at Brown University

(Mark Brown and Samuel J. Hough, communications with author).

William Knoll: *U.S.L.T.A. Service Bulletin*, June 1955, 2; September 1955, 3.

Page 190 *cup's spinner*: A letter to the editor of the *Boston Sunday Herald,* 2 August 1936, from the Concord Silversmiths Corporation said William H. Morton 'spun' the famous cup'; *Hands That Built New Hampshire* (1940) gave the honor to a William Rowan (145). See also Chapter 5.

and individual players: Starting in 1956, captains' names were added as well, partially as a tribute to Harry Hopman, according to Trengove, *Story of the Davis Cup,* 193.

Page 191 *'illegal amateur I had been'*: Kramer with Deford, *The Game,* 132.

T. Gaunt & Co.: 'Valuation of Goods,' memorandum 28 February 1984, from Garrard & Co. to International Tennis Federation; David Studham, Melbourne Cricket Club, to Catherine Zusy, 13 and 21 November 1996. Zusy, an independent fine arts curator, has been particularly helpful in tracing the Gaunt connection.

Page 192 *challenge round would be replaced*: *NY Times*, 4 May, 2 July 1971; Trengove, *Story of the Davis Cup,* 242; Bud Collins and Zander Hollander, *Modern Encyclopedia of Tennis,* 486.

linesman even massaged: Colin Dibley, interview with author.

Page 193 *'no game can afford'*: Herbert Warren Wind, 'Cupa Davis,' *New Yorker,* 4 November 1972, 59-71; *Sports Illustrated,* 23 October 1972, 22-25; *Time,* 30 October 1972, 69; Collins and Hollander, *Modern Encyclopedia of Tennis,* xvii; Erik van Dillen, interview with author.

'here in Budapest': John Davis, interview with author; Wind, *New Yorker,* 70.

Page 194 *'no national boundaries'*: DFD, 'The Establishment of an International Trophy,' *Fifty Years of Lawn Tennis in the United States*, 71.

trophy out of its misery: Murray Janoff, 'It's Time to Scrap the Cup, Pete!', unidentified clipping (1972?) with accompanying letter, John Davis to William McChesney Martin Jr., 11 February 1975, Martin Papers. In a reply two weeks later, Martin wrote that another problem with retiring the cup at the moment was that the US was currently not holding it and 'I don't think it seems very gracious to try to retire it when you are no longer in possession of it' (Martin to John Davis, 24 February 1975, Martin Papers). Pete (Dwight F. Davis Jr.) had died in 1973.

'is worth saving': Bud Collins, *NY Times,* 2 January 1977.

Page 195 *two significant changes*: *NY Times*, 8 October 1980.

'logical sequel': Trengove, *Story of the Davis Cup,* 250.

Page 196 *invited the victorious skipper*: ibid., 298; Neale Fraser to author, 3 November 1997.

pitcher and the big bowl: Brian Tobin, interview with author.

'don't tell me there's no chance,' 'Davis Cup thing is friendship': *NY Times*, 30 November 1992.

Davis Memorial Tennis Center: *SL Globe-Democrat*, 9 May 1963, 24 December 1965; Judy Dippold, center manager, communication with author.

Davis city park: 'Dwight Davis Park,' information sheet, Department of Parks, Recreation and Forestry, St. Louis; *SL Globe-Democrat*, 2 August 1962.

Page 197 *first visual image*: *Golf and Lawn Tennis*, 25 July 1900, 353.

Chapter 27 Malmö

Page 198 *have won the cup more often*: most match and player statistics in this chapter from International Tennis Federation, *Davis Cup Media Guide, 1997; Event Guide, World Group Final, 1996;* John Barrett, ed., Christine Forrest, player biographies, *ITF World of Tennis, 1997*; Rino Tommasi, *Tennis Record Book, 1997.*

Page 201 *'achieves Utopia'*: Michiko Kakutani, 'Making Art of Sport,' *NY Times Magazine,* 15 December 1996, paraphrasing author Peter Williams in *The Sports Immortals.*

watching television: *Tennis Week,* 20 February 1997, 50.

Page 202 *'so many people pulling them'*: Tom Gullikson, interview with author.

Page 204 *Longwood...now located*: Report of the Board of Governors of the Longwood Cricket Club on Permanent Grounds, 1911; miscellaneous notes and clippings Longwood Scrapbook, Longwood Cricket Club, all in Longwood CC Archives, Chestnut Hill, Massachusetts. According to the scrapbook, the club's first annual meeting in its new home was 15 January 1923. Minutes of a 1924 board meeting conveyed the club's gratitude for its original site: 'For many years the Longwood Cricket Club was able through the generosity of the Sears family to provide its members with ideal playing conditions for a nominal sum' (Robert Minton, *One Hundred Years of Longwood*, 20).

original site: Jane Otte, Winsor School, communications with author; Charles W. Hubbard to Charles E. Stratton, 11 March 1908; Resolution concerning deed of Davis Sears by the Board of Overseers of the Poor, City of Boston, 22 April 1908; Hubbard to Charles S. Hamlin, Report of Committee on Building, 29 April 1908, all in Winsor School Archives; Atlas of the City of Boston (Philadelphia: G. W. Bromley & Co., 1890) plate 38; *Boston Globe*, 21 November 1908.

Page 205 *14 grandchildren*: Dwight F. Davis III, John G. Davis (children of Dwight F. Jr.); Cynthia Colman, Molly Viscountess Norwich, Virginia Shapiro, Christopher Makins, Patricia Makins, Dwight Makins (children of Alice); Diana Martin, William M. Martin III, Cynthia Ghenea (children of Cynthia); Helena Hermes, Cynthia Hermes, Timothy Hermes (children of Helen).

none lived to see: Concord Evening Monitor, 11 September 1903, 8 May, 29 May 1905.

Page 206 *third tier*: The American silver company Reed & Barton is building three new mahogany tiers for the base. On these will be affixed the original plaques from the first two tiers, as well as blank plaques for the next 30 years (Catherine Barrett Cornwall, Reed & Barton, to author, 22 September 1998).

Page 208 *old-fashioned way*: In the 12-point tie-break, introduced in Davis Cup in 1989, at 6-6 (except in the fifth set) the match goes to whoever first wins 7 points (by 2) in the deciding game (Bud Collins and Zander Hollander, *Bud Collins' Modern Encyclopedia of Tennis*, 487).

Page 210 *'tensely emotional'*: David Miller, *Times*, 3 December 1996.

'the greatest final': Simon O'Hagan, *Independent*, 3 December 1996.

Epilogue *at the foot of a statue*: Independent, 4 December 1996; Régine Tourres, Fédération Française de Tennis, to author, 3 February 1997.

Select Bibliography

COLLECTIONS

There is no tidy, inclusive Dwight F. Davis Collection in any university library or historical society archive. Davis left no journals or collection of personal papers, and his official papers exist to a greater or often lesser degree in a variety of locations. Davis correspondence connected with his years in the Philippines can be found in files of the Bureau of Insular Affairs in the National Archives at College Park, Maryland, and in the W. Cameron Forbes Collection, Houghton Library, Harvard University. Unfortunately there seem to be no similarly extensive and easily accessible files covering his years in the War Department other than some correspondence, minimally indexed, in the Coolidge Papers, available on microfilm. Some Davis correspondence and references can be found at the Herbert Hoover Presidential Library in West Branch, Iowa, primarily in the Hoover Papers, the William R. Castle Diaries (microfilm) and the Henry L. Stimson Diaries (original in Manuscripts and Archives, Yale University Library). At the Missouri Historical Society in St. Louis, there are a few Dwight Davis letters in various collections including the William McChesney Martin Jr. Papers. There are also a few Davis letters in the Theodore Roosevelt Jr. Papers at the Library of Congress, and frequent Davis references in the Ted Roosevelt Diaries (unindexed). Some Davis letters are in the archives of the Brookings Institution in Washington, DC.

Pauline Sabin Davis left her papers to the Schlesinger Library at Radcliffe College in Boston. There is scarcely any mention of Davis in her journals, which do not cover the years of their marriage. Particularly helpful at the New York Public Library was the collection of US regimental histories and the newspaper morgue of the *New York Sun*. The *Boston Globe* morgue, made available through the good offices of Bud Collins, also produced much that was useful. On tennis matters, the excellent and extensive William M. Fischer Lawn Tennis Collection at St. John's University, Jamaica (Queens), New York, provided much information, as did the Kenneth Ritchie Wimbledon Library in London. Mary Lou Strong has efficiently preserved Holcombe Ward's scrapbooks, found at the Seabright Lawn Tennis and Cricket Club in Rumson, New Jersey. Dr. James Dwight's scrapbooks have been given to Harvard's Houghton Library. They contain no information about the Davis Cup's origins.

Material on the Davis Cup manufacturer, the William B. Durgin Co., was found at the New Hampshire Historical Society, Concord, including a file of letters from a John F. Reilly, a Durgin employee in the 1890s-1900s. In the 1940s Reilly decided to correspond with all of the former Durgin employees he could locate. He deposited their letters and reminiscences in the Concord Library, so that 'some future historian will find some of his spade work already done'. As it turned out, 'his spade' was 'her spade'. I hope John Reilly would approve of Chapter 5.

BOOKS

Newspaper and periodical articles, theses, dissertations and other unpublished material have been given full citations in chapter notes. Books on tennis, because of their number, are listed here in a separate category.

GENERAL

Ackroyd, Peter. *T. S. Eliot, A Life*. New York: Simon & Schuster, 1984.

'Annual Report of the Park Commissioner', 1908. 'Annual Report of the Park Department', 1912-1914. 'Annual Report of the Division of Parks and Recreation', 1915, 1916. In *Mayor's Message with Accompanying Documents to the Municipal Assembly of the City of St. Louis*. St. Louis: City of St. Louis.

Army War College, Historical Section. *Order of Battle of the United States Land Forces in the World War, American Expeditionary Forces*. Washington: US Government Printing Office, 1931.

Bauer, Theodore W. *History of the Industrial College of the Armed Forces*. Washington: Alumni Association of the Industrial College of the Armed Forces, 1983.

Beale, Howard K., ed. *Diary of Edward Bates, 1859-1866*. Washington: US Government Printing Office, 1933.

Brooks, Jerome. *The $30,000 Cup: The Stormy History of the Defense of the America's Cup*. New York: Simon & Schuster, 1958.

Caner, George C. Jr. *History of the Essex County Club, 1893-1993*. Manchester-by-the-Sea, Mass.: Essex County Club, 1995.

Carnes, Mark C. and John A. Garraty. *Mapping America's Past*. New York: Henry Holt, 1996.

Carpenter, Charles H. Jr. *Gorham Silver, 1831-1981*. New York: Dodd, Mead, 1982.

Carpenter, Charles H. Jr. with Mary Grace Carpenter. *Tiffany Silver*. New York: Dodd, Mead, 1978.

Carter, Robert L. *Pictorial History of the 35th Division*. St. Louis, 1933.

Commager, Henry Steele, ed. *Documents of American History*. 6th edition. New York: Appleton-Century-Crofts, 1958.

Condon, Yvonne M. 'St. Louis 1904.' In *Historical Dictionary of World's Fairs and Expositions, 1851-1988*. John E. Findling, ed. Westport, Conn.: Greenwood Press, 1990.

Critchlow, Donald T. *The Brookings Institution: Expertise and the Public Interest in a Democratic Society*. DeKalb, Ill.: Northern Illinois University Press, 1985.

Dale, Alzina Stone. *T. S. Eliot, The Philosopher Poet*. Wheaton, Ill.: H. Shaw, 1988.

Davis, Burke. *The Billy Mitchell Affair*. New York: Random House, 1967.

Eliot, T. S. *The Complete Poems and Plays of T. S. Eliot.*. London: Faber & Faber, 1969.

Garland, Joseph E. *Boston's Gold Coast, The North Shore, 1890-1929*. Boston: Little, Brown, 1981.

Gilbert, Martin. *Atlas of the First World War: The Complete History*. New York: Oxford University Press, 1994.

Gillie, Mildred Hanson. *Forging the Thunderbolt: A History of the Development of the Armored Force*. Harrisburg, Pa.: Military Service Publishing, 1947.

Gleeck, Lewis E. Jr. *The American Governors-General and High Commissioners in the Philippines*. Quezon City: New Day Publishers, 1986.

Good, James. *Capital Losses*. Washington: Smithsonian Institution Press.

Gordon, Lyndall. *Eliot's Early Years*. New York: Noonday Press, 1977.

The 'H' Book of Harvard Athletics. Vol. I, John A. Blanchard, ed. Vol. II, Geoffrey H. Movius, ed. Cambridge, Mass.: Harvard Varsity Club, 1923, 1964.

Hall, Lee. *Olmsted's America: An 'Unpractical Man' and His Vision of Civilization*. Boston: Little, Brown, 1995.

Hands That Built New Hampshire: The Story of Granite State Craftsmen, Past and Present. Federal Writers' Project. Brattleboro, Vt.: Stephen Daye Press, 1940.

Harvard College. *Class of 1900, Secretary's Report*, 1906, 1915, 1921, 1925, 1940, 1945, 1950. *Class of 1930*, 1955. Cambridge, Mass.: Harvard University Press.

Hewes, James E. Jr. *From Root to McNamara: Army Organization and Administration, 1900-1963*. Washington: Center of Military History, United States Army, 1975.

History of the Louisiana Purchase Exposition. St. Louis: Universal Exposition Publishing, 1905.

Hobbs, Leonard S. *The Wright Brothers' Engines and Their Design*. Washington: Smithsonian Institution Press, 1971.

Hodgson, Godfrey. *The Colonel: The Life and Wars of Henry Stimson, 1867-1950*. New York: Knopf, 1990.

Hofstadter, Richard. *The Age of Reform: From Byron to F.D.R.* New York: Knopf, 1955.

Hofstadter, Richard. *The Progressive Movement, 1900-1915*. Englewood Cliffs, NJ: Prentice-Hall, 1963.

Hogg, Ian V. *Armour in Conflict: The Design and Tactics of Armoured Fighting Vehicles*. London: Jane's, 1980.

Hoover, Herbert. *The Memoirs of Herbert Hoover: The Cabinet and the Presidency, 1920-1933*. New York: Macmillan, 1952.

Howard, Fred. *Wilbur and Orville: A Biography of the Wright Brothers*. New York: Knopf, 1987.

Hoyt, Charles B. *Heroes of the Argonne: An Authentic History of the Thirty-Fifth Division*. Kansas City, Mo.: Franklin Hudson, 1919.

Hunter, Julius K. *Westmoreland and Portland Places*. Columbia, Mo.: University of Missouri Press, 1988.

Hurley, Alfred F. *Billy Mitchell: Crusader for Air Power*. New York: Franklin Watts, 1964.

Kane, Joseph Nathan. *Facts About the Presidents*. New York: H. W. Wilson, 1989.

Karnow, Stanley. *In Our Image: America's Empire in the Philippines*. New York: Random House, 1989.

Kenamore, Clair, *From Vauquois Hill to Exermont: A History of the 35th Division of the U.S. Army*. St. Louis: Guard Publishing Co., 1919.

Kirschten, Ernest. *Catfish and Crystal*. Garden City, NY: Doubleday, 1960.

Levine, Isaac Don. *Mitchell: Pioneer of Air Power*. New York: Duell, Sloan & Pearce, 1943.

Lipton, Sir Thomas J., with William Blackwood. *Lipton's Autobiography*. 2nd ed. New York: Duffield & Green, 1932.

Lord, Walter. *The Good Years: From 1900 to the First World War*. New York: Harper, 1960.

Loughlin, Caroline, and Catherine Anderson. *Forest Park*. Columbia, Mo.: Junior League of St. Louis and University of Missouri Press, 1986.

Lyford, James O., ed. *History of Concord New Hampshire*. Vols. I and II. Concord: Rumford Press, 1903.

Macksey, Kenneth. *The Tank Pioneers*. London: Jane's, 1981.

Mallon, Bill. *A Statistical Summary of the 1904 Olympic Games*. Durham, NC: 1981.

Marquardt, Frederic S. *Before Bataan and After: A Personalized History of Our Philippine Experiment*. Indianapolis: Bobbs-Merrill, 1943.

Maurer, Maurer. *Aviation In the U.S. Army, 1919-1939*. Washington: Office of Air Force History, United States Air Force, 1987.

McCullough, David. *Truman*. New York: Simon & Schuster, 1992.

Morison, Elting E. *Turmoil and Tradition: A Study of the Life and Times of Henry L. Stimson*. Boston: Houghton Mifflin, 1960.

Morison, Samuel Eliot, ed. *Development of Harvard University,1869-1929*. Vol. I of Tercentennial History. Cambridge, Mass.: Harvard University Press, 1930.

Morison, Samuel Eliot. *The Oxford History of the American People*. New York: Oxford University Press, 1965.

Mount, Charles Merrill. *John Singer Sargent*. New York: W. W. Norton, 1955.

Murray, Robert K. *The Politics of Normalcy: Governmental Theory and Practice in the Harding-Coolidge Era*. New York: W. W. Norton, 1973.

Nicolay, John G., and John Hay, ed. New and enlarged edition. *Complete Works of Abraham Lincoln*. Harrogate, Tenn.: Lincoln Memorial University, 1894.

North Shore Blue Book, Containing Lists of the Summer Residents of the Principal Resorts from Nahant to Gloucester. Boston: Edward A. Jones, 1896, 1898.

The Old Executive Office Building: A Victorian Masterpiece. Washington: Executive Office of the President, Office of Administration, 1984.

Parkman, Francis, Jr. *The Oregon Trail: Sketches of Prairie and Rocky Mountain Life*. New York: A. L Burt, 1912.

Parsons, Charles S. *New Hampshire Silver*. [Exeter, NH:] Adams Brown, 1933.

Pershing, John J. *My Experiences in the World War*. 2 vols. New York: Frederick A. Stokes, 1931.

Petillo, Carol Morris. *Douglas MacArthur, The Philippine Years*. Bloomington, Ind.: Indiana University Press, 1981.

Pictorial Saint Louis. St. Louis: Dry & Compton, 1875, reprinted 1971.

Primm, James Neal. *Lion of the Valley: St. Louis, Missouri*. 2nd ed. Boulder, Colo.: Pruett Publishing, 1990.

Rainwater, Dorothy T. *Encyclopedia of American Silver Manufacturers*. New York: Crown Publishers, 1975.

Regier, C. C. *The Era of the Muckrakers*. Chapel Hill, NC: University of North Carolina, 1932; reprinted Gloucester, Mass: Peter Smith, 1957.

Report of the Secretary of War to the President, 1922-1928. Washington: US Government Printing Office.

Ross, Ishbel. *Grace Coolidge and Her Era*. New York: Dodd, Mead, 1962.

Scammell, J. M. *History of the Industrial College of the Armed Forces, 1924-1946*. [Typescript, 1946.]

Schwarz, Jordan A. *The Speculator: Bernard M. Baruch in Washington, 1917-1965.* Chapel Hill, NC: University of North Carolina Press, 1981.

Selling Quality Jewels Since 1800: A History of Shreve, Crump & Low Co. Boston, 1974.

Souvenir of the Semi-Centennial Anniversary of the Founding of the House of Saml C. Davis & Co. St. Louis, 1885.

Steffens, Lincoln. *The Shame of the Cities.* 1904. Reprint, First American Century Series, New York: Hill and Wang, 1957.

Stevens, Walter B. *History of St. Louis, The Fourth City, 1764-1909.* Vol. III. St. Louis: S. J. Clarke Publishing, 1909.

Stiles, Henry R., A.M., M.D. *The History and Genealogies of Ancient Windsor, Connecticut,1635-1891.* Vol II, Genealogies and Biographies. Hartford, Conn.: Lockwood & Brainard, 1892.

Stimson, Henry L., and McGeorge Bundy. *On Active Service in Peace and War.* New York: Harper & Bros., 1947, 1948.

Strandberg, John E., and Roger J. Bender. *The Call of Duty: Military Awards and Decorations of the United States of America.* San Jose, Calif.: Bender Publishing, 1994.

Thomson, David S. *Pictorial Biography: HST.* New York: Grosset & Dunlap, 1973.

Townsend, Kim. *Manhood At Harvard: William James and Others.* New York: W. W. Norton, 1996.

Truman, Harry S. *Memoirs. Vol. I: Years of Decision.* Garden City, NY: Doubleday, 1955.

Van Ravenswaay, Charles. *St. Louis: An Informal History of the City and Its People.* St. Louis: Missouri Historical Society Press, 1991.

Wallechinsky, David. *Sports Illustrated Presents The Complete Book of the Summer Olympics.* Boston: Little, Brown, 1996.

Warren, David B., Katherine S. Howe and Michael K. Brown. *Marks of Achievement: Four Centuries of American Presentation Silver.* New York: Museum of Fine Arts, Houston, in association with Harry N. Abrams, 1987.

Wheldon, John. *Machine Age Armies.* London: Abelard-Schuman, 1968.

Whitehouse, Arch. *Tank: The Story of Their Battles and the Men Who Drove Them from Their First Use in World War I to Korea.* Garden City, NY: Doubleday, 1960.

Winter, William C. *The Civil War in St. Louis, A Guided Tour* (For the Civil War Roundtable). St. Louis: Missouri Historical Society Press, 1994.

TENNIS

Alexander, George E. *Lawn Tennis: Its Founders and Its Early Days.* Lynn, Mass.: H. O. Zimman, 1974.

Ashe, Arthur with Frank Deford. *Arthur Ashe: Portrait in Motion.* Boston: Houghton Mifflin, 1975.

Austin, H. W. ('Bunny') and Phyllis Konstam. *A Mixed Double.* London: Chatto and Windus, 1969.

Baddeley, Wilfred. *Lawn Tennis.* The Oval Series, 3rd ed. London: Routledge, 1903.

Baltzell, E. Digby. *Sporting Gentlemen.* New York: Free Press, 1995.

Barrett, John. *One Hundred Wimbledon Championships.* London: Collins Willow, 1986.

Barrett, John, ed. *ITF World of Tennis,* 1995, 1997. London: Collins Willow.

Brookes, Mabel. *Crowded Galleries.* Melbourne: William Heineman, 1956.

Budge, J. Donald. *Budge on Tennis, with a Biography by Allison Danzig.* New York: Prentice-Hall, 1939.

Budge, Don [and Frank Deford]. *Don Budge: A Tennis Memoir.* New York: Viking Press, 1969.

Burrow, F. R. *Last Eights at Wimbledon, 1877-1926.* London: Lawn Tennis and Badminton, 1926.

Collins, Bud and Zander Hollander, ed. *Bud Collins' Modern Encyclopedia of Tennis,* 2nd ed. Detroit: Visible Ink Press, 1994.

Cummings, Parke. *American Tennis: The Story of the Game and Its People.* New York: Little, Brown, 1957.

Danzig, Allison and Peter Schwed, ed. *The Fireside Book of Tennis.* New York: Simon and Schuster, 1972.

Davis Cup by NEC Media Guide, 1996-1998. London: International Tennis Federation.

Deford, Frank. *Big Bill Tilden: The Triumphs and the Tragedy.* New York: Simon and Schuster, 1976.

Fifty Years of Lawn Tennis in the United States. New York: United States Lawn Tennis Association, 1931.

Janoff, Murray. *Game! Set! Match!* New York: Stadia Sports Publishing, 1973.

Kramer, Jack, with Frank Deford. *The Game: My 40 Years in Tennis*. New York: G. P. Putnam's Sons, 1979.

Laney, Al. *Covering the Court: A 50-Year Love Affair with the Game of Tennis*. New York: Simon and Schuster, 1968.

Little, Alan. *Wimbledon Compendium, 1994, 1995*. London: All England Lawn Tennis and Croquet Club.

Merrihew, S. Wallis. *The Quest of the Davis Cup*. Lawn Tennis Library, vol. 6. New York: American Lawn Tennis, 1928.

Metzler, Paul. *Tennis Styles and Stylists*. New York: Macmillan, 1970; Sydney: Angus & Robertson, 1969.

Minton, Robert. *One Hundred Years of Longwood*. Lynn, Mass.: H. O. Zimman, 1977.

Myers, A. Wallis, ed. *Lawn Tennis At Home and Abroad*. London: George Newnes; New York: Charles Scribner's Sons, 1903.

Myers, A. Wallis. *The Complete Lawn Tennis Player*. London: Methuen, 1908.

Myers, A. Wallis. *The Story of the Davis Cup*. London: Methuen, 1913.

Myers, A. Wallis. *Memory's Parade*. London: Methuen, 1932.

Obear, Davison. *Sixty Years of Tennis In St. Louis 1881-1941*. St. Louis, [1941].

Patten, William. *The Book of Sport*. New York: J. F. Taylor, 1901.

Perry, Fred. *Fred Perry: An Autobiography*, London: Stanley Paul, 1984.

Potter, Edward C. *The Davis Cup*. London: Thomas Yoseloff; Cranbury, N.J.: A. S. Barnes, 1969.

Phelps, Frank V., Sandra Harwitt, et al. *History of Philadelphia Tennis, 1875-1995*. Marilyn F. Fernberger, William J. Clothier, Ed Fabricius, ed. [Newport, R. I.:] International Tennis Hall of Fame, 1995.

Schickel, Richard. *The World of Tennis*. New York: Random House, 1975.

Sears, Richard D. 'Lawn Tennis in America'. In *Tennis, Lawn Tennis, Rackets, Fives*. J.M. Heathcote, C. G. Heathcote, et al., ed., 1890, 1903. Reprint, Shedfield, Hampshire: Ashford Press Publishing, 1987.

Spalding Lawn Tennis Annual, various years. New York: American Sports Publishing.

Steinkamp, Egon. *Gottfried Von Cramm, Der Tennisbaron*. Munich: Herbig, 1990.

Talbert, Bill and Pete Axthelm. *Tennis Observed: The USLTA Men's Singles Championships, 1881-1966*. Barre, Mass.: Barre Publishers, 1967.

Talbert, Bill with John Sharnik. *Playing for Life*. Boston: Little, Brown, 1958.

Tinling, Ted with Rod Humphries. *Love and Faults: Personalities Who Have Changed the History of Tennis in My Lifetime*. New York: Crown Publishers, 1979.

Trengove, Alan. *The Story of the Davis Cup*. 2nd ed., rev. London: Stanley Paul, 1991.

United States Tennis Association. *USTA Tennis Yearbook, 1997*. Lynn, Mass.: H. O. Zimman.

Wimbledon Lawn Tennis Museum. *Catalogue, The Kenneth Ritchie Wimbledon Library*. 6th ed. London: Wimbledon Lawn Tennis Museum, 1995.

Wright & Ditson's Lawn Tennis Guide, various years. Boston: Wright & Ditson.

Wynne, Brian A. and Jerry Cotter Wynne. *The Book of Sports Trophies*. New York: Cornwall Books, 1984.

Acknowledgments

A mong the many who helped with this book, seven people deserve special thanks. John G. Davis was instrumental in getting this biographical ball rolling in the first place. John Dodds, Caroline Loughlin, Frank Phelps, Anne Rolfe, Szilvia Szmuk and Margaret Winter showed exceptional interest in this project and provided assistance beyond any reasonable expectation. In addition to John Davis, other members of the Davis family who were extremely helpful in providing information and insights were: Cynthia Makins Colman, Annemarie and Dwight F. Davis III, Helen Davis Hermes, Cynthia Hermes, Tim Hermes, Dwight Makins, Cynthia Davis Martin, Alita Weaver Reed, Sam Weaver, Harry Langenberg, Sheila Smith Cochran and Pauline Smith Willis.

It is an irony of writing history, of researching the past, that those with the best stories, those whose lives and memories stretch back the furthest, are, alas, often no longer around when the resulting book is completed. Three who graciously gave time for interviews but died before this book's publication were two of Dwight Davis's sons-in-law, Lord Sherfield (Roger Makins) and William McChesney Martin Jr., and US Davis Cup player Frank Parker.

My thanks to the following libraries, archives and other organizations and to their knowledgeable and helpful members, staff and directors, past and present: American Legion National Headquarters Library (Bob Cox); Auraria Library (Frank Tapp); Bettmann Archives (Katherine Bang); Boston Athenaeum; Boston Public Library; *Boston Globe* (Jennifer Blake, Bud Collins, Mark Shechtman); Bostonian Society; British Newspaper Library; Brookings Institution (Sarah Chilton); Brown University John Hay Library (Mark Brown); Columbia University Oral History Collection (David Skey); Concord Public Library; Clark Art Institute (Marc Simpson), Connecticut Historical Society (Judith Ellen Johnson); Department of the Army – Center of Military History, Historical Support Branch (Terrence J. Gough), US Army Military History Institute (David A. Keough); Department of Defense, Protocol Office (M/Sgt. Michael Buckley); Essex County Club (Polly Hutchinson, Roland Teague); Essex Institute Library (Eugenia Fountain); French Tennis Federation (Jacques Durr, Régine Tourres); Germantown Cricket Club (Joan Bower); Gorham Co. (Sara Kirtlink, Florence Rafuse, Dave Rogers); Harvard University – Baker Library, Houghton Library, Law School Library (David Warrington), Pusey Library (Brian A. Sullivan), Schlesinger Library/Radcliffe College; Herbert Hoover Library (Dwight M. Miller, Wade Slinde, Cindy Worrell); Imperial War Museum, London (Colin J. Bruce); Indiana Historical Society Library (Leigh Darbee); Indiana State Library; Indianapolis-Marion County Public Library (particularly the social sciences reference librarians and Judy McGeath, inter-library loans).

My thanks also to: International Brotherhood of Electrical Workers/Bayberry Land (George Miller); International Tennis Hall of Fame (Jan Armstrong, Mark Stenning, Debra Teixeira, Mark S. Young II); Kansas Historical Society (Jason Westco); Kortenhaus Communications (Debbie First); Library of Congress (Jeff Flannery); National Archives (Doug Morgan, Tim Nenninger, Joe Schwarz, John Taylor, Mitch Yockelson); Longwood Cricket Club (David Bianco); Malmo Tourist Office (Lars Rudbert); Massachusetts Historical Society; Missouri Historical Society (Martha Clevenger, Jennifer Crets, Kirsten Hammerstrom, Dennis Northcott, Greta Reisel, Duane Sneddeker, Jason Stratman, Dina Young); Melbourne Cricket Club (David Studham); Mulberry Co. Ltd. (Vanessa Lunt); National Civic League (Mike McGrath); National Army Museum, London (C. Wright); National Art Library/Victoria & Albert Museum, London; National Defense University, Archives and History (Susan Lemke, Robert Montgomery); National Public Parks Tennis Association (Hollis Smith, Randy Stratton); New Hampshire Historical Society (Bill Copeley, Steve Cox, Donna-Belle Garvin, James Garvin, Kathryn Grover, Elizabeth Hamlin-Morin); New York Public Library (Thomas Bourke); Purdue University Library (Lawrence J. Mykytiuk); Reed & Barton (Catherine Barrett Cornwall); Royal Thai Embassy; Seabright Lawn Tennis and Cricket Club (Mary Lou Strong); Shreve, Crump & Low (Kevin Jenness, Ben Molinari, Jane Pritchard); St. John's University Library, Special Collections (John Ayers, Anna Ong-Shu, Angeles Ramos-Yunque, Szilvia Szmuk).

ACKNOWLEDGMENTS

And thanks to: St. Louis County Department of Parks and Recreation (Esley Hamilton); St. Louis Department of Parks, Recreation and Forestry (John Anderson), Dwight F. Davis Memorial Tennis Center (Judy Dippold); St. Louis Mercantile Library (Charles Brown, John N: Hoover); St. Louis Public Library (Kathy Smith, Laurel Yatsko); State Historical Society of Missouri; Swedish Tennis Federation (Fredik Belfrage); Tennis Australia (Neale Fraser); Tank Museum/Royal Tank Corps, Dorset (David Fletcher); Theodore Roosevelt Association (John A. Gable, Fritz R. Gordner); Tiffany & Co. (Louisa Bann, Annamarie Sandecki); United States Tennis Association (Bob Garry, Harry Marmion, Brian Walker); University of Missouri/St. Louis (William Fischetti); Washington University Archives (Carole Prietto), Law School (Colleen Erker, Ann Nicholson); Wimbledon Lawn Tennis Museum, Kenneth Ritchie Wimbledon Library (Alan Little); Winsor School (Jane Otte).

The following individuals assisted in a variety of ways: John Alexander, Anand Amritraj, Bunny Austin, Nicolas Ayeboua, Pam Brandvik, Ed Brune, Virginia and Jack Byrne, Don Budge, Bob Bremner, Dewitt Brown, William H. A. Carr, William J. Clothier, Ashley Cooper, Kathleen and Richard Cordsen, Terry County, Mary Daly, Colin Dibley, Jaroslav Drobny, Richard Dwight, Roy Emerson, Ed Fabricius, Vesle Fenstermaker, Guy Forget, Sultan Gangji, Norman Gengaults-Smith, Alex Goriansky, Valiska and Marshall Gregory, Inge Haesloop, Mary Taussig Hall, Samuel J. Hough, Lisa Hurley, Madelyn Kriplen, Marsh Kriplen, Penny Landrigan, Lisa Schnell Lanzillo, Bob Lowe, Stan Lupien, Char Lugar, Britt Marie and Nils Magnuson, Stan Malless, Allerton Delano Marshall, Malcolm W. Martin, Amy Massie, Virginia McKay, Chuka Momah, Phil Morton, Herb Motley, John Newcombe, Chris Nguyen, Maria O'Connor, William Julius Polk Jr., Richey Reneberg, Ken Rosewall, John W. Sears, Ted Schroeder, Pancho Segura, Vic Seixas, Nancy Scott, Leon Strauss, Elizabeth Wright Strelinger, Marjorie Swain, Bill Talbert, Tony Trabert, Erik van Dillen, John Van Ryn, Armando Vieira, Kate Weddington, Barry Williams, Alexander H. Whitman, Frederick Crocker Whitman, George Wright, Sidney Wood, Catherine Zusy.

I wish to acknowledge those in London who made it possible for a book about the life of Dwight Davis and the origins of his silver cup to move, at last, from idea to printed page. My thanks to the International Tennis Federation and to its leaders and staff, past and present, particularly Ian Barnes and Brian Tobin and also Debbie Bamlett, Alun James, Ann Page, Vanessa Smith, Lindi Sprenger, Christopher Stokes and Barbara Travers. Thanks also to the wise and tactful Roger Houghton, of Lucas Alexander Whitley, Writers' Agents, who gave good counsel about many things, including the book's structure, and to associate publisher Julian Shuckburgh, of Ebury Press, who patiently attempted to teach an American writer the rules of punctuation, British style.

Finally, thanks to the members of my encouraging family – particularly my husband, who supplied not only advice, affection, stability and perspective, but a shrewd first reading, knowledge of World War I rifles and innumerable carry-in dinners. And to Louis R. Lowe, who, so many years ago, first took his young daughter to see a match of world class tennis.

Index